Richard Acklam   Araminta Crace

PRE-INTERMEDIATE

Total English

Students' Book

Longman

Contents

UNIT	LESSON 1	LESSON 2
1 **24 hours** page 5	**Grammar:** likes and dislikes **Vocabulary:** daily routines and activities **Can do:** ask and talk about personal likes and dislikes	**Grammar:** Present Simple; adverbs of frequency **Vocabulary:** sleeping habits **Can do:** ask and answer questions about daily routines
2 **Music** page 15	**Grammar:** Past Simple **Vocabulary:** talking about biographies **Can do:** talk about personal events in the past	**Grammar:** *so* and *neither* **Vocabulary:** word families - nouns and adjectives **Can do:** say when you are the same as/different from, another person
3 **Taste** page 25	**Grammar:** *going to* (future plans) **Vocabulary:** food and restaurants **Can do:** tell a friend about your future plans	**Grammar:** defining relative clauses **Vocabulary:** talking about films **Can do:** write an informal letter to a friend
4 **Survival** page 35	**Grammar:** comparatives **Vocabulary:** describing people **Can do:** compare people	**Grammar:** superlatives **Vocabulary:** survival skills **Can do:** write a thank-you note
5 **Stages** page 45	**Grammar:** *should, can, have to* **Vocabulary:** times of life **Can do:** exchange opinions with a friend	**Grammar:** Present Perfect with *for* and *since* **Vocabulary:** friendship **Can do:** write a personal profile
6 **Places** page 55	**Grammar:** *will* **Vocabulary:** geographical features **Can do:** make general predictions about the future	**Grammar:** *too, too much/many, enough* **Vocabulary:** machines at home **Can do:** give explanations for choices
7 **Body** page 65	**Grammar:** First Conditional **Vocabulary:** appearance **Can do:** describe a person's physical appearance	**Grammar:** gerunds and infinitives **Vocabulary:** personality **Can do:** describe someone's personality
8 **Speed** page 75	**Grammar:** Present Simple Passive **Vocabulary:** verbs about change **Can do:** describe simple changes	**Grammar:** questions **Vocabulary:** phrasal verbs about relationships **Can do:** find out personal information
9 **Work** page 85	**Vocabulary:** work **Can do:** respond to simple job interview questions	**Grammar:** *can, could, be able to* **Vocabulary:** make/do **Can do:** talk about your abilities
10 **Wildlife** page 95	**Grammar:** phrasal verbs **Vocabulary:** phrasal verbs **Can do:** talk about people who influenced you	**Grammar:** countable/uncountable nouns **Vocabulary:** animals and zoos **Can do:** write a short contribution for a bulletin board
11 **Travel** page 105	**Grammar:** Present Perfect Simple with *just, yet* and *already* **Vocabulary:** holidays **Can do:** find out if someone would be a good travel companion	**Grammar:** verbs with two objects **Vocabulary:** greetings and presents **Can do:** make generalisations about customs
12 **Money** page 115	**Grammar:** Second Conditional **Vocabulary:** money **Can do:** say what you'd do in a hypothetical situation	**Grammar:** reported speech **Vocabulary:** education **Can do:** report what someone said to you

Communication activities page 125   Writing bank page 145   Irregular verb table page 149

LESSON 3	COMMUNICATION	FILM BANK
Grammar: Present Continuous **Vocabulary:** shops and shopping **Can do:** write an informal email to update someone on your life.	**Can do:** talk about your learning needs and ability	London **page 133**
Grammar: Present Perfect Simple (for experience) **Vocabulary:** verb/noun collocations about achievements **Can do:** talk about personal achievements and experiences	**Can do:** explain why you like a piece of music	Summer holiday **page 134**
Grammar: Present Continuous (for future arrangements) **Vocabulary:** adjectives; sense verbs **Can do:** make arrangements with a friend	**Can do:** contribute to a simple discussion	Jamie Oliver **page 135**
Grammar: indirect questions **Vocabulary:** survival English **Can do:** ask polite questions	**Can do:** agree on choices with a partner	Surviving in the Sahara **page 136**
Grammar: *used to* **Vocabulary:** habits **Can do:** describe yourself when you were younger	**Can do:** make a simple informal presentation	On Golden Pond **page 137**
Grammar: uses of *like* **Vocabulary:** describing natural places **Can do:** describe a favourite place	**Can do:** explain your preference for a holiday destination	Around the world **page 138**
Grammar: purpose/reason/result **Vocabulary:** illness and injury **Can do:** talk about illness and give advice	**Can do:** understand and talk about a magazine quiz	Carry on Doctor **page 139**
Grammar: Past Continuous and Past Simple **Vocabulary:** talking about books **Can do:** ask and answer questions about past actions	**Can do:** talk for an extended period on a familiar topic	Speed-dating **page 140**
Grammar: Past Simple Passive **Vocabulary:** crime **Can do:** write a short article	**Can do:** take part in a simple negotiation	The interview **page 141**
Grammar: the definite article *(the)* **Vocabulary:** verb + prepositions (1) **Can do:** speculate about sounds and pictures	**Can do:** participate in reaching a group decision	Wolves **page 142**
Grammar: Past Perfect Simple **Vocabulary:** travel writing **Can do:** write about a place you've travelled to	**Can do:** achieve your aim in a typical travel conversation	Gill's wild world **page 143**
Grammar: *both, neither, either* **Vocabulary:** verb + prepositions (2) **Can do:** describe similarities/differences	**Can do:** make a simple complaint in a shop/restaurant	The Ladykillers **page 144**

Do you know...?

1 Do you know these grammar terms? Complete the table with the words in bold from sentences 1–10 below.

a) pronoun	*They* (sentence 2)
b) countable noun	
c) comparative	
d) possessive	
e) modal verb	
f) auxiliary verb	
g) contraction	
h) uncountable noun	
i) article	
j) Present Perfect	

1 She is **a** doctor.
2 **They** are very generous.
3 This book is **yours**.
4 **Does** she eat meat?
5 You **can** smoke outside.
6 Keith **has written** four novels.
7 How much **water** do you drink every day?
8 Could you give this **pen** to him?
9 This watch is **cheaper** than the last one.
10 **He's** quite late.

2　**a** Do you know these parts of speech? Complete the table with the correct words from the box below.

1) noun	
2) verb	*write*
3) phrasal verb	
4) adjective	
5) adverb	
6) preposition	

> write　sister　carefully　listen　give up
> quickly　at　beautiful　look after
> cinema　green　down　happy　factory

b Complete the sentences with words from the box above.

1 My _____ is nearly three years older than me.
2 We stayed in a really _____ hotel.
3 Please don't look _____ me like that!
4 Please _____ to me very carefully.
5 I ran as _____ as I could.
6 I've decided to _____ chocolate in the New Year.

3 Do you know these pronunciation terms? Look at the words in the box and answer the questions below about each word.

> chocolate　cinema　sister　factory

1 How many syllables are there?
2 Where's the main stress?
3 Are there any syllables you don't pronounce?

4 Do you know any vocabulary related to the topic areas in the box? Make a list.

> food　work　travel　money　music
> animals　routines　body　home

5 Do you know this classroom language? Match questions 1–8 to the replies a–h below.

1 What does 'party animal' mean?
2 How do you spell 'exercise'?
3 Can you say that again, please?
4 What page is that on?
5 Could you speak up a bit please?
6 What's the answer to number 5?
7 What's our homework?
8 How do you pronounce the second word in line 4 of the text on page 26?

a) Page 13, at the end of Unit 1.
b) Do exercises 3, 4 and 5 on page 64.
c) I don't know. We should ask Mario. He's good at grammar.
d) /ˈresɪpiːz/
e) E-X-E-R-C-I-S-E
f) It's someone who likes going to parties.
g) Of course. It is quite noisy in here.
h) Sure, no problem. All of it or just the last part?

1 | 24 hours

Lead-in

1 Discuss.

1 What is your favourite time of the day/week? Why?

2 What is your least favourite time of the day/week? Why?

3 What is a typical day like for you?

2 What can you see in the photos? Use verb phrases from the box. Which phrases are not in the photos?

> chat on the phone   listen to the radio   get up early
> go to bed late   stay in bed late   have breakfast/lunch/dinner
> watch TV   check your emails   do exercise   go for a walk
> go clubbing   do nothing   catch a bus/train

3 **a** Look again at the verb phrases.

Write **D** next to the things you do every day.

Write **W** next to the things you only do at weekends.

Write **S** next to the things you sometimes do.

Write **N** next to the things you never do.

b Write more verb phrases of things you do ...

- every day.
- only at weekends.

c Compare with a partner. Do you do the same things?

Speaking

1 a Look at the quiz below. What can you see in each picture? Tell your partner.

b Match the pictures A–C with the descriptions 1–3 below.

1 This person likes staying in, eating and watching television. ☐
2 This person likes going out, dancing and meeting friends. ☐
3 This person likes reading and going to museums and art galleries. ☐

2 a Work with a partner and do the quiz.

b Check the results. Are the results true for you?

What kind of **person** are you?

A

1 It's your birthday. Do you ...

A go clubbing with friends? ○
B have dinner in a restaurant with friends? ○
C get a DVD and a take-away pizza? ○

2 It's a sunny weekend. Do you ...

A have a picnic with family and friends? ○
B visit another city? ○
C read a magazine at home? ○

3 It's your lunch break at work. Do you ...

A meet some friends and go to the gym? ○
B go to an art gallery? ○
C have a sandwich at your desk? ○

4 It's your summer holiday. Do you ...

A go clubbing in the evenings? ○
B visit old buildings? ○
C lie on the beach? ○

5 You go shopping on holiday. Do you buy ...

A some clothes for the evening? ○
B a book about the place you're in? ○
C an ice cream? ○

B

C

Mostly As:
You're a real party animal and fun to be with. Don't forget to stop and rest sometimes!

Mostly Bs:
You're a proper culture vulture and like learning something new. Don't forget to join the party sometimes!

Mostly Cs:
You're a total couch potato and usually on the sofa, doing nothing. Come on – get up and join in the fun!

Reading

3 Read the text. Is each person a 'party animal', a 'culture vulture' or a 'couch potato'?

We asked these people about their typical Saturday. Here's what they said:

I <u>don't like</u> getting up early at the weekends so I usually stay in bed late – sometimes until about 10.30a.m.! <u>I absolutely love</u> having a big breakfast on Saturdays. <u>I can't stand</u> going to the gym or doing exercise but I sometimes go for a walk in the afternoon. <u>I quite like</u> meeting friends in the park or just lying on the grass and doing nothing. <u>I'm not very keen on</u> going out on Saturday evening. I stay in and chat on the phone and get a take-away pizza.

Marek Rzeczkowska, Krakow, Poland

<u>I really hate</u> doing nothing so I get up early on Saturdays and start the day by checking my emails. <u>I really like</u> meeting friends and having breakfast in a café, so I catch a bus into town at about 9.00a.m. After breakfast, my friends and I sometimes go to an art gallery. <u>I'm quite keen on</u> most kinds of art so <u>I don't mind</u> which gallery we go to but my friends really hate modern art. I do different things on Saturday evenings. I sometimes have dinner with friends or I stay in and watch TV.

Lola Gutierrez, Sevilla, Spain

4 Complete the sentences with Marek or Lola.

Lola likes getting up early on Saturdays.

1 _____ likes having a lot to eat for breakfast.
2 _____ doesn't usually have breakfast at home on Saturdays.
3 _____ doesn't like doing any sport or exercise.
4 _____ likes doing nothing in the park.
5 _____ likes going to art galleries.
6 _____ likes chatting on the phone on Saturday evenings.
7 _____ likes watching TV in the evening.

Grammar | likes and dislikes

5 Complete the Active grammar box using the <u>underlined</u> phrases from the texts in Ex. 3.

> ### Active grammar
>
> 1 _____   ☺☺☺
>   *I really like ...*   ☺☺
>   *I quite like ...*   ☺
>
> 2 _____   ☺
>
> 3 _____   😐
>
> 4 _____   ☹
>   *I don't like ...*   ☹
>
> 5 _____   ☹☹
>   *I really hate ...*   ☹☹
>
> Use a noun or the gerund after these phrases.

6 Write sentences using the prompts. Don't forget to change the verb if necessary.

☺ /watch football on TV.
I'm quite keen on watching football on TV.

1 ☺☺☺ /my job.
2 ☹ /do crossword puzzles.
3 ☺☺ /beach holidays.
4 ☹☹ /be cold.
5 😐 /dogs.
6 ☺ /go to the cinema.
7 ☹☹ /talk on the phone in English.
8 ☺☺☺ /go dancing on Friday evenings.

Person to person

7 Make the sentences in Ex. 6 true for you. Cover the sentences and tell your partner.

Speaking and writing

8 Tell other students what kind of person you are, and why.
I think I'm mostly a party animal because I absolutely love going out with my friends.

9 **a** Write a paragraph with the title *My typical Saturday*. Use the texts in Ex. 3 to help you.

b Read your partner's paragraph. What new things do you learn about your partner?

1.2 | Goodnight

Grammar	Present Simple; adverbs of frequency
Can do	ask and answer questions about daily routines

Speaking and listening

1 a Make these sentences true for you. Compare with a partner.

1 I sleep a lot.
2 Sleep is a waste of time.
3 I can only sleep on a hard bed.

I don't sleep a lot – usually six hours a night.

b 1.1 Listen to a TV programme about sleep. Tick ✓ the things you hear.

cats ☐   dogs ☐
snakes ☐   fish ☐
babies ☐   children ☐
adults ☐   old people ☐
horses ☐

2 1.1 Listen again and answer the questions.

1 Who sleeps about a) seven hours, b) seventeen hours and c) eight hours every day?
2 What is strange about the way horses sleep?
3 What is strange about the way fish sleep?
4 In one year, the average person sleeps for: a) 2,688, b) 2,860 or c) 2,680 hours?
5 In one night, how many dreams does the average person have?

3 Discuss.

1 How often do you remember your dreams?
2 How often do you have the same dream?
3 Do you have any favourite dreams?

Vocabulary

4 a Match the questions to the answers.

1 What time do you go to bed?	a) At about 7a.m.
2 Do you have a snack before bed?	b) About eight hours.
3 What do you do to help fall asleep?	c) At about 11p.m.
4 How many hours do you sleep at a time?	d) At about 7.30a.m., after I have a shower.
5 How do you feel when you wake up?	e) I'm often a bit tired.
6 What time do you get up?	f) I usually have one in the morning.
7 What time do you have breakfast?	g) I always have a lie-in on Sundays.
8 Do you have a shower in the morning or the evening?	h) No, I don't. I never have time.
9 Do you have a nap during the day?	i) I hardly ever eat before bed.
10 Do you ever have a lie-in?	j) I sometimes listen to the radio.

b 1.2 Listen and check your answers.

c In pairs, decide what the difference in meaning is between:

1 to wake up/to get up.
2 to sleep/to fall asleep.
3 to have a snack/to have breakfast.

Grammar | Present Simple; adverbs of frequency

7 Complete the Active grammar box with *do*, *does*, *don't* or *doesn't*.

> **Active grammar**
>
> ➕ : *I usually go to bed about 10.30.*
>
> ➖ : *They _____ have a nap during the day.*
> : *He _____ have a lie-in during the week.*
>
> ❓ : *_____ you wake up early?*
> : *_____ she often have a snack before bed?*
>
> Use the Present Simple to talk about routines (things you do every day) and habits (things you do often).
>
> **Adverbs of frequency**
> *always, usually, often, sometimes, hardly ever, never*
> *100%* ————————————➤ *0%*

see Reference page 13

8 Choose the correct form.

A: (1) *Do/Does* you fall asleep quickly?

B: Yes, I (2) *do/does*. I (3) *don't/doesn't* listen to the radio, I just (4) *go/goes* to sleep immediately.

A: (5) *Do/Does* you use an alarm clock?

B: No, I (6) *do/don't*. My mum (7) *get/gets* up first, then she (8) *call/calls* me.

A: (9) *Do/Does* anyone in your family have strange sleep habits?

B: Yes, my brother (10) *do/does*. He (11) *talk/talks* in his sleep but he (12) *don't/doesn't* wake up.

9 Write true answers for you for the questions in Ex. 8.

I usually fall asleep quickly but I sometimes read a book.

Pronunciation

10 a Match the vowel sounds to the <u>underlined</u> words.

a) /uː/   b) /ə/   c) /ʌ/

A: (1) <u>Do</u> you have a nap during the day?

B: Yes, I (2) <u>do</u>.

A: (3) <u>Does</u> Jane get up early?

B: Yes, she (4) <u>does</u>.

b 🔲1·3 Listen and check. Practise the dialogues with a partner.

Person to person

11 Ask and answer the questions in Ex. 4a with a partner.

A: *What time do you go to bed?*

B: *I usually go to bed about midnight.*

---

5 Complete the text using the <u>underlined</u> phrases in Ex. 4.

> # Is sleeping a problem for you?
> ## Do you want to sleep but can't fall asleep?
> Here are some tips for happy sleeping:
>
> - (1) _____ of bread or fruit about an hour before you (2)_____.
> - Try not to (3) _____ in the day. Only sleep at night.
> - If you (4) _____ in the night, don't (5) _____ , just stay in bed and read a book.
> - Always (6) _____ in the morning, it's the most important meal of the day.

6 Which advice in Ex. 5 do you follow? Which tips do you disagree with?

I don't eat before I go to bed.

Reading

1 a Which things in the box can you find in the photos?

> staff customers shop assistant products doorman

b Discuss.

1 What is the most famous shop in your country?

2 Why is it famous? What can you buy there?

2 a Read the text. Why is Harrods famous?

All things, for all people,
EVERYWHERE

Harrods is probably the most famous department store in the UK. It's over 150 years old and it has 330 departments on seven floors. On special days, about 300,000 customers come and spend their time and money in Harrods.

More than 5,000 people from over fifty different countries work for the store. However, the staff are not just shop assistants. Harrods has its own hairdresser's, doctor's, bank, fire brigade, and much more. A huge team of people clean and look after the store. This includes checking and changing the 11,500 light bulbs on the outside of the building.

Harrods is famous for providing 'all things, for all people, everywhere'. Whatever you want, you can buy it at Harrods – from expensive jewellery and furniture, to paper and pens. Someone even bought a baby elephant called Gertie as a present for Ronald Reagan. However, many people come to Harrods just to look and not to buy and this can be a problem. Sometimes the doorman doesn't let people in because they are wearing the wrong kind of clothes!

> **On special days, about 300,000 customers come and spend their time and money in Harrods.**

b Read the text again and answer the questions.

1 How many people go to Harrods every day?

2 What different kinds of jobs are mentioned?

3 What does 'all things, for all people, everywhere' mean?

4 Who was Gertie?

5 Why does the doorman stop some people going into Harrods?

6 What do these numbers refer to?

a) 150 b) 330 c) 5,000 d) 11,500

3 Discuss.

1 Would you like to visit Harrods? Why/Why not?

2 Do you enjoy shopping? Why/Why not?

Listening

4 a **1.4** Listen to a customer survey in Harrods. Complete the chart.

Where are you from?	What are you doing in London?	What are you doing in Harrods?
Customer 1: (1) _____	working as an au pair	(2) _____
Customer 2: (3) _____	(4) _____	buying a ring
Customer 3: England	shopping	(5) _____

b Compare your answers with a partner.

Grammar | Present Continuous

5 Match sentences 1 and 2 in the Active grammar box to rules a) and b).

Active grammar

⊕ 1 *I'm working as an au pair.*
2 *My girlfriend is shopping for clothes.*

⊖ *I'm not buying anything.*
We're not staying long.

? *Are you looking for anything special?*
What are you doing in Harrods?

Use the Present Continuous for:

a) actions happening at this moment
e.g. sentence: _____

b) temporary actions happening 'around now' but not at this moment:
e.g. sentence: _____

Use the Present Simple (NOT the Present Continuous) with state verbs (e.g. *be, know, like, love,* etc.).

---

see Reference page 13

6 Use the Present Continuous to complete the dialogues.

A: I (1) _____ (wait) in the restaurant on the fourth floor. Where are you? It's 4.30! What (2) _____ (you / do)?

B: We (3) _____ (sit) on the bus. The traffic is very bad. We (4) _____ (not / move).

A: Hello. I (5) _____ (phone) from London.

B: Really? What (6) _____ (you / do) there?

A: Jenny and I (7) _____ (stay) with some friends for a week. It (8) _____ (rain) today so we (9) _____ (not / go) out.

7 Choose the correct alternatives.

1 I *do/'m doing* a Spanish evening class this term. It *starts/is starting* at 7.30 every Monday.

2 What *do you do/are you doing* these days? *Do you still study/Are you still studying?*

3 Michaela *doesn't eat/isn't eating* meat. She *doesn't like/isn't liking* it.

4 What *do you usually do/are you usually doing* in the summer holidays?

5 They *often go/'re often going* to Corsica with friends.

8 **1.5** Listen. What is happening? Make sentences with He/She ... .

9 Work in pairs.
Student A: look at the picture below.
Student B: look at the picture on page 127.

Find five more differences.

A: *Is the man buying a DVD?*
B: *No, he isn't. He's buying a book.*

Writing

10 Read the email in the Writing bank on page 145. Do the exercises.

11 Write an email to a friend you haven't talked to for a long time. Tell him/her about your life at the moment.

Hi Angela,
How are you? I've got so much to tell you ...

1 Communication

Wheel of English

1 Look at the 'Wheel of English'. Match the words and phrases in the box to the pictures.

~~grammar~~ vocabulary reading writing listening speaking and pronunciation

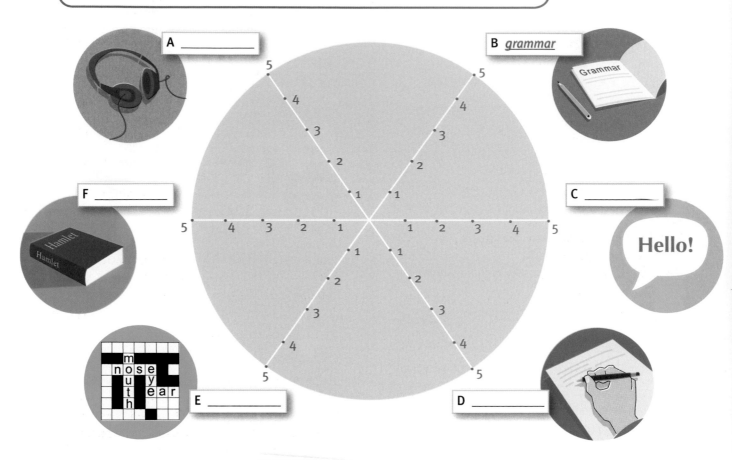

A _____

B *grammar*

C _____

D _____

E _____

F _____

2 [1.6] **Listen.**

How important is each aspect of English for Antonio? Put a cross (X) at the correct place on each part of the wheel, then join the crosses.

3 [1.6] **Listen again.**

How good is Antonio at each aspect of English? Make notes.

4 Draw your own 'Wheel of English'. Then explain it to your partner. Use language from the How to ... box.

5 Look at the Lifelong learning box. Write one more tip on how to improve each aspect of your English.

Lifelong learning

There's more than one way

There are a lot of ways to improve your English. For example:

Writing: send emails to your classmates

Listening: listen to an English language radio station

Vocabulary: make a vocabulary notebook and always keep it in your pocket

Speaking: chat on the phone to your classmates

6 Tell other students your ideas. Make a note of the three best learning tips you hear.

Present Simple

⊕ ⊖	I/You/We/They	go don't go	to bed early.
	He/She/It	goes doesn't go	
❓	Do	you/we/they get up	
	Does	he/she/it get up	early?

Yes, I do. / No, I don't.
Yes, he does. / No, he doesn't.

Use the Present Simple for routines, habits and things that are generally true.

I always call my parents on Sundays.

I often go to the cinema.

He doesn't like going to bed.

contractions: *don't = do not*; *doesn't = does not*

3rd persons: *He/She/It*: add *s* to the verb in the affirmative.

Adverbs of frequency

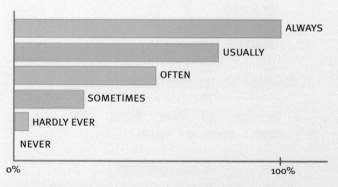

Use adverbs of frequency to say how often you do something.

I usually play the piano in the evenings.

The adverb of frequency comes after the verb *to be*.

I'm never late.

The adverb of frequency comes before a main verb.

He sometimes goes clubbing on Saturdays.

❗ Use the affirmative with *never* and *hardly ever*, not the negative.

He hardly ever stays in bed late.

Present Continuous

⊕	I He/She/It We/You/They	am is are	working.
⊖	I He/She/It You/We/They	am not is not are not	
❓	Am Is Are	I he/she/it you/we/they	having a lie-in?

Yes, I am. / No, I'm not.
Yes, you are. / No, you aren't.
Yes, he is. / No, he's not (he isn't).

Use the Present Continuous to talk about actions happening at the time of speaking and temporary actions happening around now.

I'm doing the washing-up.

He's doing a lot of exercise at the moment.

State verbs

like	love	hate	want	need	prefer
know	understand	believe	remember		

Use the Present Simple (NOT the Present Continuous) with state verbs.

I know how to play chess.

Key vocabulary

Verb–noun phrases about daily routine
catch a bus/train   chat on the phone
check your emails   go clubbing   go to bed late
go to the gym   have a lie-in   have a snack
lie on the beach   meet some friends   do exercise
do nothing   fall asleep   get a take-away pizza
get up early   go for a walk   have a nap
have a picnic   have a shower
have breakfast/lunch/dinner   listen to the radio
read a magazine   sleep   stay in bed late
wake up   watch TV

Shops
customers   doorman   products   shop assistant
staff

1 Each sentence has one word missing. Write the missing word in the correct place. Look at the symbols to help you.

I love the colour pink. ☺ ☺ ☺

I *absolutely* love the colour pink.

1   I'm quite on watching football. ☺

_____.

2   I stand science fiction films. ☹ ☹

_____.

3   I like sending text messages. ☺ ☺

_____.

4   I really the winter. ☹ ☹

_____.

5   I quite pizza. ☺

_____.

6   I absolutely going to the beach. ☺ ☺ ☺

_____.

7   I mind getting up early. 😐

_____.

8   I not very keen on dancing. ☹

_____.

2 Complete the dialogues with the correct form of the Present Simple.

A: *Do you get up* (you/get up) early?

B: Yes, I do. In the week (1) _____ (I/get up) at about 6.30.

A: What time (2) _____ (you/start) work?

B: At about 9.00. (3) _____ (I/go to bed) early too.

A: (4) _____ (you/go to bed) before ten o'clock?

B: No, I don't, but (5) _____ (I/fall asleep) in front of the TV most nights!

A: (6) _____ (you/have a snack) before you go to bed?

B: No, I don't. (7) _____ (I/have dinner) late every evening.

A: My brother is a really good swimmer.

B: (6) _____ (he/swim) a lot?

A: Yes, he does. (7) _____ (He/get up) very early and (8) _____ (swim) for two hours before breakfast. Then (9) _____ (he/go) back to the swimming pool after work.

B: (10) _____ (he/go) out with his friends much?

A: Only at weekends. (11) _____ (He/not/go) out in the week at all.

3 Complete the dialogues using one of the verbs below in the Present Continuous.

> not/get   ~~do~~   have   sit   check
> walk   watch   do

A: What *are you doing* (you) at the moment?

B: I (1) _____ on a bus with some friends.

A: What about you?

B: I (2) _____ lunch with my family.

A: (3) _____ (Jack) TV?

B: No, he isn't. He (4) _____ his emails.

A: (5) _____ (you/John) any exercise at the moment?

B: Yes, lots! We (6) _____ to work and (7) we _____ take-away pizzas at the moment.

4 Choose the correct alternatives.

I *usually go*/am usually going to work by car.

1   Listen to that man. What language *does he speak/is he speaking?*

2   It *doesn't rain/isn't raining* much in the summer here.

3   You *work/'re working* very hard today.

4   *Do you prefer/Are you preferring* tea or coffee?

5   I *stay/'m staying* at the Savoy Hotel in London for a week.

6   Who's that woman? What *does she want/is she wanting?*

5 Complete the questions with the correct verb.

> do   fall   go   have   listen   chat
> catch   wake up   ~~watch~~

Do you *watch* TV every evening?

1   How often do you _____ clubbing?

2   Do you need an alarm clock to _____ in the morning?

3   Do you _____ a snack before you go to bed?

4   Do you usually _____ to the radio at work?

5   Where do you usually _____ your homework?

6   Do you find it easy to _____ asleep?

7   How often do you _____ a bus to work?

8   How often do you _____ on the phone to your best friend?

2 | Music

Lead-in

1 What musical instruments can you see in the photos? What other instruments do you know?

2 a **2.1** Match the extracts to the types of music.

> classical   Latin   rock   house   pop   jazz

b What kind(s) of music do you like/hate?

3 a Complete the sentences using the words or phrases in the box.

> read music   really into   download   compilation CDs
> favourite band   lead singer   favourite record   last concert

1 My _____ is Coldplay. I've got all their CDs.
2 The _____ I went to was Beethoven's 9th Symphony.
3 I _____ a lot of music from the Internet.
4 I can't _____ but I can play by ear.
5 I sometimes make _____ for my friends.
6 My _____ is *Yesterday* by The Beatles.
7 I'd like to meet the _____ of Radiohead. He sounds interesting.
8 I'm _____ jazz at the moment. I love Louis Armstrong.

b Make sentences about you. Use the words or phrases in the box. Tell your partner.

I don't download music from the Internet. I don't know how to do it.

15

Reading

1 **a** Look at the photo. When do you think this pop star was famous?

   b Read the text and complete the chart.

'M' – a star for the future?

Do you know Robin Scott? No? Well, not many people do. He's the lead singer with M and a star for the future. M's new record is a huge hit at the moment. It's called *Pop Muzik* and it's already very popular in the UK and Europe.

Robin and his girlfriend, Brigit Novik, sing the lyrics. Their strange voices make it sound very different. Brigit's voice sounds like a robot!

Robin is certain to be a big star in the future. This is just the beginning for M.

May 1979

Date of article	*May 1979*
Name of band	
Lead singer	
Other singer	
Song	
Hit in ...	
Future for lead singer	

Listening

2 **a** **2.2** Listen to an interview with Robin Scott twenty-five years later. Did he become a big star?

   b Listen again and answer the questions.

   1 Where did he grow up?
   2 What kind of college did he go to?
   3 When did he make his first record?
   4 Where did he move to in the mid-seventies?
   5 How did he choose the name M?
   6 What happened in February 1979?
   7 What happened in 1989?
   8 What is he doing now?

3 **a** Discuss.

   1 How do you think Robin feels about writing a 'real classic'?
   2 Can you think of other songs which are 'real classics'?

   b **2.3** Listen to *Pop Muzik*. What do you think of it?

Grammar | Past Simple

4 **a** Complete the Active grammar box with the correct form of the verb in the Past Simple.

> ### Active grammar
>
> **Use the Past Simple for completed actions in the past.**
>
> ⊕ : We ____ a band with my brother. (form)
> : I ____ up in south London. (grow)
>
> ⊖ : I ____ very happy about my first record. (feel)
> : They ____ with me all the time. (agree)
>
> ❓ : Where ____ all ____ ? (it/start)
> : How ____ of the name M? (you/think)

b Which verbs in the Active grammar box are regular? Which are irregular?

see Reference page 23 and irregular verb table page 149

5 **a** Complete the sentences using the Past Simple.

1 I _____ (go) to a fantastic concert last night.

2 Mozart _____ (write) 600 pieces of music.

3 My brother _____ (play) his guitar all day yesterday.

4 Ten years ago my favourite band _____ (be) Oasis.

5 I _____ (make) a compilation CD for my sister's birthday.

6 My dad _____ (teach) me how to play the piano.

7 I _____ (buy) three jazz CDs last week.

b **2.4** Listen and check your answers.

6 Complete the dialogue with the Past Simple of the verbs in brackets.

A: Where (1) _____ (you/grow up)?

B: When I (2) _____ (be) very young, we (3) _____ (live) in Venice. Then when I was twelve, my family (4) _____ (move) to Milan. I (5) _____ (not/like) it at first, but when I was a teenager, I (6) _____ (love) it.

A: (7) _____ (you/go) to college when you (8) _____ (leave) school?

B: No. I (9) _____ (not/go) to college until I was twenty-two. First, I (10) _____ (get) a job in a record shop for a year and (11) _____ (save) up some money. Then I (12) _____ (go) travelling.

Pronunciation

7 **a** **2.5** Listen and repeat.

> worked believed ended moved wanted
> loved finished waited kissed

b Put the verbs into the correct column according to the pronunciation of -ed.

/t/	/d/	/ɪd/
worked		

c Add more verbs to each column.

8 **a** **2.6** Listen and write the sentences.

b In pairs, practise the sentences.

Speaking

9 **a** Prepare to interview a student about his/her life. Make questions using the ideas below and your own ideas.

- when/where born
- where grew up
- what liked/disliked about school
- what job wanted to do
- what important things happened as teenager
- what did when left school
- what important things happened after that

b In pairs, interview each other about your lives. Use the language in the How to ... box to help you. Take notes.

HOW TO ...

refer to times in the past	
1 Say when an action happened	three years/two months *ago*
	when I left school/I was fifteen
	in 1973/February 1979/the summer of 2000
	in the mid 70s/late 80s/ early 90s
	last week/month/year
2 Link an action to another action	*after* that/leaving school
	three years/five days *later*

10 Write a short biography of your partner. Use your notes from Ex. 9a.

Adriana was born in 1980. She grew up in a small village near Naples. She didn't like school but she loved music ...

2.2 The Mozart effect

Grammar	*so* and *neither*
Can do	say when you're the same as/different from another person

Reading

1 **2.7** Listen to three pieces of music by Mozart. How does each one make you feel? Use the adjectives in the box and your own words.

> happy   sad   relaxed   awake   sleepy   thoughtful

This piece makes me feel relaxed and calm.

2 Read the text about the effects of music. Match the headings to the correct paragraph.

a **Music for stress and pain**

b **Get a better score and remember more**

c **The right music to study better**

d **All kinds of music have an effect**

1 _____

Music is not just entertainment. It is medicine for both the brain and the body. Don Campbell is an expert on *The Mozart effect* and the incredible power of music. He says that all kinds of music, from Mozart to jazz, from Latin to rock can affect our learning and our health.

2 _____

Many people use music to help them feel <u>relaxed</u> after a busy day at work. Music can also reduce the stress of being ill, especially by reducing pain. The director of Baltimore Hospital says that thirty minutes of classical music has the same effect as ten milligrams of the painkiller *Valium*.

3 _____

Campbell also says that music can help you concentrate but you need the right kind of music for your mood. And you need to listen for about ten minutes before you start studying. Perhaps your mind needs relaxing or maybe you are <u>tired</u> and you want to feel more <u>energetic</u>. So you should choose the appropriate music to help you. You can use many different kinds of music to help you concentrate. Mozart's music is very popular, however, because it is very organised and it makes your brain more alert and <u>imaginative</u>.

4 _____

Music helps you to study better and it can also actually make you more <u>intelligent</u>. In one study, students who listened to Mozart before doing a test got much higher marks than those who didn't. Many studies also show that children who learn to play a musical instrument before the age of twelve have better memories for the rest of their lives.

3 Read the text again. Mark the statements true (T), false (F) or don't know (DK).

1 Music is good for our bodies and brains.
2 Don Campbell loves Mozart's music.
3 Music helps many people to relax after work.
4 Many hospitals use music to help with pain.
5 Listening to music before you study is a bad idea.
6 Only Mozart's music helps you to study.
7 The students listened to Mozart for fifteen minutes before doing the test.
8 It's a good idea for children to learn to play a musical instrument.

4 Discuss.

1 What music do you listen to?
2 What effect does it have?

Vocabulary | *word families*

5   a Match the <u>underlined</u> adjectives in the text with the definitions below.

1 _____ = good at learning and understanding things

2 _____ = can think of new and interesting ideas

3 _____ = active and can work hard

4 _____ = calm and not worried

5 _____ = feeling that you want to rest or sleep

b Complete the table. Use a dictionary if necessary.

ADJECTIVE	NOUN
relaxed	
tired	
energetic	
imaginative	
intelligent	

6   a <u>Underline</u> the main stress in the words in the table.

b   2.8 Listen and check your answers.

1 Can you work out any rules for word stress with nouns?

2 Which pairs of words have the same stress?

3 Which pairs have different stress?

Lifelong learning

Record it all!

When you're recording new vocabulary, write all the important information in your vocabulary book.

Include the stress, the part of speech, a definition and an example sentence.

Relaxed (adj.)— calm and not worried. Jazz makes me feel very relaxed.

7 Choose the correct alternatives.

1 Latin music makes me feel *energetic/energy*.

2 I don't believe that music can make you more *intelligent/intelligence*.

3 I'm a very *imaginative/imagination* person.

4 I sometimes don't go out at weekends because of *tired/tiredness*.

5 I play the piano for *relaxed/relaxation*.

6 I need to use my *imaginative/imagination* in my job.

7 Everyone has the *intelligent/intelligence* to learn a language.

8 I listen to music in the morning to give me *energetic/energy*.

9 I'm always *tired/tiredness* when I get home in the evening.

10 Jazz makes me feel *relaxed/relaxation*.

8 Make the sentences in Ex. 7 true for you.

Going for a run makes me feel energetic.

Grammar | *so* and *neither*

9   a Complete the Active grammar box.

Active grammar

Agree

1 A: *I like rock music.*   B: *So do I.*

2 A: *I've got a guitar.*   B: *So ___ I.*

3 A: *I'm not keen on him.*   B: *Neither ___ I.*

4 A: *I didn't go.*   B: *Neither ___ I.*

Disagree

5 A: *I often listen to rock music.*   B: *I ___ .*

6 A: *I've got a DVD player.*   B: *I ___ .*

7 A: *I can't play an instrument.*   B: *I ___ .*

8 A: *I don't like loud music.*   B: *I ___ .*

b   2.9 Listen and check your answers.

c Cover the answers and repeat the conversations from the Active grammar box.

see Reference page 23

10 Complete these sentences about music to make them true for you.

I really like …   I've got …   I sometimes go …
I'm …   I don't like …   I'm not …   I think …
I haven't got …

Person to person

11 Say your sentences to a partner. Respond to your partner's sentences.

A: *I really like going to see musicals.*

B: *So do I.*

12 Write a paragraph about what kinds of music you like and why.

2.3 Too much, too soon?

Grammar	Present Perfect Simple (for experience)
Can do	talk about personal achievements and experiences

Reading

1 a Discuss.

1 Why do you think Charlotte Church is famous?

2 What do you think the title of this lesson means?

b Read the introduction to the text and check your answers.

Too much, too soon?

There is no question about Charlotte Church – she was a child prodigy. <u>She had</u> a recording contract with Sony at the age of eleven and a £6 million fortune by the age of sixteen – all from singing *classical* music. <u>She's sold</u> millions of records and she's performed for the American president, the Queen and the Pope. She has achieved a lot in her short life and she has earned a huge amount of money. But the question is: *Has she done too much, too soon?*

2 a Work in pairs.

Student A: read the text on page 125. Answer questions 1–6.

Student B: read the text on page 127. Answer questions 7–12.

1 When was Charlotte born?

2 How did she get a recording contract with Sony?

3 Was her first album successful?

4 What happened to her first manager?

5 Who was her second manager?

6 How did Charlotte do in her exams?

7 When did things start to go wrong for Charlotte?

8 What happened to Charlotte's mother?

9 What did the newspapers say about Charlotte?

10 Does Charlotte think she behaved like a normal teenager?

11 How does Charlotte feel about her mother now?

12 How is Charlotte now?

b Tell your partner about your half of the text. Use the questions as a guide.

3 Discuss these questions.

1 Do you think Charlotte Church has done 'too much, too soon'?

2 Do you think parents should push their 'child prodigies'?

4 a Match words or phrases from A and B.

appear on a talent show

A	B
1 ~~appear on~~	a) too hard
2 get a	b) to go wrong
3 your parents push you	c) she goes clubbing every night
4 an album is	d) recording contract
5 things start	e) her manager
6 argue with	f) fine
7 the newspapers say	g) ~~a talent show~~
8 things work out	h) an instant success

b In pairs, use the phrases to retell Charlotte's story.

Grammar | Present Perfect Simple

5 **a** Look at the two <u>underlined</u> verb phrases in the introduction to the text. Answer the questions.

1 What tense is <u>she had</u>? Do we know when the action happened?

2 What tense is <u>she's sold</u>? Do we know when the action happened?

b Complete the rules by writing Present Perfect Simple or Past Simple.

1 Use the _____ to talk about an action or experience at a specific time in the past.

2 Use the _____ to talk about an action or experience in the past when the time is not important or not known.

6 **a** Complete the Active grammar box. What part of speech are the <u>underlined</u> verbs?

> ### Active grammar
>
> ⊕ : I've <u>written</u> a book.
> : She _____ <u>performed</u> for the American president.
>
> ⊖ : They haven't <u>sold</u> a lot of records.
> : He _____ <u>seen</u> the film.
>
> ❓ : _____ you ever <u>been</u> on TV?
> : Has she <u>done</u> too much, too soon?

b Find other examples of the Present Perfect Simple in the texts about Charlotte Church.

see Reference page 23

7 Complete the sentences with the past participles of the verbs in the box.

> be play download ~~make~~ work study
> buy meet

I've never <u>made</u> a compilation CD for my friends.

1 She's _____ the lead singer of my favourite band.

2 I've never _____ an instrument in a concert.

3 He's _____ to two rock concerts this week.

4 I've _____ in lots of music shops so I'm quite experienced.

5 They've _____ every Radiohead album.

6 She's _____ singing and piano at college.

7 I've _____ lots of jazz music from the Internet.

8 **a** Complete the dialogues with the Present Perfect Simple or Past Simple.

A: (1) _____ (you ever win) a competition?

B: Yes, I (2) _____. I (3) _____ (win) a singing competition when I was six.

A: (4) _____ (you watch) TV last night?

B: Yes, I (5) _____. I (6) _____ (see) a documentary about child prodigies.

A: (7) _____ (you ever meet) a famous person?

B: No, I (8) _____. But I (9) _____ (see) Kylie in concert last year!

A: (10) _____ (you ever play) a musical instrument in public?

B: Yes, I (11) _____. I (12) _____ (be) in a band when I was a teenager.

b **2.10** Listen and check your answers.

Person to person

9 In pairs, ask and answer the questions in Ex. 8.

Vocabulary | achievements

10 **a** Match a verb from A with a noun from B.

A	B
1 learn	a) a prize for ... (dancing/a sport)
2 make	b) to speak another language
3 start	c) an exam with distinction
4 win	d) your own company
5 pass	e) an article/a book
6 write	f) a speech to ... (thirty people)

b Which of the above have you done/not done? Which achievements are you most proud of in your life? Tell other students.

I've played the piano in a concert. I'm really proud of that.

2 Communication

My top three

1   **a** You're going to listen to a radio programme. Look at the picture. What do you think it's about?

    b **2.11** Listen to the introduction. Were you correct?

2   **a** **2.12** Listen to the rest of the programme and complete the table.

PIECE OF MUSIC	ARTIST	REASON
3		
2		
1		

    b Compare your answers with a partner.

3   Discuss.

    What do you think about the music that Ben chose?

    Which one do you like best? Why?

4   **a** Complete the sentences using the phrases in the box.

> to remind someone of (a time/a place/a person ...)
> to make someone (feel happy/feel excited/cry/smile ...)
> to remember (listening/going/feeling ...)

    1 This song _____ when I was at school.

    2 This music _____ so happy.

    3 When I first heard this record, it _____ because it was so beautiful.

    4 I _____ to this song when I was on holiday in Spain.

    b **2.13** Listen and check your answers. Repeat the sentences.

5   **a** Choose your top three pieces of music. Write notes in the table.

PIECE OF MUSIC	ARTIST	REASON
3		
2		
1		

    b Tell other students about your choices.
Use your notes and the language from Ex. 4.

Past Simple

Regular verbs

➕ : *I played jazz music all day yesterday.*

➖ : *He didn't finish his exams.*

❓ : *Why did you wait for so long?*
Did you like the last Coldplay CD?

: *Yes, I did./No, I didn't.*

Irregular verbs

➕ : *I left school in 1993.*

➖ : *They didn't come home last night.*

❓ : *Where did she grow up?*
Did he go to school with you?

: *Yes, he did./No, he didn't.*

Use the Past Simple to talk about completed actions in the past.

Use the same form for all persons (but *was/were* for the verb *to be*).

Add *-ed* to regular verbs to make the past form.

Use *didn't (did not)* to make the negative.

For list of irregular verbs see page 149.

so and neither

Use *so* and *neither* to say that we agree with, or have the same experience as someone.

Positive statement: use *so* + positive auxiliary.

Negative statement: use *neither* + positive auxiliary.

Use the opposite auxiliary to say that we disagree with, or have a different experience from someone.

➕	Agree/Disagree
I've got a new car.	*So have I./I haven't.*
I like chocolate.	*So do I./I don't.*
I hated swimming.	*So did I./I didn't.*
I'm a student.	*So am I./I'm not.*
I was keen on pop.	*So was I./I wasn't.*
➖	Agree/Disagree
I haven't got it.	*Neither have I./I have.*
I don't watch TV.	*Neither do I./I do.*
I didn't go out.	*Neither did I./I did.*
I'm not enjoying it.	*Neither am I./I am.*
I wasn't late.	*Neither was I./I was.*

Present Perfect Simple

Form: *has/have* + past participle

➕➖	I/You/We/ They She/He/It	have/haven't has/hasn't	won a prize.
❓	Have	I/you/we/they ever	heard this song?
	Has	he/she/it ever	

: *Yes, I have./No, I haven't.*
Yes, he has./No, he hasn't.

Use the Present Perfect Simple to talk about an action or experience in the general past – the specific time is not important or is not known.

❗ Don't use the Present Perfect Simple with past time expressions, e.g. *last night, two weeks ago.*

Use the Past Simple to talk about an action or experience at a specific time in the past.

A: *I've visited eleven countries in my life.*

B: *Have you ever been to the Far East?*

A: *Yes, I have. I went to Thailand in 2001.*

Key vocabulary

Music

classical   Latin   rock   house   pop   jazz
lead singer   favourite band/CD   a compilation CD
read music   download music from the Internet
be really into (something)

Word families (adjective/noun)

energetic/energy   imaginative/imagination
intelligent/intelligence   relaxed/relaxation
tired/tiredness

Achievements

learn to speak another language   make a speech
start your own company   write an article/a book
win a prize for   pass an exam with distinction

1 Complete the sentences using the Past Simple.

I _learned_ to play the piano when I was a child.
My father _taught_ me. (learn/teach)

1 He _____ his old computer and _____ a new one. (sell/buy)

2 My grandmother _____ on the pavement and _____ her arm. (fall/break)

3 I was on a special diet last week. I only _____ fruit and I only _____ water. (eat/drink)

4 When we _____ on holiday last year, I _____ a lot of photos. (be/take)

5 I _____ to a concert last night and _____ two really good bands. (go/see)

2 Complete the dialogues with the Past Simple of the verbs in the boxes.

> say   ~~do~~   go   think   meet   not/like

A: What _did you do_ (you) last weekend?

B: On Friday evening, I (1) _____ my friend Natalia and we (2) _____ to see a film. I (3) _____ it was a really good film but Natalia (4) _____ it. She (5) _____ it was boring.

> stop   like   not/like   hate   be   live

A: Where (6) _____ (you) born?

B: In Scotland. I (7) _____ in the countryside when I was a child.

A: (8) _____ (you) it?

B: No, I (9) _____ it. I (10) _____ the weather because it never (11) _____ raining!

3 Agree or disagree using *so*, *neither* or short answers.

A: I've got a headache.

B: (agree) _So have I_.

1 A: I thought that coat was very expensive.

B: (agree) _____.

2 A: I didn't like her last single.

B: (disagree) _____.

3 A: I'm doing my homework at the moment.

B: (agree) _____.

4 A: I don't go swimming much.

B: (agree) _____.

5 A: I've got really noisy neighbours.

B: (disagree) _____.

6 A: I went to a great restaurant last weekend.

B: (agree) _____.

4 Complete the sentences using the Present Perfect Simple.

Susie _has seen_ The Lord of the Rings five times at the cinema! (see)

1 I _____ of that band. (not hear)

2 _____ a marathon? (you/ever/run)

3 I _____ to Carnival in Brazil twice. (be)

4 _____ your leg? (you/ever/break)

5 She's nervous because she _____ a horse before. (not ride)

6 _____ any climbing before? (you/do)

7 I _____ all over the world. (work)

8 _____ music from the Internet? (you/ever/download)

5 Choose the correct alternatives.

A: Hello. I'd like to apply for the job of sales assistant.

B: Well, I hope you *had/'ve had* the right kind of experience. (1) *Did you do/Have you done* this kind of job before?

A: Yes, I (2) *did/have*.

B: Where?

A: Well, I (3) *had/'ve had* some experience in a record shop.

B: Oh, really?

A: Yes, I (4) *worked/'ve worked* there two years ago.

B: (5) *Were you/Have you been* a sales assistant?

A: No, I (6) *wasn't/haven't*. I (7) *was/'ve been* a cleaner.

B: Oh, I'm sorry. We need someone who (8) *had/'s had* experience as a sales assistant.

6 Find and correct the mistake in each sentence.

Who was the ~~main~~ singer of Atomic Kitten? *lead*

1 The children are full of energetic today. Let's go to the park.

2 I often listen to music in the evenings for relaxed.

3 My sister has won lots of prizes for singing when she was young.

4 You are the most intelligence people I know.

5 I was nervous about making a speak to over 200 people.

6 You don't need much imaginative to be an accountant.

7 I'd like to listen to more classic music.

8 She's really in house music.

3 Taste

Lead-in

1   What can you see in the photos? Add more words to each list.

FOOD	DRINK	PEOPLE	KITCHEN EQUIPMENT
oranges	mineral water	chef	saucepan

2   **a** Complete the sentences using the words or phrases in the box.

> cook for yourself   ~~give (something) up~~   eat out
> celebrity chefs   diet   vegetarian

Is there any food that you would like to **_give up_**? If so, why? ☐

1   Have you ever been a _____? Why/Why not? ☐

2   Do you know any special kinds of _____ for people who want to lose weight fast? Do you think they work? ☐

3   Do you often _____ ? Do you use recipes to help you? ☐

4   How often do you _____ ? What is your favourite restaurant? ☐

5   Are there any famous _____ in your country? ☐

b **3.1** Listen and match each answer to the correct question.

3   Ask and answer the questions from Ex. 2 with another student.

Reading

1 Read the text quickly. Choose the best title:

a **How to be a good cook.**

b **KerryAnn opens a new restaurant.**

c **A success story for Jamie.**

Food lovers everywhere love the hottest young celebrity chef, Jamie Oliver. One big reason is his simple, easy and, above all, tasty recipes, which he has put together in some excellent recipe books. Good food was always very important in Jamie's family. His parents had a pub in the south-east of England and, from the age of eight, he started cooking and helping the chefs.

Recently, he started a new project. He opened a restaurant called '15' in east London. He gave himself nine months to take a team of unemployed 16–24-year-olds, with almost no previous experience of cooking, and turn them into top-class chefs. Jamie says his biggest lesson is that each individual needs a different approach. Some people learn quickly and others need a bit more time.

The project also became a TV series called *Jamie's kitchen* which millions of people watched. One of the real success stories is KerryAnn Dunlop. Originally she failed her college exams but after Jamie took her on, everything changed. Now she runs her own section of the kitchen. 'Everyone is still having a really good time. We get tired sometimes but we have fun in the kitchen, and seeing everyone enjoying the meals we've prepared makes us all feel good.' And about Jamie, she says, 'He's fantastic. He's like a big brother or best friend to me now.' And what is she going to do next? 'I think I'd like to work abroad. I'm going to apply for a job in a top New York restaurant.'

'Everyone is still having a really good time. We get tired sometimes but we have fun in the kitchen'

2 Read the text again and answer these questions.

1 Why is Jamie Oliver's food successful?

2 When did Jamie start cooking?

3 Who did Jamie employ as chefs for his new restaurant?

4 What is surprising about KerryAnn's story?

5 How does she feel about Jamie?

6 Where would she like to work next?

3 **a** Match a word or phrase from **A** with a word from **B** to make phrases from the text.

a real success story

A	B
~~a real success~~ open a	restaurant chef
top-class tasty	experience ~~story~~
no previous work	abroad recipe

b Make sentences about Jamie or KerryAnn using the phrases from Ex. 3a.

KerryAnn is one of the real success stories of the project.

4 Would you like to learn to be a top class chef? Why/Why not?

Grammar | *going to*

5 **3.2** Listen to this trainee chef talk about her future plans and answer the questions.

1 What are her plans for the summer?

2 What are her plans after that?

6 **a** **3.2** Listen again and complete the sentences in the Active grammar box.

Active grammar

Use *going to* to talk about future plans and intentions.

➕ *I _____ _____ _____ work for him over the summer.*

➖ *I _____ _____ _____ _____ stay there longer than a few months.*

❓ *What _____ _____ _____ _____ do next?*

---

b Change the sentences in the Active grammar box so that they begin with *You*, *She* and *They*.

see Reference page 33

7 Correct the sentences below. There is a word missing in each sentence.

I going to be an astronaut when I grow up.

I'm going to be an astronaut when I grow up.

1 They're going visit their son in Australia in the summer.

2 What he going to do this afternoon?

3 You going to see Sarah at the weekend?

4 We're going to tennis on Sunday morning.

5 They not going to work abroad this summer.

6 When are you to come and visit me?

7 Marie-Ann isn't going catch the train.

8 **a** Write complete sentences with *going to*.

1 I/start going to the gym.

2 Rachel/not/get a new job.

3 we/visit your parents tomorrow?

4 They/not/come to dinner next week.

5 What/you/do this weekend?

6 He/call you later.

7 Where/Peter and Tania/stay?

8 Who/tell him the news?

b **3.3** Listen and check your answers. Practise saying *going to* correctly.

Person to person

9 Tell another student three things you plan to do this week. One should be false. Your partner must decide which.

Speaking

10 **a** What are your plans for the next two years? Think about these areas of your life and make notes.

---

work   travel   hobbies and sports
home   education   friends and family

b Talk about your future plans with another student. Use the How to ... box to help you.

HOW TO …	**talk about future plans**	
	Ask someone about their plans	*What are your plans for the next two years?*
1	Describe your plans	*I'm going to learn English … I'm going to get a part-time job …*
2	Give a time reference	*… this year … next year*
3	Give a reason	*because I want to work abroad. … to earn some money.*

3.2 Big Night

Grammar	defining relative clauses
Can do	write an informal letter to a friend

Listening

1 **a** Look at the photo from the film *Big Night*. Discuss.

1 What nationality do you think the two men are?

2 What do you think is the relationship between them?

3 What do you think the film is about?

b [3.4] Listen to a conversation about the film and check your answers.

2 [3.4] Listen again and complete the notes below.

1 Name of film:
It's called 'Big Night'.

2 Time/place:
It's set in ...

3 Main characters:
It's about ...

4 Problem:
The problem is that ...

5 The plan:

3 Think of a film you like. Make notes as in Ex. 2. Tell your partner about the film. Use the phrases above.

ORIGINAL MOTION PICTURE SOUNDTRAC

Pronunciation

4 **a** You can use a good English–English dictionary to check pronunciation. How is *chocolate* pronounced? Which letter is silent?

chocolate /ˈtʃɑklət/ a sweet hard brown food: *Can I have a piece of chocolate?*

b Circle the silent letters in the words below.

spaghetti   comfortable   Wednesday   vegetable   knife   island   lamb   calm   hour   yoghurt

c [3.5] Listen and check the pronunciation.

5 **a** [3.6] Listen then repeat the sentences to your partner.

1 I had lamb in yoghurt for lunch on Wednesday.

2 Would you prefer spaghetti or vegetable soup?

3 Chocolate makes me feel calm.

4 It takes an hour to get to the island.

5 For camping holidays take comfortable shoes and a penknife.

b Can you think of more words with silent letters?

Grammar | defining relative clauses

6 Look at the examples and complete the Active grammar box with the <u>underlined</u> words.

It's about two brothers <u>who</u> live in New York.
They own a restaurant <u>which</u> isn't doing very well.
Next door to 'Paradise' there's a restaurant <u>where</u> they serve terrible Italian food.

Active grammar

Defining relative clauses give information about people, things and places.

They come directly after the noun.

Use _____ for people.

Use _____ for things.

Use _____ to say what happens in a place.

You can use *that* instead of *who* or *which* (informal).

---

see Reference page 33

7 a Complete the sentences with *who, which* or *where*.

1 This is the café _____ I always buy my lunch.
2 She's the woman _____ owns the café.
3 Is that the ring _____ your son gave you?
4 This is _____ I lived as a child.
5 You are the only person _____ has noticed my new haircut.
6 Do you have the money _____ I gave you yesterday?
7 Is she the one _____ you don't like?
8 This is _____ we first kissed.

b In which sentences above can you also use *that*?

8 a Make sentences from the prompts.

The TV programme/makes me laugh the most/ *Friends*.

The TV programme which makes me laugh the most is 'Friends'.

1 Spinach/the only vegetable/I never eat.
2 The place/I feel happiest/my bedroom.
3 The village/I was born/beautiful.
4 My sister/the only person/I tell my secrets to.
5 The music/I listen to the most/jazz.
6 The thing/I like most about myself/my hair.

b Make the sentences true for you.

Lifelong learning

Describe it!

If you don't know the name of something in English, explain what you mean with these phrases.

It's the thing that you use for eating ice cream. (spoon)
It's the stuff that you drink on special days, like weddings. (champagne).
It's the person who runs the kitchen in a restaurant. (chef)

Use *thing* for countable nouns, *stuff* for uncountable nouns and *person* for people.

---

9 Student A: look at page 125.
Student B: look at page 127.

Writing

10 Look at the Writing bank on page 145. Then complete the letter below.

Dear Tania,

Sorry for not (1) _____ recently but things have been incredibly busy. We've finally moved into the house which I told you about. It's great but it needs lots of work! We haven't been out much but we did go and see 'Big Night'. It's fantastic! Have you seen it?

The main (2) _____ I'm writing is because I'm organising a surprise party for Stephanie's birthday. We're having it at the local Spanish restaurant where I think I took you for lunch once. Anyway, if you're not doing anything on the evening of 25th (8pm), please come! We'd love to see you and catch up.

Hope (3) _____ OK with you.

Simon x

11 Read the letter again. Put the things which Simon does into the correct order.

a He gives his news
b He invites Tania to a party
c He says he hopes Tania is well
d He apologises

12 Write a short letter to a friend. Give your news and invite him/her to a party.

3.3 It's the place ...

Grammar	Present Continuous (for future arrangements)
Can do	make arrangements with a friend

Reading

1 Discuss.

    1 What are your favourite and least favourite foods?

    2 Say what you think of the foods in the photos.

2 Mark the adjectives positive (+) or negative (–). Which take *absolutely* and which take *very*?

> delicious   tasteless   tasty   disgusting
> mouth-watering   horrible

3 Read the text and answer this question.

What were the results of the research?

4 Read the text again and mark these sentences true (T) or false (F).

    1 Researchers asked the people to give the place marks out of ten.

    2 People in the residential home for the elderly liked the food.

    3 Customers in the restaurant liked the food.

    4 The place is always more important than the food.

    5 The food was exactly the same in all the different places.

    6 The food got the highest marks in the army training camp.

5 Decide on the correct meaning of the underlined words or phrases in the text.

    1 a) extremely good b) extremely bad

    2 a) times b) places

    3 how something a) tastes b) feels

    4 how something a) looks b) sounds

    5 a) a bad score b) a good score

    6 a) a meal b) a waiter

6 Discuss.

    1 Is the place you eat food important for you?

    2 Where do you eat your meals at home?

Were school dinners really so bad?

Don't spend lots of money on [1] top quality cooking; just make sure you like the place where you have it. A new report says that the enjoyment of a meal doesn't depend on what you eat, but where you eat it.

Researchers prepared the same meal in ten different [2] locations and asked the people eating it to give it marks out of ten for the taste, [3] texture and [4] appearance of the food. When they served 'chicken à la king' in a residential home for the elderly, it got [5] low marks. However, when they served it to customers in a four-star restaurant, the reaction was very different. The customers said it tasted delicious.

'The results show that in many cases the location is actually much more important than the food,' said Professor John Edwards of Bournemouth University. Edwards and his team took great care to make sure that all the meals would be as similar as possible. They used exactly the same kind of chicken, they stored the dishes in the same kind of plastic bags and served them all with the same type of rice. The meal got the highest marks in every category – taste, texture, appearance – at the restaurant. Interestingly, bottom marks went to the [6] dish when they served it in an army training camp. As one of the soldiers said, 'It tastes awful and smells disgusting!'

(adapted from *The Week*)

Vocabulary | sense verbs

7 Match the sentences below to the pictures.

1 This **tastes** delicious! ☐
2 You **look** nice! ☐
3 That **sounds** awful! ☐
4 You **feel** hot! ☐
5 This doesn't **smell** great. ☐

A

B

C

D

E

8 Use *look, sound, smell, taste* and *feel* to give your opinion about the following.

> fresh coffee   being in love
> a Ferrari   Madonna
> your shoes   old milk
> chillies   cigarettes

I love fresh coffee, but it smells better than it tastes.

Grammar | Present Continuous for future arrangements

9 **a** **3.7** Listen to the dialogue. What arrangement does the woman have for this evening?

b Listen again and complete the Active grammar box.

Active grammar

Form the Present Continuous with: *be* + verb + *-ing*

What _____ you doing tonight?

I _____ going out for dinner with Marcin.

He _____ coming with us.

Use the Present Continuous to talk about future arrangements (a time and place is decided).

Use *going to* when you have a plan or intention but no arrangement yet.

---

see Reference page 33

10 **a** Make sentences using the Present Continuous.

1 I/not do/anything/tonight.
2 Karen/go to a restaurant/next week.
3 He/not go out/this weekend.
4 We/watch TV/at home/tonight.
5 they/spend this summer/by the beach?
6 I/play football/tomorrow night.

b Make the sentences above true for you or your classmates.

Patricia isn't doing anything tonight.

Speaking

11 Look at the How to ... box. Think of other phrases to replace the <u>underlined</u> ones.

HOW TO ... **make arrangements**

A Check if someone is free	<u>*What are you doing on*</u> *Friday night?*
B Reply	*Nothing. Why?* *I'm busy, I'm afraid. I'm <u>seeing Jo</u>.*
A Make a suggestion	<u>*Why don't we*</u> *try the Indian restaurant?*
B Accept/reject	<u>*Great idea!*</u> *Oh! I'm <u>not very keen on</u> Italian food.*
A Arrange to meet	<u>*I can meet you*</u> *at the restaurant at 7p.m.*
B Confirm	*Perfect!* *8p.m. <u>would be better for me</u>.*

---

12 Write your diary for next weekend. Then make arrangements with three different classmates.

3 | Communication

Design a restaurant

1 Tell other students about one of your favourite restaurants. Describe:

- the kind and quality of food
- the size of the restaurant
- the quality of service
- the prices
- the kind of people who go there and the general atmosphere

2 **a** **3.8** Listen to a man talking about his plans. What is he going to do?

b Listen again and complete the tasks.

1 Mark the following things on the plan of the restaurant below.

> toilets   kitchen   restaurant area
> main entrance

2 Complete the menu opposite.

THE *art* RESTAURANT

Starters

Goat's cheese salad

Garlic mushrooms on toast

Main courses

Vegetarian pasta

Roast chicken and vegetables of the day

Desserts

Apple tart with cream / ice cream

Cheese and biscuits

3 **a** Work in groups. You're going to open a new restaurant. Discuss the following:

- the location
- what size and how the space is going to be organised
- the name of the restaurant
- decoration
- a sample menu
- any special features
- prices
- what kind of music (if any)
- how to attract clients

b Tell other groups your ideas. Vote for the group with the best chance of success.

going to (future plans)

Use *going to* to talk about something you intend or plan to do (you have already decided to do it).

A: *Are you going to see Sally this week?*

B: *I don't know. I'm going to phone her this evening.*

+	I He/She/It We/You/They	am is are	going to	see Maria on Saturday.
−	I He/She/It We/You/They	am is are	not going to	
?	Am Is Are	I he/she/it we/you/they	going to	see her?

Yes, I am./No, I'm not.

We often use future time expressions with *going to* (*this afternoon, tonight, tomorrow, next week*, etc.).

Defining relative clauses

Defining relative clauses give us more information about a noun.

They answer the questions: *Which person? Which thing? Which place?*

Defining relative clauses come immediately after the noun in the main clause.

Use *who* to talk about people, *which* to talk about things and *where* to talk about places.

This is the book which you want.

She's the teacher who I like.

That's the shop where I bought these shoes.

That can be used instead of *who* or *which*.

The young man that/who I work with never stops talking.

Tom bought the jacket that/which we saw yesterday.

! Don't use commas before or after defining relative clauses.

Present Continuous (future arrangements)

Use the Present Continuous to talk about personal arrangements or fixed plans. They often involve other people and the time/place has been arranged.

When are you starting your new job?

She isn't coming to my birthday party.

+	I He/She/It We/You/They	am is are	meeting	Alan at 7p.m.
−	I He/She/It We/You/They	am is are	not meeting	
?	Am Is Are	I he/she/it we/you/they	meeting	him?

Yes, I am./No, I'm not.

! *Going to* and the Present Continuous can be used to express similar ideas. Choose depending on what you mean.

I'm going to see Phil again. (a decision has been made but no arrangement)

I'm going to see Phil tonight at the tennis club. (an arrangement has been made with Phil)

With the verbs *go* and *come*, we usually use the Present Continuous.

I am going to Australia as soon as I have saved enough money.

Key vocabulary

Food and drink

tomato   onion   ice cream   mineral water
orange juice   lamb   spaghetti   chocolate
vegetable   yoghurt

Cooking and eating

cook for yourself   give (something) up   eat out
celebrity chef   diet (noun)   vegetarian
top-class chef

Adjectives

delicious   tasteless   tasty   disgusting
mouth-watering   horrible

Sense verbs

look   feel   sound   smell   taste

1 Answer the questions below with *going to* and the word in brackets.

Have you finished the report? *(tomorrow)*

No, I'm going to finish it tomorrow.

1 Have you had something to eat? (later)
2 Have you taken the dog for a walk? (after dinner)
3 Have you bought Mary a birthday present? (at the weekend)
4 Have you painted the spare bedroom? (on Tuesday)
5 Have you cleaned the bathroom? (in the morning)

2 Make questions with *going to* for each situation.

Your friend tells you that she is going into town.

What *are you going to* buy?

1 Your friend has said he definitely wants to give up smoking.
   When _____?
2 Peter tells you that it's Jane's birthday next week.
   Are _____ present?
3 Your friend has bought a painting.
   _____ put it?
4 You see a friend filling a bucket with hot water.
   Are _____ car?

3 Make one sentence from two. Use *who, which* or *where*. (You may sometimes need to leave out a word.)

This is the car. I would like to buy it.

This is the car which I would like to buy.

1 A waiter brought us our food. He was very friendly.
   The _____.
2 This is a restaurant. John asked me to marry him here.
   This _____.
3 A train goes to the airport. It runs every twenty minutes.
   The _____.
4 Some men robbed the post office. They escaped in a black BMW.
   The _____.
5 This is the corner of the road. The accident happened here.
   This _____.

4 Find and correct four Present Continuous mistakes in this conversation.

A: Hi Tim! What do you do this evening?
B: Not a lot. Actually, I'm probably have a quiet evening at home alone.
A: Why don't you come round to my house? I inviting a few friends over for dinner.
B: I'm not sure. I'm quite tired.
A: How about tomorrow night?
B: I'm go to see a film with my brother. Why don't you come too?
A: Great! I'd love to.

5 Look at the diary extract. Write complete sentences about what the person is doing on each day.

She's having a day off on Monday.

Monday

DAY OFF!   11am Dentist
           2pm lunch with Jenny
           6.30 pm Italian class

Tuesday

10am presentation to Sales Reps.
3pm meeting with Marketing Director.
6pm phone USA office
8pm cinema with Nathan

6 Choose the correct word or phrase to complete the sentences.

tasty   vegetarian   ~~disgusting~~   recipe
cooker   low marks   work abroad   chef
smells

Yuk! This food is absolutely *disgusting*.

1 We've just bought a new electric_____.
2 Who is the new _____ at that restaurant?
3 I want to be a _____ but I like meat too much.
4 I'd love to _____ – perhaps in New York.
5 That meal gets _____ from me. It was horrible!
6 That looks very _____. Can I have some?
7 It _____ great. How does it taste?
8 I'm cooking for Ruth tonight. Do you know a _____ for chicken and spinach?

4 Survival

Lead-in

1   Describe the photos. What words do you associate with each?

sailing: sea, cold, boat, loneliness

2   **a**   Match the phrases in the box with the definitions.

> physical/mental strength   control your fear   rely on
> a challenge   achieve your goal

1   _____ : make yourself feel less frightened
2   _____ : succeed in getting the result you wanted or hoped for
3   _____ : something new, exciting or difficult to do
4   _____ : trust or depend on someone or something
5   _____ : the physical or mental ability to deal with difficult situations

b   **4.1**   Listen and check your answers.

3   Discuss.

1   Which activities in the photos need a) mental strength, b) physical strength or c) both?
2   What are you afraid of? E.g. flying, crowded places, heights, etc. Do you do anything to help control your fear? If yes, what?
3   What are your goals at the moment? How will you achieve them?
4   Do you enjoy a challenge at work/in your leisure time?
5   Who or what do you rely on most in times of need?

Reading

1 Look at the people in the photos and the headings in the text. What goals do you think they achieved? Read the text and check your ideas.

Going UP

Most people can hold their breath long enough to dive to the bottom of a swimming pool, but on 17 August 2002, Tanya Streeter went a lot, lot deeper. The 29-year-old held her breath for 3 minutes 26 seconds and became the world free-diving champion. She dived 160 metres below the surface of the sea (that's further than three football pitches). During the dive her lungs shrank[2] to the size of oranges. Her heart slowed to fifteen beats a minute and she sang her national anthem in her head to control her fear. Tanya says that her mental strength is more important than her physical strength. 'I am a very determined person. When I decide to do something, I do it. "Redefine your limits" is my motto[3].'

In 1953, Sir Edmund Hillary and Tenzing Norgay climbed to the top of Mount Everest. The next challenge was to climb it without bottled oxygen. This was the goal of Austrian climbers Peter Habeler and Reinhold Messner. Doctors said they were crazy and told them not to try it. They tried it anyway.
On 8 May 1978, they were about 800 metres from the top of Everest. They woke at 3a.m. and began preparing. It took them two hours to get dressed. Every breath was precious[1] and they used their hands to communicate. Climbing was slow. Messner thought he was going to burst like a balloon. At 8,800 metres, they stopped and lay down every few steps because of the lack of oxygen. But between one and two in the afternoon they achieved their 'impossible' goal. They reached the top of Mount Everest without oxygen.

Going DOWN

Glossary
[1] *precious* = very valuable and important
[2] *to shrink* (Past = *shrank*) = to get smaller
[3] *motto* = a phrase that expresses your beliefs

2 Read the text again. Mark the statements true (T), false (F) or don't know (?).

1 Habeler and Messner didn't listen to their doctors. ☐
2 It took them two hours to go 800 metres. ☐
3 The main problem was breathing. ☐
4 They were given an award for their achievement. ☐
5 Tanya Streeter holds the world record for holding her breath. ☐
6 She has a good trainer. ☐
7 She was afraid during her dive. ☐
8 She didn't know how to control her fear. ☐
9 She feels that being physically strong isn't the most important thing. ☐

3 Discuss.

How would you feel about diving a long way under the sea and climbing a mountain like Mount Everest?

Vocabulary | describing people

4 **a** Replace the <u>underlined</u> phrases with the verb *to be* and an adjective from the box.

> determined intelligent confident ~~brave~~ ambitious generous talented reliable

My brother <u>isn't afraid of anything</u>. His hobby is mountain climbing.

My brother *is brave*. His hobby is mountain climbing.

1 My aunt <u>gives her time and money to other people</u>. She gave me £200 at Christmas!

2 Jane <u>feels sure</u> that she will pass her end-of-year exams.

3 Sarah <u>can understand things quickly</u>. She's got lots of qualifications.

4 Petra <u>always does what she says she will do</u>. She won't be late.

5 Joe <u>wants to be successful and powerful</u>. He wants to be a manager.

6 My dad <u>never lets anyone/anything stop him</u>. He's decided to run a marathon and I'm sure he'll do it.

7 Sam <u>has a lot of natural ability</u> as a writer. She won a short story competition in June.

b **4.2** Listen and check your answers.

5 **a** Tell another student about people you know who have each of the characteristics above.

My friend's really generous. He always lends me money.

b What kind of people do you think a) Habeler and Messner and b) Tanya Streeter are? What words do you think describe them?

Grammar | comparatives

6 Look at these sentences and discuss how you make comparative forms. Then complete the Active grammar box.

*Habeler and Messner are **stronger** and **fitter than** most people.*

*Free-diving is **more dangerous than** you think.*

Active grammar

	Adjective	Comparative
One-syllable adjectives	*long* *big*	*longer (than)* *bigger (than)*
Two-syllable adjectives	*boring*	_____
Two-syllable adjectives ending in -y	_____	*happier (than)*
Three-syllable adjectives	*interesting*	_____
Irregular adjectives	_____ *good*	*worse (than)* _____
Modifiers	_____	*(a bit/much) taller (than)*
(not) as... as	*kind*	*(not) as kind as*

see Reference page 43

7 Make the comparative form of the adjectives in Ex. 4.

reliable – more reliable than

8 **a** Compare the pictures below. Make two sentences about each. Use the words in the box and *a bit/much* and *not as ... as*.

> tall expensive funny

b **4.3** Listen and check your answers.

c Listen again. What do you notice about the pronunciation of *than* and *as*? Repeat the sentences with good pronunciation.

Person to person

9 Work with another student. Find five differences between you. Tell other students. Use comparatives.

She is quieter than I am.

Vocabulary | survival skills

1 **a** Match a word or phrase in the box with the underlined words or phrases below.

> abilities   deal with
> place to sleep outside
> try very hard   nature
> something difficult to do

1 How long do you think you could survive in the wilderness?

2 What survival skills do you have?

3 Could you build a shelter in a forest?

4 What is the biggest challenge in your life at the moment?

5 Do you always push yourself in difficult situations?

6 Do you cope with new situations well (e.g. living in a different city)?

b In pairs, ask and answer the questions above.

Listening

2 **a** Look at the advert. What do you think a survival school is?

b [4.4] Listen to a talk by David Johnson, the chief instructor at the Hillside Survival School. Check your answer to Ex. 2a.

3 [4.4] Listen again and complete the notes opposite.

4 Discuss.

1 Would you like to go on one of the courses at the Hillside Survival School? Why/Why not?

2 How would you feel about doing the activities you can see in the photos?

Hillside SURVIVAL SCHOOL
Learn to cope in the wilderness!

THE HILLSIDE SURVIVAL SCHOOL – David Johnson

David's previous work: (1) _____
His 'aims': help people discover nature/outdoor life;
2) _____

Basic survival course:
How long for? (3) _____
When does it take place? (4) _____
Cost? (5) _____

Extreme survival course:
When does it take place? (6) _____
Cost? (7) _____

Minimum age: (8) _____
Full payment by: (9) _____
Discounts for: (10) _____

Grammar | superlatives

5 Read these notes about the courses. Does each person feel positive or negative?

A big thank-you for helping to make it the <u>most exciting</u> birthday I've ever had! I would love to do it again.

Chris

Hi David

Just a quick email to say we really enjoyed the weekend. It was probably the <u>hardest</u> thing we've ever done but it was also great fun. Thanks a million for an experience we will never forget (even though you said our shelter was the <u>worst</u> you've ever seen)! □

Best wishes,

Catherine and Emma

I had a fantastic time. I enjoyed it a lot more than I expected and learnt a great deal. I think David's the <u>best</u> teacher in the world!

Dorinda

6 Look at the <u>underlined</u> words in Ex. 5. How do you form superlatives? Complete the Active grammar box.

Active grammar

Short adjectives (one syllable) =
(*the*) + adjective + _____

Long adjectives (two or more syllables) =
(*the*) + _____ + adjective

Two-syllable adjectives ending in -*y* =
(*the*) + adjective without -*y* + -*iest*

Irregular adjectives:

good = _____   *bad* = _____

Before superlatives we use *the* or a possessive adjective.

the oldest building
my best friend

After superlatives we normally use *in* before the names of places and groups of people. In most other cases we use *of*.

see Reference page 43

7 Find and correct two mistakes in each sentence.

1 Simon is most experienced person of our office.
2 Which is the large city of Africa?
3 Today is the most hot day on the year.
4 My sister is the intelligentest person at our family.
5 This is the more valuable in all the paintings.
6 Tim is the fitter player at our team.

8 **a** Turn to page 37. Make the superlative form of the adjectives in Ex. 4a.

b Write sentences using the superlative form of the adjectives.

This/comfortable chair/the house.

This is the most comfortable chair in the house.

1 This/exciting holiday/I ever have.
2 Everest/high/mountain/the world.
3 What/good department store/New York?
4 This/wet day/the year so far.
5 This/boring film/ever see.
6 Football/popular sport/Brazil.
7 This/difficult exam/I ever take.

Pronunciation

9 **a** <u>Underline</u> the words in each sentence in Ex. 8b which would normally be stressed.

This the most <u>comfortable</u> <u>chair</u> in the <u>house</u>.

b **4.5** Listen and check your answers.

Person to person

10 Discuss.

1 What is the most dangerous situation you have ever been in? What happened?
2 What is the most interesting place you have been to?
3 Who is your best friend? Why is he/she your best friend?
4 Who is the most famous person you have ever met or known?

Writing

11 **a** Look at the thank-you notes in Ex. 5. Write down the useful phrases that could be used in any thank-you note.

A big thank-you for ...

b Think of a real reason for a thank-you note. Write the thank-you note.

Reading

1 a What words come to mind when you think about the English?

b Read the text. Circle the topics in the box which are mentioned.

> drinking tea   football   English food
> driving habits   being polite   libraries
> the weather

Looking at ... England

There are ideas about England and the English which are just not true. England does not stop for afternoon tea every day, although the English do drink a lot of the liquid (hot, with milk) and although the weather is very changeable, it doesn't rain all the time!

Also, there's lots of good food in England. No, really! In the major cities you'll be spoilt for choice, with the cuisine of almost every nationality on offer. Indian food is a particular favourite of the English. To find proper English food, try eating in a traditional pub.

The famous English politeness is everywhere. The English use 'Please', 'Thank you' and 'Sorry' more than most nationalities. For example, if you step on someone's foot, they'll probably say 'Sorry' to you! If you make a complaint, it's also usual to begin with 'Sorry' as in: 'I'm sorry, but this soup is cold.'

You may think it strange on the London Underground that people don't talk to each other, even when crowded together in the rush hour. Silence is usual as people read their books or newspapers. That doesn't mean English people are unfriendly. It just means you might have to get to know them first!

2 Read the text again. Mark the statements true (T) or false (F).

1 The English don't like their tea to be hot.
2 You get a lot of different types of weather in England.
3 Indian food is very popular in England.
4 You can only find typical English food in good English restaurants.
5 The English often use 'Sorry' to begin a complaint.
6 The English like to talk to people they don't know on the Underground.

3 Did anything in the text surprise you? Tell your partner.

Lifelong learning

Survival tips

How can you survive in English outside the classroom? If you want to use/understand English, where can you go for help? Tell other students.

I can ask my friend. He's very good at English!

Listening

4 **4.6** Listen to five dialogues. Match each one to a situation.

> in a restaurant   in a clothes shop
> on a bus   in a bank   in a taxi

5 a **4.6** Listen again and answer the questions.

Dialogue 1: Where does she want to go? What does she ask the driver?

Dialogue 2: What does the customer ask for? What does the assistant do?

Dialogue 3: What does the customer want to know? What does the customer decide to do?

Dialogue 4: Where does the passenger want to go? What does she offer to do?

Dialogue 5: What does the customer ask for? How does she want to pay?

b Look at the tapescripts on p.156. Practise saying them with another student.

6 Choose a different situation and write a short conversation.

Grammar | indirect questions

7 Look at the Active grammar box. Complete rules a) and b) and answer questions 1–2 below.

Active grammar

Use indirect questions when you want to be polite.

Direct question	Indirect question
How far **is** the station?	Do you know how far the station **is**?
Where **can** I **get** a taxi?	Can you tell me where I **can get** a taxi?
What time **does** the train **arrive**?	Do you know what time the train **arrives**?
Is the museum open?	Do you know **if** the museum **is** open?

a) Questions with verb *to be*:

Direct: question word/phrase + verb *to be* + subject

Indirect: indirect phrase + question word + _____ + _____

b) Questions with main verbs:

Direct: question word + auxiliary verb + subject + verb

Indirect: indirect phrase + question word + _____ + _____

1 What happens to the auxiliaries *do/does/did*?

2 How do you make *Yes/No* questions indirect?

---

see reference page 43

8 a Make these questions indirect. Use the words in brackets.

How long does the journey take? (Do/know?)

Do you know how long the journey takes?

1 How much is that? (Can/tell?)

2 Where can I get an application form? (Do/know?)

3 Do you have any 1st class stamps? (Can/tell?)

4 How far is it to the library? (Do/know?)

5 Is there a post office near here? (Can/tell?)

6 What's the time? (Do/know?)

7 Where do I get off the bus? (Can/tell?)

b **4.7** Listen and check your answers. Repeat them with similar intonation.

Speaking

9 a You're going to do a survey for a market research company. With a partner, choose a topic for the research from the box.

> free-time activities   holidays   Internet use   shopping   food   favourite films

b Write questions for your survey.

Can you tell me what you do in your free time?

c Look at the How to ... box, then conduct your survey.

HOW TO ... be polite in English

Use polite words/phrases	*Excuse me, could I ask you a few questions?*
	Sorry, but I don't think you understood my question.
	Can you say that again, please?
Use indirect questions	*Can you tell me what kinds of films you like?*

---

10 Report your findings to the class.

Maria uses the Internet every day.

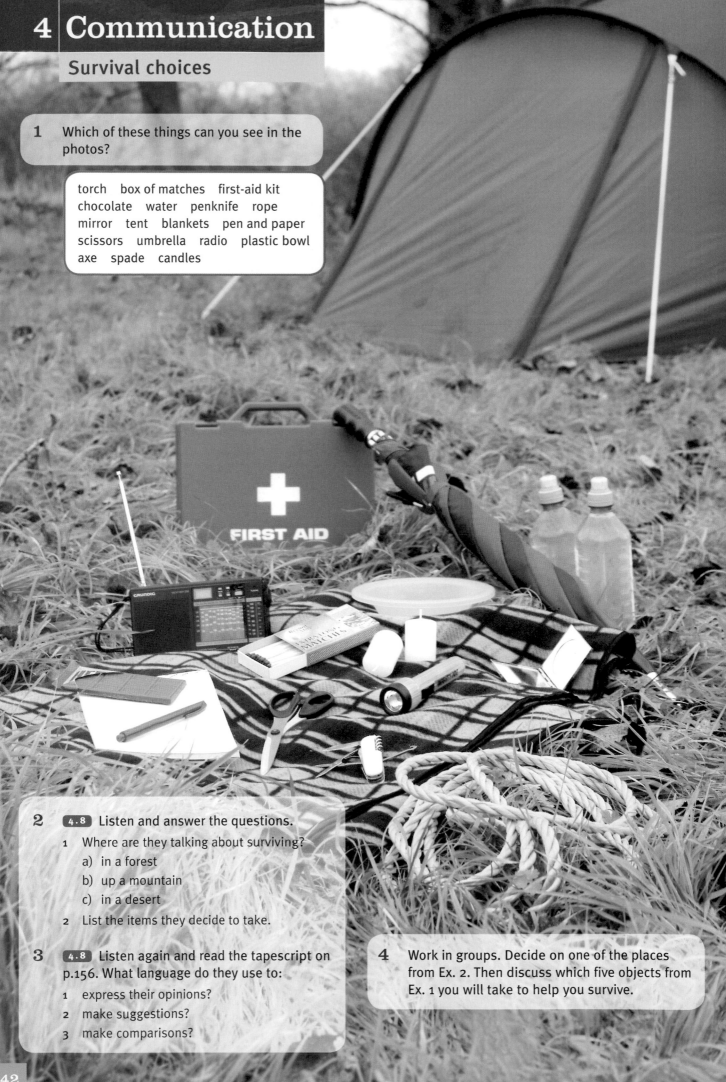

4 Communication

Survival choices

1 Which of these things can you see in the photos?

> torch   box of matches   first-aid kit
> chocolate   water   penknife   rope
> mirror   tent   blankets   pen and paper
> scissors   umbrella   radio   plastic bowl
> axe   spade   candles

2 **4.8** Listen and answer the questions.

1 Where are they talking about surviving?
   a) in a forest
   b) up a mountain
   c) in a desert
2 List the items they decide to take.

3 **4.8** Listen again and read the tapescript on p.156. What language do they use to:

1 express their opinions?
2 make suggestions?
3 make comparisons?

4 Work in groups. Decide on one of the places from Ex. 2. Then discuss which five objects from Ex. 1 you will take to help you survive.

Comparatives and superlatives

One-syllable adjectives

Adjective	Comparative	Superlative	Spelling
hard	harder (than)	the hardest	ends in consonant: + -er; the -est
nice brave	nicer (than) braver (than)	the nicest the bravest	ends in -e: + -r; the -est
fit big	fitter bigger	the fittest the biggest	vowel + consonant: double consonant

Their garden is **larger than** ours.

Brian is **the thinnest** boy in the class.

Two- or more syllable adjectives

Adjective	Comparative	Superlative	Spelling
happy easy	happier (than) easier (than)	the happiest the easiest	two syllables ends in -y: y changes to i
boring interesting	more boring (than) more interesting (than)	the most boring the most interesting	two or more syllables: no change

The beach is **more crowded than** yesterday.

It's **the easiest** way to do it.

She is **the most famous** person I know.

Irregular adjectives

Adjective	Comparative	Superlative
bad	worse (than)	(the) worst
good	better (than)	(the) best
little	less (than)	(the) least
far	farther/further (than)	(the) farthest/furthest

(not) as ... as

We can also make comparisons with *(not) as ... as*.

Marta is **as tall as** Tom but she isn't **as tall as** Rachel.

Before superlatives

We use *the* or a possessive adjective.

the least expensive

my oldest son

After superlatives

We usually use *in* with places and groups of people:

Which is the highest mountain **in** the world?

Who is the youngest manager **in** the company?

We use *of* in most other cases:

She is the cleverest **of** my three sisters.

We often use the Present Perfect Simple:

He's the most interesting person I'**ve** ever **met**.

Indirect questions

Use indirect questions to make a question more polite.

*Who are **those people**?*

***Can you tell me** who **those people** are?*

*When will **you** arrive?*

***Do you know** when **you** will arrive?*

! Use the word order of positive statements.

Can you tell me what time this shop opens?

! Do not use the auxiliaries *do/does/ did*.

How much do the tickets cost?

Do you know how much the tickets cost?

Use *if* or *whether* for indirect *Yes/No* questions.

*Do you know **if/whether** Mr Barnard is in his office?*

Key vocabulary

Survival

achieve your goal   challenge   control your fear
cope with new situations   physical/mental strength
push yourself   rely on   shelter   skills
survive in the wilderness

Survival equipment

axe   blankets   box of matches   candles
first-aid kit   mirror   penknife   tent   torch   rope
scissors   spade

Describing people

ambitious   brave   confident   determined
generous   intelligent   reliable   talented

4 Review and practice

1 Complete these sentences with comparatives. Use the adjectives in the box.

> quiet   bad   exciting   ~~old~~   far   happy

Her CV says she is only twenty-three years old. I thought she was _older_.

1 This café is very noisy. Can we go somewhere _____?
2 That film sounds really boring. *Murder city* sounds _____.
3 My job is quite good. It could be a lot _____.
4 You seem _____ today – you looked quite sad yesterday.
5 The house was _____ from the station than I thought.

2 Complete the sentences below with a comparative and *not as ... as*.

Sarah is 1.65 metres. I am 1.70 metres. (tall)
I'm _taller than_ Sarah. Sarah _isn't as tall as me_.

1 The gold watch is €180. The silver watch is €100. (expensive)
The gold watch ... . The silver watch ... .
2 The Brighton train leaves at 3.30p.m. The London train leaves at 3p.m. (late)
The Brighton train ... . The London train ... .
3 Health is very important to me. Money is not very important to me. (important)
Health ... . Money ... .
4 White bread tastes good. Brown bread tastes very good. (good)
Brown bread ... . White bread ... .

3 Complete these sentences with superlatives. Use the adjectives in the box.

> tall   friendly   expensive   fast   ~~long~~   hot

It's _the longest_ film I've ever seen. It lasted for four hours!

1 This jacket cost €350. It was _____ one in the shop!
2 August is usually _____ month in the UK. The temperature goes up to around 24 °C.
3 Sam is _____ boy in the class. He is nearly two metres tall.
4 This is _____ car I've ever had. It goes from 0–100 kilometres per hour in seven seconds.
5 Michael is _____ man I've ever met. He loves to meet new people.

4 Complete the sentences using *one of* + a superlative + *in/of*.

She's a very funny person. She's _one of the funniest people in_ *my family*.

1 It was a very hot day. It was _____ the year.
2 Susie's a very good swimmer. She's _____ Scotland.
3 Harry's an intelligent boy. He's _____ his school.
4 It's a very old house. It's _____ the town.
5 It was a bad shock. It was _____ my life.
6 Marcos is a really brave soldier. He's _____ the army.

5 Add a word to each sentence to make it correct.

Can you tell me where the bathroom ⌃*is*?
1 You know why he isn't home yet?
2 Do you know I can pay by credit card?
3 Can you tell me I can find a garage?
4 Can you tell whose car this is, please?
5 Do you know time the next train for Manchester leaves?

6 Ask about the following things using *Do you know ...?* or *Can you tell me ...?*

What time/shops close?
Do you know what time the shops close?
1 where/find/cheap hotel?
2 Internet café/near here?
3 how much/taxi to the airport?
4 where/I/buy/map of Britain?
5 need visa/go to Ireland?

7 Complete the sentences using the words or phrases below. There are four extra words.

> intelligent   reliable   brave   ~~challenge~~
> achieve my goal   skills   torch   tent
> scissors   shelter

John likes to have a new _challenge_ to stop him getting bored.

1 Oh no! My _____ isn't working. I forgot to get new batteries.
2 My car is very _____. It never breaks down.
3 I'd like to _____ of cycling across Germany by the end of next year.
4 Have you got any _____? I want to cut this string.
5 What are the main _____ that you need to survive in the desert?

5 | Stages

Lead-in

1 Look at the photos. What are they doing? How old are the people?

They are getting married.
She's in her early/late/mid-twenties, thirties.

2 **a** What do you think the age range is for each time of life?

A baby is from birth to about one year old.

> baby   toddler   child   teenager   adult   (be) middle-aged
> pensioner   (be) old/elderly

b Compare with a partner. Do you agree?

3 What is the typical age in your country to do the things below?

> have children   rebel against your parents   get a job
> get engaged   have your first kiss   look after your grandchildren
> retire   get married   graduate from university
> earn a good salary   learn to drive a car   get a place of your own

4 Describe your life or the life of an older person.

My grandmother was born in Seville in 1942. When she was a child,
she moved to Madrid. She lived there until her twenties and got
married at twenty-six.

5.1 Turning eighteen

Grammar	*should, can, have to*
Can do	exchange opinions with a friend

Reading

1 Discuss.
1 What has/have been the best year(s) of your life so far? Why?
2 Describe the situations in the photos. Have you ever had similar experiences?

2 **a** Work in groups of three. Read your text and tick (✓) the subjects mentioned.
Student A: read about Wong Fei below.
Student B: read about Isabel on page 125.
Student C: read about Gregor on page 130.

	WONG FEI	ISABEL	GREGOR
the army			
education			
free time			
career			
money			
family			

b Take turns to tell your partners about your text. Listen and complete the table for the other two people.

3 Discuss.
1 Who has the hardest life: Wong Fei, Isabel or Gregor? Why?
2 Who has the easiest life? Why?
3 Who are you most similar to?
4 What were you doing when you were eighteen?

FROM ADOLESCENT TO ADULT

Fei is an only child and lives with her family in Shanghai. She is studying law at Jiaotong University and she will turn eighteen in a few weeks.

My goals are to get my degree, to go to England to study marketing and then to come back and find a good job. China is changing and you can get rich now in China.

When I'm earning a good salary, I'd like to do more travelling but I have to take care of my parents too. They're going to retire soon. They've given me a good life and I have to do the same for them. This is the way things are in China and it should be the same everywhere.

Normally, when you get married, you're only allowed to have one child. However, because I'm an only child, I can have two children if I marry another only child. Anyway, at the moment it's all a dream because I'm single.

I like reading stories on the Internet. I also like reading fashion magazines like *Vogue*. Perhaps my favourite thing is to go shopping with friends. We don't have much money but it's fun to look in the windows and think about what we're going to buy when we are rich!

Wong Fei, China

Grammar | *should, can, have to*

4 Read the sentences in the Active grammar box and complete the explanations.

> ### Active grammar
>
> I **have to** take care of them.
> I **don't have to** share my bedroom.
> You **can** earn more money abroad.
> My parents **can't** afford that.
> It **should** be the same everywhere.
> She **shouldn't** do this but she enjoys it.
>
> ### Explanations
>
> Use _____ to say something is possible.
> Use _____ to say something is necessary.
> Use _____ to say something is a good idea. (opinion)
> Use _____ to say something is not possible.
> Use _____ to say something is not necessary.
> Use _____ to say something is not a good idea. (opinion)

see Reference page 53

5 Choose the best alternatives.

1 I *can't/don't have to* go out. I'm too busy.
2 We *don't have to/can't* catch a taxi. I'll drive.
3 I *have to/can* go into the army for a year. I don't have a choice.
4 You *shouldn't/don't have to* smoke during meals – it's annoying.
5 I *should/have to* do more exercise. I'm putting on weight.
6 You *can/should* see the doctor at 5p.m. on Thursday. That's the earliest time she is free.

6 Complete these sentences with *should(n't)*, *can('t)* or *(don't) have to*.

I *have to* get good grades so I can go to college.

1 You _____ spend the night at my flat. We have a spare bedroom.
2 Young people in my country _____ do military service. It stopped last year.
3 I think everyone _____ vote at elections. It's our duty as citizens.
4 Maria _____ come if she doesn't want to.
5 I think people _____ come to work in jeans. It looks really bad.
6 In the UK children _____ stay at school until they're sixteen. It's the law.

Pronunciation

7 [5.1] Listen to these sentences.

1 She <u>shouldn't</u> ask that.
2 She <u>shouldn't</u> do that.
3 I <u>can't</u> afford that.
4 I <u>can't</u> buy that.

Is the final *t* of *shouldn' t* and *can' t* pronounced:
a) before a word that starts with a vowel?
b) before a word that starts with a consonant?

8 Make sentences about your country using the prompts. Include your opinion.

people/vote

In Poland, people can vote when they are eighteen years old but they don' t have to vote. I think everyone should vote.

1 children/help with the housework
2 people/look after their parents
3 teenagers/pay to go to university
4 children/leave school

Listening and speaking

9 [5.2] Listen to two dialogues. Which statements are they discussing?

1 Eighteen is too young to get married.
2 Teenagers only worry about girlfriends/ boyfriends and money.
3 Young people should do military service.

10 [5.2] Listen again. Tick (✓) any phrases in the How to... box that you hear.

HOW TO...	**exchange opinions with a friend**	
	1 Give your opinion	*I think /I don't think ...* *In my opinion ...*
	2 Explain why	*because ...* *I mean ...*
	3 Ask for an opinion	*What do you think?* *Don't you think so?*
	4 Agree/ disagree	*I don't know.* *I'm not so sure ...* *You're probably right ...*

11 Choose a statement from Ex. 9. Exchange opinions with a partner.

5.2 Old friends

Grammar	Present Perfect Simple with *for* and *since*
Can do	write a personal profile

Grammar | Present Perfect Simple with *for* and *since*

1 Read this extract from a website. What is its purpose?

 **Friends Together**

Member profile | Contact options | Search

Tina Armstrong

What I'm doing now

Since I left school, I've travelled a bit and had a few different jobs including working on a cruise ship in the Caribbean. <u>I've worked for the same company for the last two years</u> and I really like it. It's a big advertising firm and I'm an Accounts Manager.

I've lived in Birmingham since 2002 and have a lovely flat near the centre which I share with Gerald, my cat!

I haven't seen anyone from school for ages, so send me a message. I'd love to hear from you!

Send an email to Tina
Send an ecard to Tina
Send a voice message to Tina

2 Look at the <u>underlined</u> words in the text and answer the questions.

1 When did Tina start her job?
2 Does she still work there?

3 Complete the Active grammar box with the past participle of the verbs in brackets.

Active grammar

Form the Present Perfect Simple with:
subject + *have/has* + past participle

➕ : *My dad has _____ (be) in hospital **for** a week.*

➖ : *We haven't _____ (see) her **since** university.*

❓ : *Have you _____ (live) in Paris **for** long?*

Complete the rules below with *for* or *since*.

1 Use _____ to refer to the start of the action.

2 Use _____ to refer to the time period of the action.

see Reference page 53 and irregular verb list page 149

4 **a** Read the dialogue between Tina and an old friend, Martin. Complete using *for* or *since*.

Tina: I'm so glad you emailed. It's been ages (1) _____ I saw you!

Martin: I know. Well, I've been in Poland (2) _____ almost two years. I'm teaching English there.

Tina: So, are you enjoying it?

Martin: Yes, it's great. Especially (3) _____ I met this woman called Dorota. We've known each other (4) _____ about six months now. She works in the same school as me.

Tina: Oh! That's great … so, when are you both coming to the UK?

b **5.3** Listen and check your answers.

5 Write replies using the words in brackets.

Do you often go to the theatre? (No/ages)

No, I haven't been for ages.

1 Do you often see Sarah? (No/last Christmas)
2 Do you usually have a summer holiday? (No/years)
3 Do you often play tennis? (No/last summer)
4 Do you usually work at the weekend? (No/months)

Person to person

6 Choose three things/people from the box below. Tell another student how long you have known the people or had the things.

> your best friend   your shoes   your teacher   your watch
> your oldest friend   your mobile phone   your doctor

Vocabulary | friendship

7 Match the words or phrases in A with the correct definition in B.

A	B
1 a colleague	a) have a good relationship
2 an old school friend	b) someone you work with
3 get in touch	c) have no more contact
4 go out (with someone)	d) start having contact
5 get on well (with someone)	e) someone you were at school with
6 lose touch	f) have a romantic relationship

8 Complete Tina's story with the correct form of the words or phrases from Ex. 7. Use one of the words or phrases twice.

> Martin is (1) _____ of mine. I first met him at secondary school. We (2) _____. In fact, we were best friends. But then, when I went to university we (3) _____ and I didn't hear from him for ages. About a year ago, I registered with *Friends Together*. Martin saw my profile and (4) _____ again. He was in Poland at that time and he (5) _____ with a woman called Dorota. She was his (6) _____ – they worked at the same school. Their relationship didn't last and Martin moved back to the UK. We've seen each other a few times. Martin says he'd like us to (7) _____ with each other but I'm not sure. I think he needs more time to forget about Dorota.

9 Work with a partner. Look at the pictures. Decide on a possible order.

10 Take it in turns to tell your partner the story. Try and use the phrases from Ex. 7.

Writing

11 Read Tina's profile in Ex. 1 again. Which of the following topics does she mention?

> friends she's in touch with
> work/study   relationships
> free-time activities   home
> hopes for the future

12 Write your own profile. First make notes about what information you want to include. Then write your profile.

> Since school:
>
> Free time ⟨ learned to ski
>   played in band
>
> Study ⟨ Business Studies
>   English (school in UK)
>
> Relationships – got engaged!

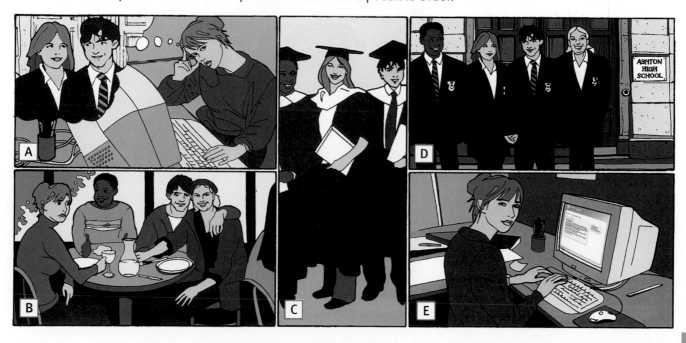

5.3 The truth about ageing

Grammar	*used to*
Can do	describe yourself when you were younger

Speaking and listening

1   **a** In pairs, ask and answer the questions in the quiz.

   b **5.4** Listen to the answers. Do any of them surprise you?

2   Which statement do you most agree with?

   1   How long you live depends on your lifestyle (diet, exercise, smoking, etc.).

   2   How long you live depends on your genes.

3   **a** **5.5** Listen to an extract from a radio programme. Which of the statements above does it say is probably true?

   b Listen again. Mark the statements true (T) or false (F).

   1   Most very old people have always had very healthy lifestyles.

   2   Jeanne Calment holds the record for being the oldest person ever.

   3   She stopped smoking two years before she died.

   4   Many experts think that some people have genes that protect them from some diseases.

   5   Jeanne Calment got cancer when she was about fifty years old.

   6   Some people think that eating much less every day will increase your lifespan.

4   Discuss.

   Would you like to live to 120 years old? Why/Why not?

Grammar | *used to*

5   Match the person to the reason they give for living a long time.

   physical exercise   mental exercise   thinking positively

AGEING
HOW MUCH DO YOU KNOW ABOUT IT?

1   **On average, which nationality lives the longest?**
   a) the Japanese
   b) the Italians
   c) the Swedish

2   **What was the average lifespan two thousand years ago?**
   a) twenty-six years
   b) thirty-six years
   c) forty-six years

3   **By 2050, what percentage of the world's population will be sixty-five or older?**
   a) 2%   b) 10%   c) 20%

4   **On average, which groups of people live longer?**
   a) smokers or non-smokers?
   b) single people or married people?
   c) pet owners or non-pet owners?

'I'm 89 years old. I used to do a lot of sport but I don't do any now. The most important thing for me is to feel good about life and laugh every day.'

'I'll be 85 on my next birthday. The thing that keeps me young is dancing. I didn't use to do any physical exercise but now I dance every day.'

'I can't believe it but I'm 87! I used to smoke but I gave up when I was 55. I don't do much exercise, but I like to keep my brain active. I love chess.'

6 Look at the quotes in Ex. 5 and complete the Active grammar box with *use* or *used*.

Active grammar

Used to is for habits and situations in the past which don't happen now.

➕ I _____ to play tennis.

➖ She didn't _____ to play tennis.

❓ Did you _____ to play tennis?

---

see Reference page 53

7 Make complete sentences with *used to* or *didn't use to*.

1 (I/have/long hair) _____ but now it's short.
2 (I/not like/olives) _____ but I do now.
3 **A:** (you/play any sports) _____ at school?
4 (we/be friends) _____ but we're not now.
5 **A:** (they/live together) _____?
  B: No, they didn't.
6 (Paul/work for me) _____ but now he's my boss.
7 (Zuza/not be interested in fashion) _____ but now she loves it.

8 a Look at the pictures and use the prompts below to make sentences about Thomas.

20 YEARS AGO	NOW
~~do a lot of sport~~	~~not do any sport~~
have a lot of hair	not have much hair
be quite slim	be overweight
not have a girlfriend	be married
have a bicycle	have a car
not have much money	get a good salary

Thomas used to do a lot of sport. Now he doesn't do any.

b [5.6] Listen and check your answers.

Pronunciation

9 a [5.6] Listen to the sentences from Ex. 8 again. How do you pronounce *used to* and *didn't use to*?

b Practise saying the sentences with the correct pronunciation.

Person to person

10 Tell your partner about when you were younger. Think about the following:

hopes and fears	sports
likes and dislikes	pets
hair and clothes	music

I used to want to be a pilot but now I'm afraid of flying!

Vocabulary | habits

11 a Match a verb from A with a noun phrase from B.

A		B	
1	eat	a)	a heavy smoker
2	eat	b)	mentally active
3	be	c)	physical exercise
4	be	d)	junk food
5	drink	e)	to bed very late
6	do	f)	a lot of water
7	think	g)	healthily
8	go	h)	positively

b Discuss.

1 Which of the verb phrases do you think are good habits? And which are bad?

2 Which of the things did you use to do? Which do you do now?

5 Communication

This is your life

1 What do you know about the actors in the photos?

2   **a** **5·7** Listen to the first part of a programme called *This is your life*. Which actor is it about?

  b **5·8** Now listen to the rest of the programme. What is the importance of the information below?

> six years old   wash dishes   long hair and a beard
> twenty-one   1980 $350 million

He lived with his grandparents until he was six years old.

3   **a** You're going to make a short presentation about your partner. First, ask your partner questions to complete the fact-file about him/her.

· · · · · · · · · · · · · Fact-file · · · · · · · · · · · ·

Name: _____

Year and place of birth: _____

Lives in: _____

Marital status: _____

Friends say he/she is: _____

b Now prepare questions about the topics below.

> favourite memories
> hobbies   career
> successes in life
> language-learning history
> appearance in the past

What is your favourite memory from your childhood?

c Interview your partner using your questions above. Make notes for your presentation.

4   **a** Use the fact-file and your notes to prepare your presentation.

b Make your presentation to the class.

Today on ' This is your life' we are talking about a woman who ...

5 Reference

should, can, have to

Form: modal verb + infinitive

+	I/You/ He/She/It/ We/They	should can	wait.
−	I/You/ He/She/It/ We/They	shouldn't can't	smoke.
?	Should/ Shouldn't Can/Can't	I/you/he/ she/it/we/they	go?

! Do not use the auxiliary *Do/Does* when making the question form with *should* or *can*.

Should I wear a hat to the wedding?

NOT: ~~Do I should wear a hat to the wedding?~~

Use *should(n't)* when you think something is a good/bad idea.

You should wear smart clothes for your job interview.

You shouldn't go to bed late before an important exam.

Use *can't* when something is impossible.

I can play tennis on Saturday morning.

I can't unlock the door with this key.

Form: model verb + infinitive

+	I/You We/They He/She/It	have to has to	work.
−	I/You We/They He/She/It	don't have to doesn't have to	come.
?	Do Does	I/you/we/they have to he/she/it have to	leave?

Use *have to* when something is necessary and there is no choice.

I have to get up early tomorrow because my train leaves at 7a.m.

Use *don't have to* when something is not necessary and there is a choice.

In Britain, you don't have to vote.

Present Perfect Simple with *for* and *since*

Use the Present Perfect Simple with *for* and *since* to talk about actions or states which started in the past and continue to now.

I've lived in this country for six years.

I haven't seen Maria since last summer.

How long have you been at this school?

Use *for* when we give the length of the time.

for three years, for a week, for half an hour, for ages …

Use *since* when we give the beginning of the time.

since 1996, since this morning, since 10.30.

used to

Form: *used to* + infinitive

+	I/you/ he/she/ we/they	used to	play the piano.
−	I/you/ he/she/ we/they	didn't use to	do any exercise.
?	Did	I/you/ he/she/ we/they	use to	live in the countryside?

Used to refers to regular activities and states in the past that don't happen now.

Tina used to play the violin but now she doesn't.

I didn't use to like London but now I love it.

Key vocabulary

Times of life
adult   baby   (be) middle aged   (be) old/elderly
child   pensioner   teenager   toddler

Life activities
earn a good salary   get a job
get a place of your own   get engaged/married
graduate   have children   learn to drive   retire

Friendship
lose touch   get in touch   go out (with someone)
old school friend   colleague
get on well (with someone)

Good and bad habits
a heavy smoker   be mentally active
do physical exercise   eat healthily   eat junk food
go to bed very late   think positively

1 Rewrite these sentences using *should(n't)*, *can('t)* or *(don't) have to*.

It's a good idea to join a gym if you want to get fit.

You should join a gym if you want to get fit.

1 In the UK it is necessary to wear seatbelts in the back of a car.

In the UK you _____.

2 It's possible for me to do my homework while I watch TV.

I _____.

3 It's a good idea to go to Germany to improve your German.

You _____.

4 It's necessary to show your student card to get a reduction.

You _____.

5 It's not necessary to drive me to the airport. I'll get a taxi.

You _____.

6 It's not a good idea to drink coffee just before you go to bed.

You _____.

7 It's not possible for me to finish this report today.

I _____.

2 Five of these sentences have mistakes in them. Find the mistakes and correct them.

You don't have take the dog for a walk. ✗

You don't have to take the dog for a walk.

1 I can't to lift this box. It's really heavy.

2 Do he have to work this weekend?

3 You should change your office chair. It's not good for your back.

4 They doesn't have to wear school uniform.

5 Do you should take a coat with you?

6 Can you help me paint the hall this weekend?

7 Are you sure you have take all your certificates to the interview?

3 Complete the following sentences with *for* or *since*.

I've known Susie *since* we were at primary school.

1 She's lived in London _____ years!

2 We haven't had this car _____ very long.

3 They've worked _____ 2005.

4 I've had this watch _____ last summer.

5 Ken and Jo have gone out together _____ nearly a year.

4 Read the situations. Put the information into one sentence using the Present Perfect Simple.

Sam works for our company. He joined six months ago.

Sam has worked for our company for six months.

1 I play the guitar. I learnt when I was a child.

2 My parents live in Bristol. They moved there in April.

3 I have a dog. I got him two years ago.

4 I know Jack quite well. I met him in October.

5 Ten years ago they had a holiday. They didn't go on holiday after that.

6 She drives a car. She passed her driving test in 2001.

7 I study English. I started studying three years ago.

8 He saw Angie five years ago. He didn't see her after that.

5 Find and correct the mistakes in five of these sentences.

I didn't use like my piano teacher. ✗

I didn't use to like my piano teacher.

1 They used to go to the same school.

2 Did you use play football at school?

3 She didn't to get good marks at school.

4 Where you use to live before you came here?

5 He didn't use to enjoy golf very much.

6 I used like my job more than I do now.

7 Did you use to eat a lot of junk food?

8 My parents didn't use have a television.

6 Choose the correct alternatives.

1 My parents are middle-*aged/-ages* now.

2 He used to be a *heavy/big* smoker.

3 Mick and Joanne *got/had* engaged last week.

4 I got *on/in* touch with an old friend via the website.

5 I haven't seen Bill for ages. We *lost/missed* touch when he went abroad.

6 I was a well-behaved teenager. I never rebelled *on/against* my parents.

7 I'd like to get a *piece/place* of my own when I'm old enough.

8 I think it's good to be mentally *action/active* at all stages of your life.

6 | Places

Lead-in

1 **a** Look at the photos. Discuss. Which continent do you associate with each photo?

b In which continents are these countries?

> Spain   Italy   Brazil   France   Japan   Britain   Canada
> Egypt   Germany   the United States   Poland   Portugal
> Australia   Kenya   China   Mexico

c Which countries have you visited/would you like to visit?

2 **a** Write the nationality for each country.

Spain – Spanish

b **6.1** Mark the stress, then listen and check the pronunciation.

3 Check the meaning of the underlined words or phrases. In pairs, answer the questions.

1 What is the capital of Australia?
2 Which major city is situated in Europe and Asia?
3 Where are the remains of the Parthenon?
4 What are the main tourist destinations in your country?
5 Which region in your country is an area of natural beauty?
6 What is the most beautiful landscape you've ever seen?

Listening

1 a Complete the map with the words in the box. Which words **can't** you use?

> mountain   lake   beach   island   sea   ocean
> forest   desert   river

b [6.2] Listen and check your answers.

2 a In pairs, decide on the correct information about New Zealand.

1 The population is *4 million/40 million*.

2 The number of sheep is *4 million/ 40 million*.

3 The capital of New Zealand is *Auckland/Wellington*.

4 The official languages are *English and Maori/ English and Chinese*.

5 The national symbol is a *kiwi bird/kiwi fruit*.

6 You can do water sports in *North Island/ South Island*.

7 You can go skiing in *North Island/South Island*.

b [6.3] Listen to the tour guide information and check your answers.

3 Discuss with other students. Which island in New Zealand would you most like to visit? Why?

Reading

4 Read the text and choose the best title.

a   The magic of New Zealand

b   New Zealand's tourist nightmare

c   The new New Zealand

Map labels:
Ninety Mile ①
Auckland
Matamata
NORTH ISLAND
Tongariro ②
TASMAN
③
Wellington
SOUTH ISLAND
Queenstown
Kawarau
⑤
Wakatipu
⑥
SOUTH PACIFIC
④
Stewart
⑦

For years, many people thought that New Zealand was famous for sheep, rugby and
5 . . . more sheep. But suddenly these islands have a new image. They are now one of the most fashionable tourist
10 destinations in the world. And all because of a film, or actually three films. *The Lord of the Rings* was filmed in New Zealand
15 and it's a wonderful advert for the country. People now want to visit New Zealand to see the places in the film. Tourism in New Zealand is doing very well – that's the LOTR effect. Some tourists come just to see the film locations. For example,
20 there's a beautiful place called Matamata just south of Auckland. 250 tourists come here every day. They pay thirty dollars each to see the remains of Hobbiton village from the first *The Lord of the Rings* film. Tours of the various film locations are very popular.

5 Read the text again. Mark the statements true (T) or false (F).

1 Only one of *The Lord of the Rings* films was made in New Zealand.

2 They are making advertisements using the New Zealand countryside.

3 You can only see part of the Hobbiton village at Matamata.

4 Many tourists go to meet the actors there.

5 Tourism increased immediately after the films came out.

6 Holiday experts say numbers of holidaymakers will soon start to go down.

6 Find these <u>underlined</u> words and phrases in the text and say what they refer to.

they (line 7): *refers to the islands of New Zealand*

1 it (line 15):

2 that (line 18):

3 they (line 21):

4 it (line 27):

5 these things (line 33):

7 Discuss with a partner.

1 What are some positive and negative effects of tourism in your country?

2 Would you like more tourism in your country? Why/Why not?

In the two weeks after the first film came out, holiday
25 bookings went up more than twenty percent. Experts think that the number of tourists will double in the near future and <u>it</u> won't stop there. Some people think that New Zealand will soon have over three million tourists a year. But there are some questions
30 about all this success. Will tourism change the natural beauty of the landscape? Will it affect the wildlife? And will tourists still want to visit New Zealand if <u>these things</u> happen?

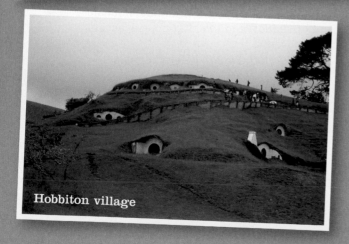

Hobbiton village

Grammar | *will*

8 Look at the Active grammar box and complete the examples.

> **Active grammar**
>
> Use *will* (+ verb) to make predictions about the future.
>
> The negative of *will* is *won't* (*will not*).
>
> ➕ *The number of tourists _____ _____ in the near future.* (double)
>
> ➖ *It _____ _____ there.* (not stop)
>
> ❓ *_____ tourism change the natural beauty of the landscape?*

see Reference page 63

9 Complete the sentences with *will* ('*ll*) or *won't* and a verb from the box.

> like   be   pass   rain   get   go   see   hurt

1 I don't want to go to that beach. It _____ very busy today.

2 We haven't got much money so we _____ on holiday this year.

3 I _____ the whole country in two weeks. It's too big.

4 I think Katya _____ the tour guide job. She's got a lot of experience.

5 Don't worry about your driving test. I'm sure you _____.

6 The weather doesn't look very good. Do you think it _____?

7 Don't be scared of my dog. He _____ you.

8 Do you think Anna _____ the present we bought her?

Pronunciation

10 a ▶ 6.4 Listen. Write the sentences you hear.

b Repeat the sentences. What is the difference in pronunciation between *want* and *won't*?

c Make the sentences true for you. Tell your partner.

Person to person

11 Go to page 130 and follow the instructions.

6.2 Frontier house

Grammar	*too, too much/many, enough*
Can do	give explanations for choices

Listening

1 **a** Look at the photo and read the text. What is the programme *Frontier house* about?

Frontier house
Channel 4 • 7.30p.m.

Can modern people cope with nineteenth-century life?

The Clune family from California decided to find out. For six months the parents and their four children lived like Americans in the Wild West 100 years ago.

What did they find difficult? How did the experience change them? Watch *Frontier house* and find out how modern people cope with old-fashioned life.

b In pairs, try and predict what each family member will find difficult about being in *Frontier house*.

Father	
Mother	
Teenage girls	
Boys (aged nine and eleven)	

2 **a** **6.5** Listen to two people talking about *Frontier house* and check if your predictions in Ex. 1b were correct.

b Listen again and circle the correct alternatives.

1 They lived in the style of people in about *1818/1880*.
2 The nearest shop was *six/sixteen* kilometres.
3 The father became *thinner/ill*.
4 The mother *missed/didn't miss* her make-up.
5 At first, the children *liked/didn't like* having so much to do.
6 The girls missed *shopping/TV* the most.
7 At the end of the experience, Tracy said her clothes were *more/less* important to her.

3 **6.6** What do you think happened when they went home? Listen and check your ideas.

4 Discuss.

1 Would you like to be in a TV programme like this? Why/Why not?
2 Which country would you like to live in for six months, a) now? b) 100 years ago? Give your reasons.

Grammar | *too, too much/many, enough*

5 **a** Look at the two sentences. Is the meaning the same or different?

He was *too weak* to do all the physical work.
He *wasn't strong enough* to do all the physical work.

b Match the rules (1–5) with the examples in the Active grammar box.

Active grammar

1 Use *too* with adjectives and adverbs.
2 Use *too much* with uncountable nouns.
3 Use *too many* with countable nouns.
4 Use *(not) enough* after adjectives and adverbs.
5 Use *(not) enough* before nouns.

A *They weren't warm enough.*
B *I'm too tired to do any more work today.*
C *I had too much time and nothing to do.*
D *They often didn't have enough food.*
E *There were too many things to do.*

see Reference page 63

6 Correct the mistake in each sentence.

1 The weather here is too much cold for me.

2 I'm not going on holiday this year because it'll cost too many money.

3 She's not enough old to get married.

4 He didn't get the job because he didn't have experience enough.

5 The children are making too noise.

6 I didn't have enough of time to finish the exam.

7 The town isn't enough near to walk from here.

7 Complete these sentences using the words in brackets and *enough*, *too*, *too much* or *too many*.

My coat isn't *warm enough* for me. (warm)

1 I'm hungry. I didn't have _____ this morning. (breakfast)

2 I'm very tired. I went to bed _____ last night. (late)

3 I'm not _____ to run a marathon. (fit)

4 I'm very busy today. I've got _____ to do. (things)

5 I didn't have _____ to do my homework yesterday. (time)

6 I often spend _____ on clothes. (money)

7 Most English people speak _____ for me to understand. (quickly)

8 This tea is _____ to drink. (hot)

Person to person

8 In pairs, discuss if the sentences in Ex. 7 are true for you.

Vocabulary | machines at home

9 Match the words and phrases in the box with the pictures.

> answerphone   CD-walkman   DVD player   dishwasher
> freezer   fridge   hairdryer   mobile phone   radio
> washing machine   vacuum cleaner

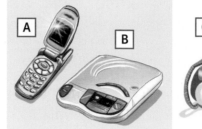
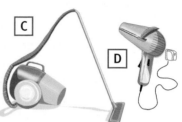

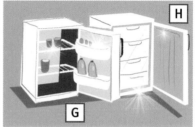

10 a Choose five things from Ex. 9 and write a definition for each one.

dishwasher: a machine that washes plates and cups

b Use your definitions to test other students.

A: *What's a machine that washes plates and cups?*

B: *A dishwasher.*

Speaking

11 [6.7] Listen to two friends doing a task. What is the task? What do they agree on?

12 In pairs, do the same task. Use the How to ... box to help you.

HOW TO ...	**talk about choices**	
	1 Say your choice	*I'd like to choose . . .* *I think we should take . . .*
	2 Give a general reason . . .	*because . . .* *The main reason is that . . .*
	3 Add a personal reason	*I couldn't live without it!* *I'm too lazy to . . .*

Reading

1 What do you know about Nelson Mandela? Write down as many facts as you can and compare with a partner.

He was in prison for a long time.

2 a Match the pictures on the charity leaflet with the phrases.

> water plants
> plant seeds
> harvest the fruit/
> vegetables
> get rid of weeds

b Discuss.

How do you think the words above are connected with Nelson Mandela?

3 Why do you think the title of the leaflet is *Garden of Freedom*? Read the leaflet and check your ideas.

4 Read the leaflet again and answer the questions.

1 Who started the garden in Kabwe prison?

2 How did gardening help Mandela?

3 What is the main reason for the garden at Kabwe prison?

4 Why did Mandela start his garden?

5 Where did Mandela make his garden?

6 Who helped him to make the garden?

7 Why was the garden a 'small taste of freedom'?

8 What does Mandela compare the garden to?

5 Would you like to read *Long Walk to Freedom* by Nelson Mandela. Why/Why not?

Garden of Freedom

The charity *Seeds for Africa* has started its first prison vegetable garden at Kabwe Prison in Zambia. There are 500 prisoners at Kabwe Prison and the prison garden will give them fresh vegetables to eat. More importantly, the prison staff hope that the garden will increase the prisoners' self-esteem[1]. The Kabwe Prison garden was inspired by Nelson Mandela who spent twenty-seven years in prison in South Africa. Gardening helped Mandela to increase his self-esteem.

'My garden was my way of escaping what surrounded us. I looked at all the empty space we had on the roof and how it got sun the whole day.

I decided I'd like to start a garden and after years of asking, I received permission[2]. I asked for sixteen large oil drums and asked the staff to cut them in half for me. They then filled each half with soil, and created thirty-two giant flowerpots.

A garden was one of the few things in prison that I could control. It gave me the simple but important satisfaction of planting a seed, watching it grow, watering it and then harvesting it. It was a small taste of freedom. In some ways, I saw the garden as being like my life. A leader must also look after his garden; he too, plants seeds and then watches, cultivates[3], and harvests the result.'
(adapted from *Long Walk to Freedom* by Nelson Mandela)

To find out more about the prison garden and other projects go to **www.seedsforafrica.org**

> **Glossary**
> [1] *self-esteem* = good feeling about yourself
> [2] *receive permission* = someone in authority says you can do something
> [3] *cultivate* = prepare and use land for growing plants

Grammar | uses of *like*

6 a Match the questions (1–4) with the answers (A–D) in the Active Grammar box.

> ### Active grammar
>
> 1 *What do you like doing in your free time?*
> 2 *What would you like to do today?*
> 3 *What is your garden like?*
> 4 *What does your garden look like?*
>
> A *I'd like to start a garden.*
> B *I like gardening.*
> C *It's full of colourful flowers.*
> D *It's very peaceful.*

b Match the definitions with the different uses of *like*.

1	want or want to do	a)	be like
2	enjoy	b)	like
3	appearance	c)	look like
4	character or characteristics	d)	would like

see Reference page 63

7 a Write questions using *like/look like/would like to/be like.*

Do you enjoy gardening?

Do you like gardening?

1 Tell me about your best friend.
2 Do you want to go out tonight?
3 Tell me about your best friend's appearance.

b In pairs, answer the questions.

8 Find and correct the mistake in each question.

What ^{is}⟨your town like?

1 Would you like visiting South Africa?
2 What the weather like today?
3 What do you like to doing at weekends?
4 Which famous person would you like meet?
5 What sports do you like play?
6 Are you look like your mum or your dad?
7 Where would you like go on your next holiday?

Pronunciation

9 **6.8** Listen to the questions in Ex. 8. Mark the words which have the main stress.

What is your town like?

Person to person

10 Ask and answer the questions in Ex. 8 with a partner.

> ### Lifelong learning
>
> *Brainstorm!*
>
> Writing is a process with different stages. The first stage is often brainstorming. When you brainstorm, you write down anything you can think of connected to the task/question. Look at Ex. 11a. Take five minutes to brainstorm your ideas.

Writing

11 a What is your favourite natural place (e.g. a garden, a beach, a forest)? What's it like? Make notes about this place.

b Tell your partner about your favourite place.

12 Read the description in the Writing bank on page 147. Do the exercises then write about your favourite place.

6 Communication

Where shall we go?

1 Match the photos with the cities. What do you know about each city?

> Edinburgh   Rio de Janeiro   Barcelona
> St Petersburg   Cairo

2 **a** ⟨6.9⟩ Listen to two people deciding where to go on holiday. Which city do they choose?

	BARCELONA	CAIRO	EDINBURGH	RIO DE JANEIRO	ST PETERSBURG
Daytime temperature (March)	12 °C	17 °C	4 °C	26 °C	−2 °C
One night's stay	€40	€15	€60	€30	€30
Meal in a restaurant	€22	€7.5	€30	€15	€7.5
Famous for ...	[parks, museums, beaches, nightlife]	[ancient sites, shopping]	[palaces/castles, shopping, museums, nightlife]	[beaches, cafés, nightlife, music]	[palaces/castles, museums]
Not famous for ...	[ancient sites]	[nightlife, beaches]	[beaches]	[museums]	[nightlife, beaches]

Key:
- 🌳 parks
- Ⓜ art galleries/museums
- 〰 beaches
- 🏃 nightlife
- 🛍 shopping/markets
- 🏰 palaces and castles
- ☕ cafés
- 🎵 music
- 🏛 ancient sites

b Listen again. Tick (✓) the reasons for their decision.

1 Linda thinks there aren't enough interesting things to do in Edinburgh.
2 They both think there aren't enough beaches in Edinburgh.
3 Edinburgh isn't warm enough for Harry.
4 Barcelona is too cold for Linda.
5 They both think Edinburgh is too expensive.

3 Imagine you have a week's holiday in March.

1 First, decide which city you'd like to go to. Make notes on where, and why. Also make notes on why you don't want to go to the other cities.

2 In groups, decide on one city to visit. Try to convince other students that your choice is best. Tell them why you decided not to go to the other cities.

will

Use *will* (+ infinitive) to make predictions about the future.

⊕	I/You/ He/She/It/ We/They	will	go.
⊖	I/You/ He/She/It/ We/They	won't	go.
❓	Will	I/you/ he/she/it/ we/they	go?
	Yes, I will./No, I won't.		

We often use *I (don't) think* and *I hope* with *will* when making predictions.

I think Manchester United will win the Cup.

I hope it'll be sunny tomorrow.

Use *I don't think he'll ...* NOT ~~I think he won't ...~~

We can also use *will* for making promises and spontaneous decisions.

Well, OK. I'll be there in five minutes.

I'll do the washing-up when I've finished this.

uses of *like*

Like has different meanings depending on the grammar of the sentence.

1 *like* = enjoy something in general

 Use *like* + gerund.

 A: *What do you **like** do**ing** at the weekend?*

 B: *I **like** go**ing** to the mountains.*

2 *would like* = want something or want to do something

 Use *would like* + infinitive or a noun

 A: *What **would** you **like to do** this weekend?*

 B: *I'd **like to see** 'The Lord of the Rings'.*

 C: *I'd **like a** quiet **night** at home.*

3 *be like* = asking about character or characteristics

 Don't use *like* in the answer.

 A: *What **is** your town **like**?*

 B: *It's quite big and very busy.*

4 *look like* = asking about appearance

 Don't use *like* in the answer.

 A: *What does your father **look like**?*

 B: *He's tall and he's got black hair.*

too, too much/many, enough

Use *too* or *not enough* when something is a problem.

*His suitcase was **too** heavy to carry.*

*He wasn't strong **enough** to carry his suitcase.*

too	Use *too* with adjectives. *I went to bed **too late** last night.*
too much	Use *too much* with uncountable nouns. *There's **too much noise** in here.*
too many	Use *too many* with countable nouns. *There are **too many books** on that shelf.*
enough	Use *enough* after adjectives and adverbs. Use *enough* before nouns. *That bag isn't **big enough**.* *He didn't play **well enough**.* *Sorry, I didn't have **enough time**.*

Use *very* when something is difficult but not impossible.

*His suitcase was **very** heavy but he carried it.*

Key vocabulary

Countries and nationalities

Australia/Australian   Brazil/Brazilian   Britain/ British   Canada/Canadian   China/Chinese Egypt/Egyptian   France/French   Germany/German Italy/Italian   Japan/Japanese   Kenya/Kenyan Mexico/Mexican   Poland/Polish   Portugal/ Portuguese   Spain/Spanish   the United States/ American

Describing places

(be) situated in   landscape   natural beauty region   the capital of   the remains of tourist destination

Geographical features

mountain   lake   beach   island   sea   ocean   river forest   desert

Machines at homes

answerphone   CD-walkman   dishwasher DVD player   freezer   fridge   hairdryer   radio mobile phone   vacuum cleaner   washing machine

1 **Choose the correct alternative.**

1 I think *I go/I'll go* to South Africa for my next holiday.

2 At the weekend, *I usually like/I'll usually like* playing tennis.

3 A: Can you phone me later?
   B: Yes, *I don't forget/I won't forget.*

4 I'm really tired. I think *I go/I'll go* to bed.

5 What time *do you/will you* get up at the weekend?

6 Do you think *it's/it'll be* sunny tomorrow?

7 Tina often *arrives/will arrive* late for school.

8 A: Would you like sugar in your coffee?
   B: Yes, *I have/I'll have* two, please.

2 **Complete the sentences using 'll/won't and a verb from the box.**

> ~~close~~   not/forget   have   help   pay
> phone   stay   not/walk   come

It's cold in here. I think I*'ll close* the window.

1 A: What would you like?
   B: I _____ a ham sandwich, please.

2 I promise I _____ to buy some milk.

3 A: Where's Dan?
   B: I don't know. I _____ him now.

4 I _____ home today – it's too wet.

5 A: Do you want to go out tonight?
   B: No, I think I _____ in.

6 Thanks for the money. I _____ you back tomorrow.

7 A: This homework is too difficult.
   B: I _____ you.

8 A: Do you want to come with us to the free concert?
   B: No, I don't think I _____. It finishes too late.

3 **Put the words in the correct order.**

got go on money to haven't enough holiday I
I haven't got enough money to go on holiday.

1 food to The eat too was hot

2 tea isn't enough There my sugar in

3 far to walk too home here It's from

4 get She's old married not enough to

5 pool the There many in too people were

6 too chocolate eat Don't much

7 shop enough in store There this aren't assistants department

8 always her quickly dinner eats She too

4 **Make one sentence from two.**

We couldn't swim in the river. It was too cold.
The river was too cold for us to swim in.

1 I can't carry this suitcase. It's too heavy.
   This suitcase _____ .

2 We couldn't sleep in the hotel. It was too noisy.
   The hotel _____ .

3 I can't eat this food. It's too spicy.
   The food _____ .

4 Nobody could do the homework. It was too difficult.
   The homework _____ .

5 I can't reach the top shelf. It's too high.
   The top shelf _____ .

5 **Look at the answers and write the questions using the prompts.**

(you/at the weekends)
A: *What do you like doing at the weekends?*
B: I like going shopping with my friends.

1 (you/for your next holiday)
A: _____?
B: I'd like to go to Costa Rica.

2 (your street)
A: _____?
B: It's quiet but there's a lot of rubbish.

3 (your cat)
A: _____?
B: She's small and completely white.

4 (you/do this evening)
A: _____?
B: I'd like to see that new film.

5 (your new shoes)
A: _____?
B: They're red and they've got very high heels.

6 **Put the letters in the correct order.**

Tokyo is the *capital* (aticpla) of Japan.

1 I couldn't dry my hair because my _____ (drahirrye) was broken.

2 I travelled in the _____ (sedret) last year but it was too hot for me.

3 You should keep ice cream in the _____ (zerefer).

4 I love diving in the Pacific _____ (necOa).

5 I do too much washing-up. I need a _____ (wehadissrh).

6 If I'm not in, leave a message on my _____ (narseweponh).

7 We set off at 6a.m. and reached the top of the _____ (anomtuni) at 1p.m.

7 Body

Lead-in

1 **a** Put these words in the correct column in the table.

> ~~hair~~ waist elbow face wrist ear nose back knee
> stomach finger thumb lips toe ankle eye mouth

HEAD	TORSO	ARM/HAND	LEG/FOOT
hair			

b **7.1** Listen and check your answers.

2 **a** Check you understand the meaning of the <u>underlined</u> phrases below.

1 Most men don't spend enough time on their <u>physical appearance</u>.
2 Most women <u>look like</u> their mothers and most men look like their fathers.
3 It's normal to <u>put on weight</u> as you get older.
4 <u>Going on a diet</u> is bad for your health.
5 You can learn about someone's <u>personality</u> by studying his/her face.
6 Small, everyday things can <u>make</u> people very <u>stressed</u>.

b Discuss the statements above.

Reading and speaking

1   Discuss.

1   Do you read any 'celebrity' magazines or watch programmes about celebrities? Why/Why not?

2   Who is the woman in the photos?

3   What do you know about her?

4   Do you think she looks different in the two photos? Why?

2   Read the text quickly. Check your answers to questions 2–4 above.

The perfect body

Most people were surprised when Renée Zellweger got the part of Bridget in the film *Bridget Jones's Diary*. The film is about a young woman who worries about work, her weight and men. Zellweger is a slim American woman – completely different from Bridget who is English and overweight.

So, what did Zellweger do to get the part right? She had lessons to improve her English accent and she put on about eleven kilos. For several months she didn't do any exercise and she ate a lot of pizza, peanut butter sandwiches and chocolate. Although it was fun at first, she often felt quite sick.

Zellweger put the weight on because she thought it was important to be as real as possible. She was surprised, however, by people's criticisms. People criticised her for being fat when she put on weight for the film. Then they criticised her again for being too skinny when she lost weight after the film. She realised it's almost impossible to have the perfect body in the eyes of the media.

So why did she do it? Well, money was probably one reason. On top of her $15 million salary, she earned $225,000 for every kilo she put on. That's an extra $2.5 million! And it didn't stop there. A British slimming magazine paid her $3.5 million to lose all the weight again. So perhaps Zellweger doesn't need to care about the criticism when she earns all this money!

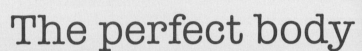

She realised it's almost impossible to have the perfect body in the eyes of the media.

3   Read the text again and mark the sentences true (T), false (F) or don't know (?).

1   Most people thought Zellweger was the wrong person for the part of Bridget Jones. ☐

2   Zellweger was unsure about taking the part of Bridget. ☐

3   She learnt to speak like an English person. ☐

4   She ate a lot and exercised a lot. ☐

5   She put on weight to feel like Bridget Jones. ☐

6   She earned $2.5 million for every kilo she put on. ☐

7   She earned more money to lose weight than to put it on. ☐

4   Read these opinions. Which one(s) do you agree with and why?

a (People worry too much about weight.

b (Putting on eleven kilos is dangerous.

c (I would do the same in her situation.

Vocabulary | appearance

5 **a** Put the words and phrases in the box in the correct column.

> slim tall beautiful skinny fat
> (un)attractive handsome ugly
> medium height thin good-looking
> short overweight muscular

WEIGHT/BUILD	HEIGHT	ATTRACTIVE OR NOT
slim	tall	beautiful

b What's the difference between:

1 slim and skinny?

2 fat and overweight?

3 handsome and beautiful?

6 **a** **7.2** Look at the pictures. Listen to two people playing 'Guess who … ?'. Which two people are they describing?

b Listen again. Complete the How to … box.

<table>
<tr><td rowspan="6" style="writing-mode:vertical">HOW TO …</td><td colspan="2">**modify adjectives**</td></tr>
<tr><td>With positive adjectives</td><td>*He's very/_____ good-looking.*
He's quite/_____ muscular.</td></tr>
<tr><td>With negative adjectives</td><td>*She's really/_____ skinny.*
He's a bit/_____ overweight.</td></tr>
<tr><td>With comparative adjectives</td><td>*She's much/_____ more attractive than most.*
She's a bit/_____ taller than average.</td></tr>
</table>

c Play 'Guess who…?' with a partner using the pictures above.

Grammar | First Conditional

7 **7.3** Listen and answer the questions.

1 What product is the advert for?

2 Is the product for men, women or both?

8 Choose the correct alternatives for the rules in the Active grammar box.

Active grammar

The First Conditional talks about a <u>possible</u>/ <u>impossible</u> situation in the future.

If you use the cream once a day, you'll have softer skin.

You'll notice the difference if you use the cream twice a day.

Make the First Conditional with:
If + <u>Present Simple</u>/<u>Present Continuous</u> + *will* (*won't*) + verb

The '*if* clause' comes <u>first</u>/<u>either first or second</u>

---

see Reference page 73

9 **a** Complete these First Conditional sentences with the correct form of the verbs in brackets.

1 If you _____ (eat) a lot of junk food, you _____ (put) on weight.

2 You _____ (not/sleep) well tonight if you _____ (drink) all that coffee.

3 If he _____ (not/call) you, what _____ (you/do)?

4 He _____ (not/have) any money left if he _____ (buy) any more DVDs.

5 If you _____ (not/start) training now, you _____ (not/be able) to run the marathon.

6 _____ (you/call) me if your bus _____ (be) late?

b **7.4** Listen and check your answers. Repeat the sentences with the same intonation.

Person to person

10 **a** Complete these sentences about you.

1 If I have time tomorrow, …

2 If it rains this weekend, …

3 If I don't go out this evening, …

4 If my English is good enough next year, …

b Compare your sentences with a partner.

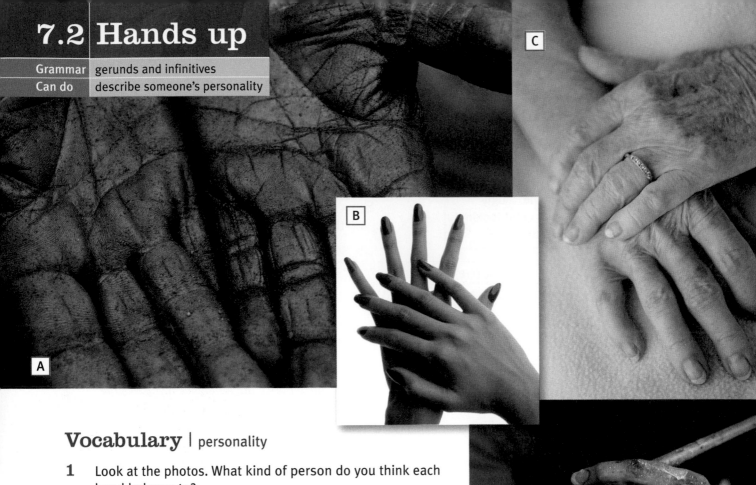

Vocabulary | personality

1 Look at the photos. What kind of person do you think each hand belongs to?

I think hand D belongs to an artist.

2 **a** Match the adjectives in the box with the underlined phrases in the sentences.

> ambitious   hard-working   reserved   open   organised
> unreliable   chatty   sensitive

1 People with long fingers are <u>easily upset</u>.
2 People with short fingers are <u>happy to talk about feelings</u>.
3 People with straight fingers <u>make lots of lists and plans</u>.
4 People with a long first finger <u>work hard</u>.
5 People with a long ring finger <u>don't do what they say they will do</u>.
6 People with a thumb that bends back <u>are easy to talk to and talk a lot</u>.
7 People with a thumb that doesn't bend back <u>don't talk about feelings or problems</u>.
8 People with a long thumb <u>really want to be successful</u>.

b Test your partner. Say a definition and your partner should say the correct word.

A: *Someone who's easily upset?*
B: *Sensitive.*

Pronunciation

3 **a** [7.5] Listen to the words in the box in Ex. 2a and mark the stress.

b [7.6] Listen and write the questions that you hear.

c Ask and answer the questions with a partner.

Listening

4 **a** [7.7] Listen to two friends, Helen and Daniel, talking. Does Daniel …

a agree with everything Helen says?
b agree with some of what she says?
c disagree with most of what she says?

b Listen again and tick (✓) the sentences in Ex. 2a which are true for Daniel.

5 Discuss with a partner. What do you think of this way of analysing people's personalities?

Grammar | gerunds and infinitives

6 Look at the examples in the Active grammar box and choose the correct alternatives.

> ### Active grammar
>
> I **want to look** at the shape of your fingers.
>
> They **seem to be** fairly straight.
>
> I really **enjoy** talk**ing** about my feelings.
>
> You **avoid** tell**ing** people about your feelings or problems.
>
> Some verbs are followed by the <u>gerund/infinitive with to</u>, e.g. *enjoy, avoid,* _____
>
> Some verbs are followed by the <u>gerund/infinitive with to</u>, e.g. *want, seem,* _____

see Reference page 73

7 **a** Choose the correct form.

1 He **offered** *to read/reading* my palm.

2 I've **decided** *not to be/not being* so lazy in the future.

3 I'm **considering** *to learn/learning* German.

4 Have you **finished** *to write/writing* your essay?

5 She's **hoping** *to be/being* a director soon.

6 I can't **afford** *to go/going* to that restaurant.

7 She **promised** *not to be/not being* late.

8 Carol **missed** *to see/seeing* Megan after she left work.

b Add the verbs in **bold** in Ex. 7a to the appropriate list of verbs in the Active grammar box.

Person to person

8 **a** Complete these sentences about your partner. Don't ask him or her, just guess.

1 He/She really wants _____ after the lesson.

2 He/She's decided _____ for his/her next holiday.

3 He/She really enjoys _____ at the weekends.

4 He/She usually avoids _____ because he/she doesn't like it.

5 He/She's considering _____ next year.

b Say your sentences to your partner and find out if they are true or not.

Reading and speaking

9 **a** Read the information below and decide what type of hands you have got.

Texture of hands

SOFT HANDS
Soft hands can mean that the person is calm but sometimes rather lazy. They are often not very ambitious.

HARD HANDS
People with hard hands sometimes get angry easily. They are often very ambitious and energetic.

Shape of hands

POINTED HANDS
This means the person is artistic, sensitive and kind. Often these people work with fashion or hairdressing.

SQUARE HANDS
People with square hands are usually hard working, organised and reliable. They are often good with money and business.

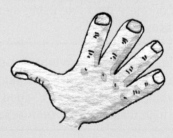

b Tell your partner about his/her personality using the information from Ex. 2a and the text above. Talk about the things in the box.

> texture of hands   shape of hands
> fingers   thumb

c How accurate do you think the information is about your personality?

7.3 Doctor, doctor

Grammar	purpose/reason/result
Can do	talk about illness and give advice

Listening

1 Look at the *Doctor, doctor* jokes and discuss the questions.

1 Do you think they are funny?
2 Do you have *Doctor, doctor* jokes like this in your language?

2 **7.8** Listen to two friends, Kate and Chris, telling *Doctor, doctor* jokes. What's the 'problem' in each one?

3 Do you know any other jokes? Tell your jokes and listen to your partner's jokes. Use the sentences in the How to ... box below.

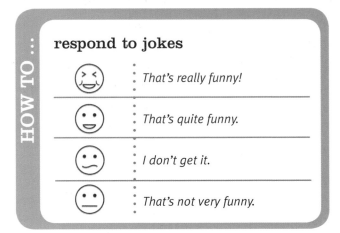

5 Match these suggestions with the correct symptoms in Ex. 4a.

Why don't you go to the dentist? *toothache*

1 Why don't you hold a cold wet cloth on your forehead.
2 You should sleep on a hard mattress.
3 You should keep a bucket near you.
4 Have you tried sucking a cough sweet?
5 Have you tried taking an aspirin?
6 Have you tried putting cotton wool in your ears?

Vocabulary | illness and injury

4 **a** Complete the table using these words and phrases.

> flu   a headache   a broken arm/leg   a cold
> a sore throat   earache   a pain in my chest
> stomachache   feel sick   food poisoning
> a high temperature   toothache   backache

ILLNESS	INJURY	SYMPTOM

b We say 'feel' sick. What verb do we use for all the other phrases?

c **7.9** Listen and check your answers.

6 **a** **7.10** Listen and repeat this dialogue with a partner.

A: I've got a really bad sore throat.
B: Have you tried sucking a cough sweet?
A: Oh, that's a good idea. Thanks.
B: That's OK. I hope you feel better soon.

b Write similar dialogues with your partner using the phrases from Ex. 4a and 6a.

c Practise in pairs.

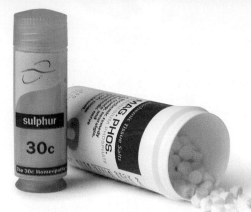

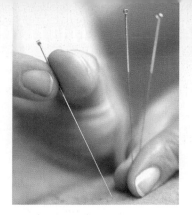

Reading and speaking

7   Look at the photos and discuss the questions.

1   What do you know about (a) homoeopathy and (b) acupuncture?

2   What experience have you had of either of them?

8   Work in pairs.

Student A: read the text on page 125 and complete your half of the table.

Student B: read the text on page 130 and complete your half of the table.

	HOMOEOPATHY	ACUPUNCTURE
Beliefs		
Typical session		
Treatment		
What it treats		
Cost		

9   **a**   Work in pairs. Tell your partner about your text. Complete the table about your partner's text.

b   Discuss.

Which would you prefer to use for the following illnesses/injuries – a homoeopath, an acupuncturist or a traditional doctor? Why?

1   flu

2   a broken arm

3   a pain in your chest

4   backache

Grammar | purpose/reason/result

10   Read the letter below. What do you think Rick's problem was?

Dear Rick

Thanks for your letter. This is a common problem <u>because people don't stand</u> or sit in the right way. There are lots of things you can do <u>so you don't need</u> to worry.

First, make sure you get the right chair <u>to support</u> your back. Secondly, think about changing your mattress. You should sleep on a hard mattress <u>in order to keep</u> your back straight during the night.

You should also take regular breaks <u>so that you change</u> your sitting position. You should do exercise every day too. <u>In order not to make</u> your back worse, don't go running. Go swimming or do yoga instead.

Good luck!

Doctor Darren

11   **a**   Look at the <u>underlined</u> words or phrases in the letter. Complete the Active grammar box by writing *infinitive* or *subject + verb*.

> ### Active grammar
>
> Giving a reason
> *because* + <u>subject + verb</u>
>
> Explaining a result
> *so* + _____
>
> Expressing purpose
> *to* + <u>infinitive</u>
> *in order (not) to* + _____
> *so that* + _____

see Reference page 73

b   Find and correct the mistake in each sentence.

1   I eat a lot of garlic because don't want to get flu.

2   I'm careful when I lift boxes that I don't hurt my back.

3   I drink water in order to feel sick on car journeys.

4   I did a lot of yoga today so feel very relaxed now.

5   I want to buy a special chair help me sit properly.

6   I usually drink milk order to get rid of a stomachache.

Writing

12   **a**   Write a short letter to Doctor Darren asking for advice about a problem.

b   Read your partner's letter. You are Doctor Darren. Write a reply giving advice.

c   Read your partner's reply. Do you think he/she gave you good advice?

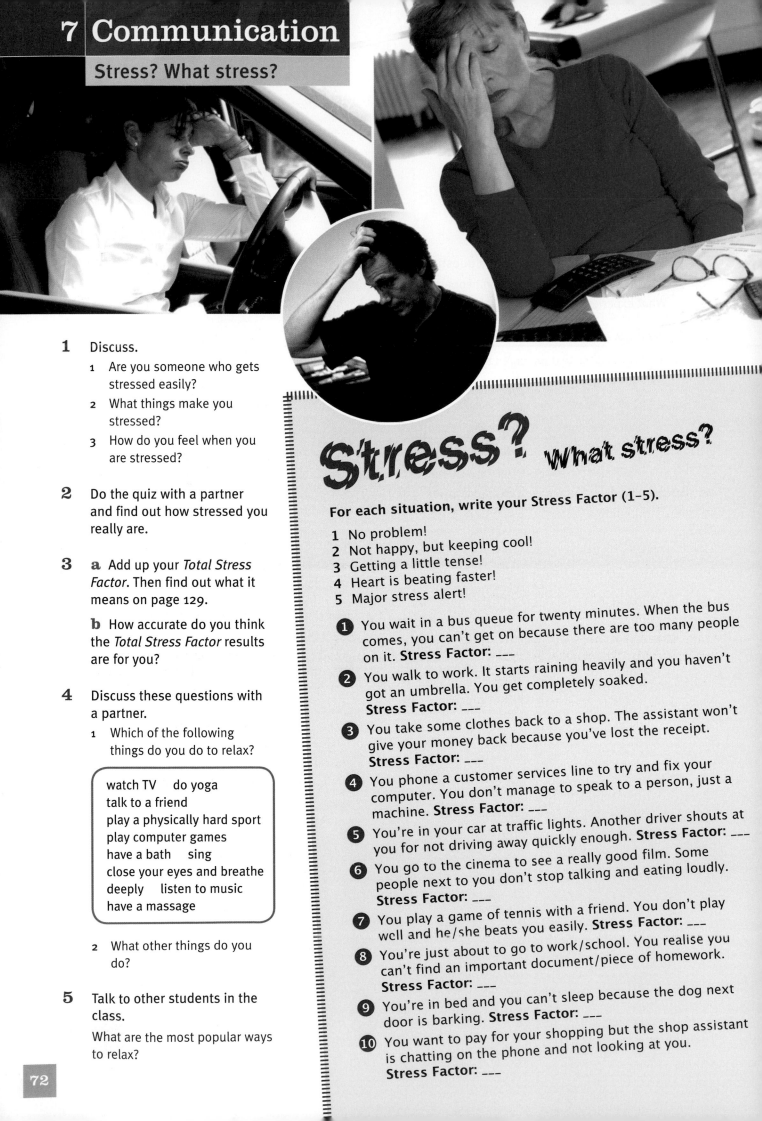

1 Discuss.

1 Are you someone who gets stressed easily?

2 What things make you stressed?

3 How do you feel when you are stressed?

2 Do the quiz with a partner and find out how stressed you really are.

3 **a** Add up your *Total Stress Factor*. Then find out what it means on page 129.

b How accurate do you think the *Total Stress Factor* results are for you?

4 Discuss these questions with a partner.

1 Which of the following things do you do to relax?

watch TV   do yoga
talk to a friend
play a physically hard sport
play computer games
have a bath   sing
close your eyes and breathe
deeply   listen to music
have a massage

2 What other things do you do?

5 Talk to other students in the class.

What are the most popular ways to relax?

Stress? What stress?

For each situation, write your Stress Factor (1-5).

1 No problem!
2 Not happy, but keeping cool!
3 Getting a little tense!
4 Heart is beating faster!
5 Major stress alert!

1 You wait in a bus queue for twenty minutes. When the bus comes, you can't get on because there are too many people on it. **Stress Factor:** ___

2 You walk to work. It starts raining heavily and you haven't got an umbrella. You get completely soaked. **Stress Factor:** ___

3 You take some clothes back to a shop. The assistant won't give your money back because you've lost the receipt. **Stress Factor:** ___

4 You phone a customer services line to try and fix your computer. You don't manage to speak to a person, just a machine. **Stress Factor:** ___

5 You're in your car at traffic lights. Another driver shouts at you for not driving away quickly enough. **Stress Factor:** ___

6 You go to the cinema to see a really good film. Some people next to you don't stop talking and eating loudly. **Stress Factor:** ___

7 You play a game of tennis with a friend. You don't play well and he/she beats you easily. **Stress Factor:** ___

8 You're just about to go to work/school. You realise you can't find an important document/piece of homework. **Stress Factor:** ___

9 You're in bed and you can't sleep because the dog next door is barking. **Stress Factor:** ___

10 You want to pay for your shopping but the shop assistant is chatting on the phone and not looking at you. **Stress Factor:** ___

First Conditional

Use the First Conditional to talk about a possible situation in the future.

If + Present Simple, *will* + verb

We don't use *will* in the '*if* clause'.

If we leave at 9.30, we'll be late.

NOT: ~~If we'll leave at 9.30, we'll be late.~~

The '*if* clause' can come first or second.

When the '*if* clause' is first, we need a comma at the end of the clause.

If I don't go to bed now, I'll be too tired tomorrow.

He'll fail his exam if he doesn't work harder.

We can also use other modal verbs in the 'result' clause (not just *will*), e.g. *may, might, could*.

*If I finish this soon, I **might** go and see Tony.*

*Bobby **may** bring his son, if he comes on Sunday.*

*If you want to go out tomorrow, you **should** do your homework now.*

We can also use other time words (with a present tense) to talk about the future, e.g. *when, as soon as*.

***When** I see him, I'll tell him.*

***As soon as** he arrives, we'll have dinner.*

Gerunds and infinitives

Some verbs are followed by the gerund and some are followed by the infinitive (with *to*).

Verbs followed by the gerund include:

enjoy, avoid, imagine, consider, finish, miss

*I **enjoy** playing tennis.*

*I can't **imagine** going to the moon.*

*Would you **consider** working part time?*

Verbs followed by the infinitive (with *to*) include:

want, seem, offer, decide, hope, afford, expect, promise

*I **want to see** that new film.*

*He **decided to start** piano lessons.*

*I'm **hoping to go** to university next year.*

Purpose/reason/result

Expressing purpose

We use these structures to express purpose:

to + infinitive
in order (not) to + infinitive
so that + subject + verb

In order to is more formal than *to* and *so that*.

I'm writing to you <u>in order to complain</u> about the meal.

I'd like to talk to the manager <u>to explain</u> the problem.

I've got a bottle of water with me <u>so that I don't get</u> thirsty.

Giving a reason

We use *because* + subject + verb to give reasons:

I'm studying very hard <u>because I've got</u> my exams in two weeks.

Explaining a result

We use *so* + subject + verb to explain results:

We booked early <u>so we got</u> very good seats in the theatre.

Key vocabulary

Parts of the body

head hair face eye nose ear mouth lips
torso back stomach waist arm elbow wrist
hand finger thumb leg knee foot ankle toe

Describing appearance

beautiful attractive unattractive handsome
good-looking ugly tall medium height short
thin slim skinny fat overweight muscular

Describing character

chatty organised sensitive hard-working
unreliable reserved open ambitious

Illnesses and injuries

flu a cold food poisoning a broken arm or leg

Symptoms

a headache a sore throat a pain in my chest
feel sick earache stomachache
a high temperature backache toothache

1 Find the missing word in each sentence.

If I eat any more, I be sick.

If I eat any more, I'll be sick.

1 We'll be late we don't leave now.
2 If it rains, we not play tennis this afternoon.
3 You buy me a newspaper if you go shopping later?
4 If I don't see Holly today, I phone her.
5 You put your hand on the cooker, you'll burn yourself.
6 I won't meet you at the cinema I don't finish my work.
7 If you lend me five pounds, I pay you back tomorrow.
8 If you get home before me, you make the dinner?

2 Write First Conditional sentences using the prompts.

she/eat all that cake/be sick

If she eats all that cake, she'll be sick.

1 they/offer me the job/take it
   _____.
2 I/have a party/pass my exam
   _____.
3 you/not use sun cream/get burnt
   _____.
4 I/be late for work/not get up now
   _____.
5 we/not invite her/she be upset
   _____.
6 I/see Jon/not tell him about the party
   _____.
7 you/not have any money left/buy those jeans
   _____.
8 we/not leave now/be late
   _____.

3 Choose the correct alternatives.

I expect passing/(to pass) my driving test.

1 I enjoy *going/to go* to the cinema.
2 I promise *not telling/not to tell* anyone.
3 He offered *washing/to wash* the dishes.
4 I considered *doing/to do* a computer course.
5 She's decided *going/to go* running every day.
6 They miss *living/to live* with their parents.
7 I hope *seeing/to see* you soon.
8 He avoided *talking/to talk* to girls as much as possible.

4 Complete the sentences with the gerund or infinitive (with *to*) form of the verbs in brackets.

We've decided *to eat* (eat) at home this evening.

1 I'm considering _____ (go) to Thailand for my next holiday.
2 I'm hoping _____ (lose) about four kilos by the end of March.
3 Gabriela offered _____ (help) me with my homework.
4 We'll leave at 10 to avoid _____ (arrive) in the dark.
5 I want _____ (do) a lot of work this weekend.
6 Let me know when you've finished _____ (talk) on the phone.

5 Choose the correct alternatives.

I'm getting a new computer (so that)/to I can work at home.

1 I'm going to bed now *so/because* I'm very tired.
2 She always walks to work *in order to/so that* keep fit.
3 I always write lists *because/so that* I don't forget anything.
4 My car broke down *so/in order to* I was late for the party.
5 I use an alarm clock *in order not to/so that* wake up late.
6 He always buys theatre tickets early *because/to* get good seats.

6 Complete the sentences using the words and phrases in the box. Two of them cannot be used.

chatty   feel sick   muscular   sensitive
high temperature   ambitious   reliable
reserved   sore throat   skinny

My brother is always talking. He's so *chatty* .

1 I think she's too thin. She's very _____ now.
2 I've got a terrible _____ and I've nearly lost my voice.
3 You can always trust Mick. He's very _____ .
4 James goes to the gym almost every day. He's getting very _____ .
5 She's quite _____ at first and doesn't say much.
6 I was in bed with a really _____ yesterday. It was nearly 40 °C.
7 My sister is very _____ . She wants to be the Director in two years.

8 Speed

Lead-in

1 **a** Look at the photos. What can you see? What is the connection?

b Complete the sentences using the correct phrase from the box.

> a top speed of   speed limit   fastest-selling   can run at

1 Cheetahs _____ 80 kilometres an hour.
2 A Mclaren Formula One car has _____ 400 kilometres an hour
3 The _____ on motorways in Spain is 100 kilometres an hour.
4 The album *No strings attached* by *NSYNC is the _____ pop album in the USA ever.

2 **a** Two of the sentences above are false. Discuss which ones.

b **8.1** Listen and check your answers.

3 **a** Check you understand the meanings of the <u>underlined</u> phrases.

1 Are you the type of person who is always <u>in a hurry</u>?
2 Do you usually arrive <u>on time</u> for things? How do you feel if you're late?
3 What time is the <u>rush hour</u> in your town? What is it like?
4 Do you usually <u>speed up</u> or <u>slow down</u> when you see an amber traffic light? Why?
5 Do you think <u>speed cameras</u> on roads are a good idea? Why/Why not?

b Ask and answer the questions with a partner. Which of you lives a 'faster' life?

Reading

1 Look at the photos and discuss.

'The Slow Movement is a group of people who want to change modern life.'

1 What do you think they don't like about modern life?

2 What changes do you think they want?

2 Read the text quickly. Choose the best title.

a Let's go! A guide to living the fast life.

b Slow down! How to go slow and live more.

c Red, amber, green! Different speeds for different people.

Food

Fast facts:

65 million fast-food meals are eaten in the USA every day.

In 1970, Americans spent about $6 billion on fast food. It is now more than $110 billion a year and this figure continues to <u>rise</u>.

In 1968, McDonald's had about 1,000 restaurants. Today it has about 28,000 around the world and this number <u>goes up</u> by almost 2,000 each year.

Slow tips:

Make your own food. It's tastier, better for you and you'll enjoy doing it. Sit down and eat with other people. Don't eat 'on the go' or at your desk.

Communication

Fast facts:

Over fifty million text messages are sent each day in the UK.

An average office worker deals with forty-six phone calls, twenty-five emails, sixteen voicemails, twenty-three items of post and nine mobile phone calls every day.

Slow tips:

Write one long email instead of three short ones.

Switch your mobile phone off or leave it at home sometimes.

Travel

Fast facts:

Over 400 million cars are currently used around the world.

London rush-hour traffic drives at an average of thirteen kilometres per hour.

Two out of three people speed up when the traffic lights turn amber.

Slow tips:

Leave your car at home if you can, and walk. Your fitness will <u>improve</u> and you'll probably get there quicker.

Spend at least twenty minutes a day in a garden or park. Sit, think, look at the trees, talk, read, enjoy the sky.

3 Correct the sentences.

The amount of money spent on fast food in the US is going ~~down~~ *up*.

1 The text recommends having lunch in front of your computer.

2 British people send more than fifty million emails every day.

3 The text says you should have your phone with you all the time.

4 The maximum speed of cars in London's rush hour is thirteen kilometres an hour.

5 Most people slow down when the traffic lights turn amber.

6 The text says driving is probably quicker than walking.

7 The text suggests relaxing at home for twenty minutes each day.

4 Look again at the 'Slow tips' from the text and work with a partner.

1 Do you do the things they suggest? Do you think they are good ideas? Why/Why not?

2 Write one more tip for each section. Tell other students your tips.

Grammar | Present Simple Passive

5 **a** Look at the examples in the Active grammar box and choose the correct alternatives.

> ### Active grammar
>
> Most sentences in English are **active**.
> Form: <u>subject</u>/<u>object</u> + verb + <u>subject</u>/<u>object</u>.
>
> *Americans spend more than $110 billion on fast food every year.*
>
> Use the **passive** when who/what causes the action is unknown or not important.
>
> *65 million fast-food meals are eaten every day in the USA.*
>
> Form: <u>am</u>/<u>is</u>/<u>are</u> + <u>infinitive</u>/<u>past participle</u>
>
> *These burgers are made from 100% beef.*

b <u>Underline</u> two more examples of the Present Simple Passive in the text in Ex. 2.

see Reference page 83

6 Complete the sentences with a verb from the box in the Present Simple Passive.

> employ   include   catch   charge
> use   deliver

1 Pizzas _____ in twenty minutes or you get your money back.
2 Service _____ in the bill.
3 Many people _____ by speed cameras.
4 London Underground _____ by thousands of people every day.
5 Millions of people _____ in the fast-food industry.
6 Customers _____ 35 yen per minute to eat in the Totenko restaurant in Tokyo.

7 **a** **8.2** Listen and write the questions.

b Try to write full answers. Then check the information on page 130.

Vocabulary | verbs about change

8 Look at the three <u>underlined</u> verbs in the text in Ex. 2 and answer these questions.

1 Which two verbs have similar meanings?
2 Which verb means *to get better*?

9 Look at the words and phrases in the box. Label them 'A' for changes in quantity or 'B' for changes in quality.

> improve/deteriorate   rise/fall
> get better/get worse   go up/go down

10 **a** Choose the correct word or phrase in each sentence.

1 The number of fast-food restaurants is *going up/getting better* steadily.
2 The quality of food that most people eat in the UK has *got worse/fallen* recently.
3 The amount of traffic has *risen/improved* over the last few years.
4 The average speed in cities has *deteriorated/fallen* in the last thirty years.
5 The air quality in most cities is *deteriorating/going down* rapidly.
6 The price of air travel has *deteriorated/gone down* in the last ten years.

b **8.3** Listen and check your answers.

Speaking

11 **a** Look at the topics in the box below. Make notes about the changes in your area/country.

> quality/number of fast-food restaurants
> wages   air quality   traffic

b Tell your partner about the changes. Use the language in the How to ... box to help you.

<table>
<tr><td rowspan="11" style="writing-mode: vertical-rl;">HOW TO ...</td><td colspan="2">talk about simple changes</td></tr>
<tr><td>What change?</td><td>Prices have gone up ...
Air quality has deteriorated ...</td></tr>
<tr><td>How fast?</td><td>... dramatically
... steadily
... slightly</td></tr>
<tr><td>When?</td><td>... recently.
... in the last two years.
... since they built the new factory.</td></tr>
</table>

Vocabulary | phrasal verbs – relationships

1 Write the phrasal verbs in the questions next to the correct definitions.

1 Do women ever <u>ask</u> men <u>out</u> in your country?

2 What do you think is the minimum time you should <u>go out with</u> someone before you get married?

3 Do you think couples who marry young often <u>grow apart</u>? Why/Why not?

4 If your partner never did housework, would you <u>put up with</u> it? Why/Why not?

5 For what reasons do people usually <u>split up with</u> their partner?

6 What different ways do people use to <u>get over</u> the end of a relationship?

PHRASAL VERB	DEFINITION
A _____	be someone's partner
B _____	stop being someone's partner
C _____	slowly stop having a good relationship
D *ask someone out*	invite someone to go on a date with you
E _____	stop feeling sad about an ex-partner
F _____	accept a bad situation without complaining

2 Complete the sentences with the correct form of the phrasal verbs from Ex. 1.

1 Pete _____ me _____ yesterday. He wants to take me to a restaurant.

2 Jade's been single since she _____ her boyfriend last year.

3 Oliver never does the washing-up and Maria just _____ it.

4 When my sister got divorced, she found it difficult to _____ her ex-husband.

5 Linda and Guy are a couple. They started _____ each other last month.

6 We used to be good friends but we've _____ over the last year.

3 Discuss the questions in Ex. 1.

Speed Date Scorecard

Your name:

Oliver Wren

Number:	Name:	Yes (tick)	Comments:
12	Miranda		
13	Wendy	✓	Funny and interesting
14	Caroline		

Reading

4 **a** Look at the photo. What do you think 'speed-dating' is?

b Read the letter and check your answers.

SpeedDate

Dear **Rachel**,

Thank you for booking a place at our next speed-dating event.

What to expect:
Speed-dating is a fast way to meet a new partner! There are twenty men and twenty women and you have *just three minutes* to talk to each person. After three minutes, if you like the person, put a tick by his or her name on your card. Then move on and talk to the next person. At the end, give us your card. If you ticked someone who also ticked you, we will give you each other's email addresses.

A few tips:
Don't start every conversation with 'What do you do?' This gets very boring. And don't ask too many questions which can be answered with 'yes' or 'no'.
Ask interesting questions, like 'How would your best friend describe you?' or 'What was the last CD you bought?'.

When?
Saturday 16th January. Arrive at 7.00 p.m.

Where?
Attica Club, 24 Hawkley Street, London.

Happy dating!

Julia Jones
Manager

5 Read the letter again and answer the questions.

1 How many people are there at this event?

2 How long do you get to speak to each person?

3 What should you do with your card?

4 Whose email addresses will you get?

5 What type of question shouldn't you ask?

6 What questions should you ask?

6 Discuss with other students.

1 What do you think about speed-dating?

2 Do you think it might be a good way to get a boy/girlfriend?

Listening

7 a **8.4** Listen to two dialogues at a speed-dating event. Which pair followed the advice in the letter?

b Listen again and write the name of the person (Melanie, Steve, Rachel and Kieron) who ...

1 is a teacher.

2 is an architect.

3 likes his/her job.

4 has never done speed-dating before.

5 is friendly.

6 has a teach-yourself Italian CD.

7 loves Italy.

Grammar | questions

8 Read the Active grammar box and choose the correct alternatives to complete rules 1–3.

Active grammar

These are two main types of questions:

Yes/No questions, e.g. *Do you enjoy your job?*

Wh-/How questions, e.g. *How would your best friend describe you?*

Find two more *Yes/No* questions and three more *Wh-/How* questions in the tapescript on page 159.

Make questions by changing the word order.

1 When the main verb is *to be*, put the verb <u>before</u>/after the subject.

What's your name?

2 With the Present Simple and Past Simple, put *do/does/did* <u>before</u>/after the subject.

Where do you live?

3 With other tenses, put the auxiliary verb or modal verb (*have, be, can, would,* etc.) <u>before</u>/after the subject.

Have you done speed-dating before?

---

see Reference page 83

9 Correct the mistake in each question.

1 What kind of weather you like best?

2 What your favourite kind of holiday?

3 What you going to do this weekend?

4 Do you can cook a really good meal?

5 You are good at making things?

6 You do collect anything unusual?

7 What you dream about last night?

8 How many countries you have visited in your life?

10 With a partner, write six more interesting questions to ask someone at a speed-dating event.

Speaking

11 a Imagine you are at a party. Talk to other students and find out some interesting information about each person. You only have two minutes with each person.

b Report back to the class. What did you find out? What was the most interesting question you were asked?

8.3 The curious incident

Grammar	Past Continuous and Past Simple
Can do	ask and answer questions about past actions

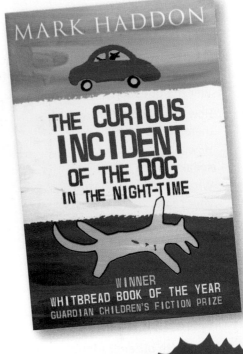

Reading

1 Discuss.

1 What books have you read recently?

2 Do you have a favourite author(s)? Who is it/are they?

2 **a** Look at the cover of the novel *The curious incident of the dog in the night-time* by Mark Haddon. What do you think the book is about?

b Read the first extract from the novel and answer the questions.

1 In what way is Christopher unusual?

2 Who do you think Siobhan is?

3 Why do you think he didn't understand the four pictures at the end of extract 1?

Extract 1

My name is Christopher John Francis Boone. I know all the countries of the world and their capital cities and every prime number up to 7,057.

Eight years ago, when I first met Siobhan, she showed me this picture

:(

and I knew that it meant 'sad', which is what I felt when I found the dead dog.

Then she showed me this picture

:)

and I knew that it meant 'happy', like when I'm reading about the Apollo space missions, or when I am still awake at 3a.m. or 4a.m. in the morning and I can walk up and down the street and pretend that I am the only person in the whole world.

Then she drew some other pictures

:) :) :| :o

but I was unable to say what these meant.

3 **a** Look at the picture. What do you think is happening?

b Read the second extract and answer the questions.

1 Why does Christopher like the police?

2 Who do you think Mrs Shears is?

3 Why does he find it difficult to answer the policeman's questions properly?

4 What do you think happens next?

Extract 2

Then the police arrived. I like the police. They have uniforms and numbers and you know what they are meant to be doing. There was a policewoman and a policeman. The policewoman had a little hole in her tights on her left ankle and a red scratch in the middle of the hole.

The policewoman put her arms round Mrs Shears and led her back towards the house.

I lifted my head off the grass.

The policeman said, 'Would you like to tell me what's going on here, young man

I sat up and said 'The dog is dead.'

'How old are you?' he asked.

I replied, 'I am 15 years and 3 months and 2 days.'

'And what, precisely, were you doing in the garden?' he asked.

'I was holding the dog,' I replied.

'And why were you holding the dog?' he asked.

This was a difficult question. It was something I wanted to do. I like dogs. It made me sad to see that the dog was dead.

I like policemen, too, and I wanted to answer the question properly, but the policeman did not give me enough time to work out the correct answer.

4 Read the last extract on page 130 and answer the questions.

   1 Did he commit the crime?

   2 Why does he make a 'groaning' noise?

   3 Why does he hit the policeman?

5 Discuss.

   1 What do you think happens next?

   2 Would you like to read this book? Why/Why not?

Grammar | Past Continuous and Past Simple

6 **a** Complete the Active grammar box by writing Past Simple or Past Continuous.

> ### Active grammar
>
> Use the _____ to talk about an action in progress at a particular time in the past.
>
> *I was holding the dog.*
>
> *I wasn't doing anything.*
>
> Use the _____ to talk about complete actions in the past.
>
> *Did you kill the dog?*
>
> *I didn't kill the dog.*
>
> Use the _____ to talk about a longer action interrupted by another action.
>
> *He was sitting on the grass when the policeman arrived.*

b Look at the three extracts again and find five examples of the Past Continuous.

see Reference page 83

7 Complete the sentences using the verbs in brackets. Use the Past Simple and the Past Continuous.

   1 I _____ (walk) home when I _____ (meet) Sarah.

   2 Marek _____ (take) a photo of me when I _____ (not/look).

   3 I _____ (read) a magazine when the train _____ (arrive).

   4 How fast _____ (you drive) when the accident _____ (happen)?

   5 When I last _____ (see) Emma, she _____ (work) in a restaurant in Paris.

   6 I _____ (tell) her what to do but she _____ (not/listen).

8 Complete the sentences using your own ideas. Use the Past Simple or the Past Continuous.

   1 I cut my finger while I _____.

   2 I was playing the piano when my friend _____.

   3 While we were watching a video, my brother _____.

   4 Debbie broke her leg while she _____.

   5 While I was living in France, I _____.

9 Guess what other students were doing at 8.30a.m., 2.00p.m. and 11.00p.m. last Saturday.

   A: *Were you having your breakfast at 8.30a.m.?*

   B: *No, I wasn't. I was asleep!*

Pronunciation

10 **a** `8.5` Listen and write the sentences.

b Listen again. How do you pronounce *was/were*? Practise the sentences.

Speaking

11 **a** Work in groups of four. Two As and two Bs.

Student As: look at page 126.

Student Bs: look at page 128.

Follow the instructions.

b Report back. Did Student As commit the crime?

Writing

12 Read the story in the Writing bank on page 147. Do the exercises.

13 Write a story starting with the words *It all happened last summer …*

Race to the finish

START

What's the top speed of a McLaren Formula One car?

Are you interested in motor racing? Why/Why not?

'Choice'

What's the name of the fastest-selling pop album in the USA?

What kind of music do you like?

Go back two spaces.

'Choice'

How many fast-food meals are eaten in the US every day?

Do you like eating fast food? Why/Why not?

'Choice'

How many text messages are sent in the UK every day?

Go back three spaces.

What is your favourite form of communication? Why?

'Choice'

What is the average speed of traffic in London's rush hour?

Do you prefer travelling by car or using a bicycle? Why?

Go back two spaces.

'Choice'

How many minutes do you have for each date at a speed-dating event?

How would your best friend describe you?

'Choice'

How old is Christopher Boone?

What is your favourite book of all time? Why?

'Choice'

FINISH!

1 Read the rules of the game below.

How to play …

RACE TO THE FINISH!

① Play in groups of three or four.

② Each player puts a counter at the starting line. Take turns to throw a dice and move around the board.

③ Answer the questions on the red squares. If you can't, go back one space. The red squares are all related to this unit.

④ Speak for one minute, without stopping, about the questions on the blue squares. If you can't, go back one space.

⑤ If you land on a 'Choice' square, the other players choose a question for you to answer or talk about.

⑥ The winner is the player who reaches the finish line first!

2 Before you play the game, in your group write seven 'Choice' questions for another group. The questions can be about general topics or facts you've learnt in this book.

What's the best holiday you've ever had?

What's the capital of New Zealand?

3 Play the game.

Present Simple Passive

In active constructions, the subject is the person or thing that does the action. Use the passive when the person (or thing) who does the action is not important or not known.

Form: *am/is/are* + past participle

*Most computers **are made** in Asia.*

*The gates **are locked** at 6:00p.m.*

We also use the passive when the object of the active sentence is the main focus. Use *by* to say who did the action.

*Most text messages are sent **by** teenagers.*

The object of active sentences becomes the subject of passive sentences. Compare:

Active: *She cleans **my room** every day.*

Passive: *My room is cleaned every day.*

Questions

There are two main types of questions:

Yes/No questions: *Do you like watching football?*

Wh- questions: *What did you do last weekend?*

The most common *Wh-* question words are:

what, where, when, who, why, which, whose and *how.*

We often put *Wh-* question words together with other words:

e.g. *what time, what kind, how much, how many, how often, how long, which one.*

***What time** does your train leave?*

***How long** have you lived here?*

Word order

1 When the main verb is *to be*, put the verb before the subject.

   *Where **were you** yesterday?*

2 When there is a main verb (with no auxiliary verb), we put *do/does/did* before the subject + infinitive.

   ***Do you like** playing computer games?*

3 For verbs with an auxiliary, we put the auxiliary verb (*have, will, can, would,* etc.) before the subject.

   ***Can you play** the piano?*

Subject questions

When we are asking about the subject of a sentence, the verb comes after the question word (and we don't use an auxiliary).

***Who left** the door open?*

NOT: ~~Who did leave the door open?~~

***Which one tastes** better?*

NOT: ~~Which one does taste better?~~

Past Continuous

➕ ➖	I/He/She/It	was wasn't	waiting ...
	You/We/They	were weren't	
❓	Was Were	I/he/she/it you/we/they	eating ...
	Yes, No, Yes, No,	I/he/she/it you/we/they	was. wasn't. were. weren't.

Use the Past Continuous to talk about an action or situation that was in progress at a particular time in the past.

Adam was cooking when I got home.

I was waiting for the bus at half past six.

Past continuous actions are not complete at that time in the past. To talk about completed actions at a particular time in the past, use the Past Simple.

I sent David an email yesterday.

Martin cooked dinner last night.

We often use the Past Continuous:

to set the scene at the beginning of a story.

It was raining heavily. Julia was walking quickly towards the cinema.

to talk about a longer action interrupted by another action.

I was watching TV when he arrived.

Key vocabulary

Speed

a top speed of   speed limit   fastest-selling
be able to run at   be in a hurry   arrive on time
rush hour   speed up   slow down   speed camera

Verbs about change

go up   go down   rise   fall   improve   deteriorate
get better   get worse

Phrasal verbs about relationships

ask someone out   go out (with someone)
put up (with someone)   split up (with someone)
get over (someone)   grow apart

1

Complete the sentences with the Present Simple Passive form of the verbs in the box.

> cover   invite   cut down   lock   ~~make~~
> serve   clean   recycle   open

Cheese *is made* from milk.

1   The rooms in this hotel _____ at 10.00a.m. every morning.
2   You _____ to Paul and Sheila's wedding.
3   All the paper in this box _____.
4   Thousands of trees _____ every year.
5   Most of the Earth's surface _____ by water.
6   The park gates _____ at 6.00p.m.
7   Breakfast _____ from 7.00 to 9.00a.m.
8   Sometimes, important public buildings _____ by the Queen.

2

Complete the sentences using the Present Simple Passive or the active form of the verbs in brackets.

My house *is painted* (paint) every year.

1   You _____ (not pronounce) the 'k' in knife.
2   Photos _____ (take) of speeding cars by speed cameras.
3   John _____ (not invite) to parties very often.
4   Fifty people _____ (employ) in the new factory.
5   People _____ (not use) this bus route much.
6   At least three trains a day _____ (cancel) at this station.
7   Glass _____ (make) from sand.
8   Many sports _____ (play) on this field on Saturday.
9   The shop _____ (close) for lunch every day.

3

Write the words in the correct order to make questions.

working/Why/today/Sam/isn't

Why isn' t Sam working today?

1   you/Have/a cheetah/ever/seen
2   coming/are/time/your friends/What
3   to work/you/always/Why/do/drive
4   lived/How long/in/that flat/she/has
5   last/see/a good film/did/When/you
6   tonight/Are/do/your homework/you/to/ going
7   you/Would/to dinner/like/tomorrow/to/come
8   going/are/on holiday/year/Where/next/you

4

Write the questions.

My favourite drink is …
What *is your favourite drink*?

1   I like eating … for breakfast.
    What _____?
2   We usually go to … for our holidays.
    Where _____?
3   She played the … as a child.
    What _____?
4   I bought a …
    What _____?
5   My mother can … really well.
    What _____?
6   I'm going to start driving lessons in …
    When _____?
7   They were late for school … last week.
    How many times _____?

5

Complete the paragraphs with the Past Continuous or Past Simple form of the verbs in brackets.

At about 6.30 yesterday evening, I *was cycling* (cycle) home from work. It (1) _____ (rain) and a lot of people (2) _____ (drive) too fast. Suddenly, a car (3) _____ (stop) in front of me. I (4) _____ (not hit) the car but I (5) _____ (fall) off my bicycle. Luckily, I (6) _____ (not / be) hurt.

A couple of years ago, I (7) _____ (walk) home along a dark street. Somebody (8) _____ (follow) me and I was quite frightened. I (9) _____ (start) to run but when I (10) _____ (look) back, I (11) _____ (see) my friend Daniel. I was so happy!

6

Replace the underlined word with the correct word.

I really like him. I hope he asks me <u>up</u> soon. *out*

1   Katie's had flu for three days but she's <u>going</u> better now.
2   You must slow <u>up</u> – the lights are turning red.
3   Tom's so lazy! Why do you put <u>on</u> with it?
4   I never drive into Lisbon during the rush <u>time</u>. It's too busy.
5   Why don't you relax? You're always <u>at</u> a hurry.
6   Dan was driving over the speed <u>maximum</u> when the police stopped him.
7   Jane and I were best friends at school. We've grown <u>away</u> now.

9 Work

Lead-in

1 **a** Match the jobs in the box with the photos. Which job isn't shown?

> plumber   firefighter   fashion designer   sales rep.   lawyer

b **9.1** How do you pronounce the jobs above? Listen and check.

c Do you have a job? How do you say it in English? Find out what jobs three other students do. If you don't know what they are, ask the student to explain.

2 Discuss these questions with a partner.

1 Look again at the jobs in the box. Which one would you most/least like to do? Why?

2 Do you have a 'dream job'? What is it? Why is it your 'dream job'?

3 **a** Put the phrases below in a logical order. Compare with other students.

I think you have to prepare a CV first ...

> get promoted   be offered a job   run your own company
> apply for a job   work long hours   resign   have an interview
> prepare a CV   take a job

b Which of these things have you done? Tell another student about your experiences.

Listening

1 a Discuss what is happening in each picture.

b [9.2] Listen to three people's stories. Match the stories with the pictures.

2 [9.2] Listen again. In which story does the person ...

1 not have an interview?
2 need a drink?
3 have to react quickly?
4 behave rudely towards the interviewer?
5 still feel embarrassed about what happened?
6 not know they should throw something?

3 a Work in groups of three. Each student reads one of the stories in the tapescript on page 159. Make notes about the important points.

b Tell the story to your group.

Vocabulary | work

4 a What is the difference in meaning between these words?

1 an employer/an employee
2 an interviewer/an interviewee
3 an application form/a CV
4 experience/qualifications
5 a salary/a bonus
6 a receptionist/a secretary
7 a company/a factory
8 a managing director/a sales rep.

b Choose the correct alternatives.

1 Most of our *employers/employees* have been with the company since we started last year.
2 A good *managing director/sales rep.* knows how to listen to people and give them the products they need.
3 I'm afraid we need someone for this job with much more *experience/qualifications*.
4 It's very important that a good *receptionist/secretary* should be welcoming to visitors.
5 If we reach our sales targets, we will get a 20 percent *salary/bonus*.
6 A good *interviewer/interviewee* knows how to ask good questions to find out about people.
7 I must fill out the *application form/CV* for that job at CoffeeCo. today.

A

B

STAFF ONLY

MANAGING DIRECTOR

C

Pronunciation

5 a [9.3] Listen and mark the main stress on each word or phrase in Ex. 4a.

an empl<u>o</u>yer/an employ<u>ee</u>

b Say each word or phrase to your partner.

6 Discuss these questions with a partner.

1 What qualities make a good interviewer/ secretary/sales rep./managing director?
2 What information should you include in a CV? What order should it be in?
3 What is a typical salary in your country for a secretary/a sales rep.?
4 Would you rather have a high salary and no bonus, or an average salary and possible bonuses?
5 When was the last time you were an interviewee? How did you feel?

Reading

7 **a** Discuss.

What must you do to be successful in a job interview? Make a list under these headings:

1 Before the interview
2 During the interview
3 After the interview

b Compare your list with other students. Do you have the same points?

8 Read the advice below. Tick (✓) the points in your list that are mentioned.

HOW TO GET THAT JOB!

Before the interview

- Find out as much as you can about the company.
- Think about questions which the interviewer might ask you. Plan how to answer them.
- Dress smartly.
- Don't be late. If you are very early, have a coffee in a local café and look at your notes.
- Switch off your mobile and take two or three slow, deep breaths before you go in.

During the interview

- When you walk in, shake hands firmly with the interviewer, look them in the eyes, and say 'Pleased to meet you'.
- Answer the questions in a confident, firm voice. Don't speak too quietly, too quickly or be too hesitant.
- Answers should not be one word or one sentence, but also should not be too long.
- When answering questions, maintain eye contact with the interviewer. If there is more than one interviewer, give them equal attention.
- Give clear, direct answers to questions. If you don't know something, say so.
- Don't lie.

- At the end of the interview, you might be asked: 'Are there any questions that you would like to ask us?' Make sure you have one or two good questions ready.
- Above all, be positive and show enthusiasm for the job.

After the interview

- If you didn't answer a question well in the interview, don't be afraid to phone up soon afterwards and say something like: 'I don't think I explained myself very well in the interview. What I wanted to say was …' This will show enthusiasm and it will remind them of you.

---

9 Read the advice again. Answer these questions.

1 What research do you need to do before the interview?
2 What kind of clothes should you wear to the interview?
3 What should you do if you arrive very early?
4 What should you do just before you enter the interview room?
5 What should you do and say when you meet the interviewer?
6 How long should your answers to questions be?
7 How should you answer questions?
8 Where should you look when you answer questions?
9 What should your general attitude in the interview be?
10 What should you do after the interview?

10 Discuss.

1 Do you disagree with any of the points? If so, which ones? Why?
2 Do you think you are good or bad at job interviews? Why?
3 Would you rather work for yourself or work in a company? Why?

Speaking

11 Look at page 131 and work in pairs. Student A is the interviewee. Student B is the interviewer.

Wayne Rooney

Keira Knightley

Reading

1 Look at the photos. What do you think these young people have in common?

2 **a** Read the first part of the text below to check your ideas.

b Read the rest of the text on page 131. How does Carl feel about his success?

BOY WONDER

Internet entrepreneur Carl Churchill describes himself as 'a normal 19-year-old'. Except that his Internet technology (IT) company is currently making £1 million a year. What's more, __A__

The Rich List 2020 is a list of twenty young people who are expected to make a lot of money – many millions – by 2020. Other names include famous actors like Keira Knightley and football stars, such as Wayne Rooney. But at the very top of the list, is Carl Churchill. He is expected to make an amazing £100 million by 2020.

3 The following sentences have been removed from the text. Decide where each one should go (A–D).

1 I think it's important to save for the future.
2 And, finally, a few hours' sleep at the house he owns in Milton Keynes.
3 His name is on *The Rich List 2020*.
4 The main things it does are to help big businesses connect to the Internet, check emails for viruses and block spam, all at very high speeds.

4 Read the whole text again. Mark the sentences true (T) or false (F).

1 Carl Churchill thinks he is a bit different from other teenagers.
2 *The Rich List 2020* consists of young people who have already made a lot of money.
3 To be so successful, Carl needs to work long hours.
4 Carl doesn't have as much of a social life as his friends.

5 Discuss.

1 Would you like to have Carl's lifestyle and work routine? Why/Why not?
2 What are the pros and cons of making a lot of money in your teens?

Vocabulary | *make/do*

6 Look at the examples of things we 'make' and things we 'do' in the box. Put these words or phrases in the correct list below.

> nothing   an effort
> progress   your best
> an appointment
> someone a favour
> a mistake   research
> a complaint

make: *money, a decision*

do: *business, homework*

7 **a** Find five examples of these phrases in the text in Ex. 2.

b Complete the questions below with *make* or *do* in the correct form.

Are you generally good or bad at *making* decisions? Does it depend on the kind of decision?

1 How do you feel if you know you've _____ a mistake while you're speaking in English?
2 When was the last time you _____ someone a favour? What was it?
3 Have you ever _____ a complaint in a restaurant or shop? If so, what happened?
4 When you have holidays, do you enjoy _____ nothing or do you like to be active?
5 In which areas do you think you are _____ most progress in your English?

c Ask and answer the questions.

Carl Churchill

Grammar | *can, could, be able to*

8 Read the Active grammar box and choose the correct alternatives.

> ### Active grammar
>
> Use *can/could/be able to* to talk about ability in the present.
>
> *John can work all night without sleeping.*
>
> Use *can/could/be able to* to talk about ability in the past.
>
> *He couldn't afford to buy a new car last year.*
>
> Use *can/could/be able to* to talk about ability in the future.
>
> *I hope the business will be able to grow.*

see Reference page 93

9 a Complete the sentences with *can/can't, could/couldn't, will/won't be able to*.

1 David _____ play the piano quite well now.

2 I _____ get to sleep last night. I kept thinking about work.

3 I _____ lift this box. It's too heavy. _____ you help me?

4 Ann _____ write simple computer programs by the time she was twelve.

5 They looked everywhere for Suzie's ring but they _____ find it.

6 _____ you hear what Paul was saying? It was very noisy in the restaurant.

7 I'm sorry, but we _____ come to the party. We're on holiday in Spain that weekend.

8 _____ help me move into my new flat on Saturday?

b 9.4 Listen and repeat sentences 1–6 with the correct pronunciation of *can*/kən/or/kæn/, *can't*/kɑːnt/, *could*/kʊd/and *couldn't*/kʊdənt/ in each one.

10 Look at the table. In pairs, say how well Melissa *could*, *can* and *will be able to* play the guitar, swim, cook and paint.

✗✗ = not at all   ✗ = not very well
✓ = quite well   ✓✓ = very well

	A	B	C	D
5 years ago	✗	✗✗	✓	✗✗
Now	✓	✗✗	✓	✗
5 years from now	✓✓	✗	✓✓	✗

5 years ago she couldn't play the guitar very well.

> ## Lifelong learning
>
> *Setting targets!*
>
> Make a list of things:
>
> 1 you couldn't do one year ago in English, e.g. order a meal in a restaurant.
>
> 2 you can do now in English, e.g. describe free-time interests.
>
> 3 you want to be able to do a year from now, e.g. read short newspaper articles.
>
> Plan how you are going to improve. Give yourself tasks to do and dates to do them.

Person to person

11 a For each activity in Ex. 10, tell another student how well you …

1 could do it in the past.

2 can do it now.

3 hope you will be able to do it in the future.

b Choose two other activities to describe in the same way.

9.3 Crime doesn't pay
| Grammar | Past Simple Passive |
| Can do | write a short article |

Vocabulary | crime

1 Look at the words and phrases in the box and answer the questions below.

> judge   thief   jury   police officer

1 Who **steals** things?
2 Who **arrests** criminals?
3 Who decides if a **criminal** is **guilty** or **innocent**?
4 Who can decide what **punishment** to give a criminal, e.g. a **fine** or a **prison sentence**?

2 Check you understand the meaning of these questions. Discuss them with a partner.

1 What punishment would you give …
   a) a thief who stole some CDs from a shop?
   b) a businessman who avoided paying £1,000 of taxes?
2 Would you consider being a police officer? Why/Why not?
3 Have you ever done jury service? Would you like to?
4 Do you agree with the idea that people are 'innocent until proven guilty'?
5 What do you think of the prison system in your country?

Listening

3 You are going to listen to a news story. The words or phrases below are from the story. Discuss with a partner. What do you think it is about?

> thief   car showroom   expensive new car
> absolutely spotless   prison sentence

4 **9.5** Listen to the story and compare your ideas.

5 **9.5** Listen to the story again. Mark the sentences true (T) or false (F).

1 Peter Blain was sent to jail for six years.
2 Police caught him while he was trying to leave the country.
3 People who work in car showrooms think that he wants to buy a new car.
4 He damages the cars he steals.
5 He makes money from his crimes.
6 He does it to feel like an important businessman.
7 His wife says that his sentence won't affect their marriage.

6 Discuss.

1 What do you think about Peter Blain's punishment? Was it too short/too long?
2 Do you think a different punishment would be better?

Grammar | Past Simple Passive

7 Read the Active grammar box and choose the correct alternatives.

> ### Active grammar
>
> Use the <u>active</u>/<u>passive</u> form to say what the subject did.
>
> *Peter Blain stole new cars.* (Peter Blain = subject)
>
> Use the <u>active</u>/<u>passive</u> to say what happened to the subject.
>
> *36 cars were stolen.* (36 cars = subject)
>
> Use the passive when who/what causes the action is unknown or not important.
>
> *He was arrested.*
>
> **Form:** *was/were* + past participle
>
> *I wasn't given anything to eat.*
>
> *What punishment were they given?*

8 Find five examples of the Past Simple Passive in the tapescript on page 159.

see Reference page 93

9 Complete the sentences with a verb from the box in the Past Simple Passive.

> arrest   paint   clean   invent   send   meet

1 All the employees _____ a letter by the Managing Director.
2 The bicycle _____ over 150 years ago.
3 We _____ at the airport by a holiday rep.
4 Two men _____ by police after stealing £2,000.
5 This car _____ last week and now look at how dirty it is!
6 The outside of the house _____ white last year.

10 Complete the sentences with the Past Simple Passive.

1 A: We _____ (not / give) very long to do our test.
   B: How long _____ (give)?
   A: Only an hour!
2 A: Someone broke into my flat but my computer _____ (not / take).
   B: What _____ (take)?
   A: My wallet and some CDs.
3 A: This house _____ (not / build) recently.
   B: When _____ (build)?
   A: At least twenty years ago.

11 Circle the correct alternatives in the text below.

Germany's worst bank robber (1) *gave/was given* a one-year suspended sentence* after a judge (2) *felt/was felt* sorry for him. The court (3) *told/was told* how Marko N., 28, (4) *waited/was waited* outside the bank for three hours trying to get over his nerves. He then (5) *ran/was run* into the bank with a woolly hat over his face. Unfortunately, he couldn't see anything. He (6) *took/was taken* off the hat in front of the security camera and demanded money from the cashier. He was holding a cigarette lighter in the shape of a gun. She just (7) *told/was told* him to go away. Finally, he ran off and (8) *arrested/was arrested* by police outside the bank. He (9) *took/was taken* in a van to the nearest police station. 'Give up being a bank robber,' the judge told him. 'You have no talent for the job.'

Glossary
* *suspended sentence* = you only go to prison if you commit another crime

Writing

12 Divide the text in Ex. 11 into three paragraphs: Introduction/The story/Conclusion. Use the How to ... box to help you.

HOW TO ...

write a short article	
Introduction: what is the important news?	*A man and woman were arrested last night after ...*
The story: tell the story from the beginning. Use sequencers like *then, next, finally.*	*Then he tried to get into the house ...* *Finally, he was caught ...*
Conclusion: finish with something funny or a quote.	*The criminal said he didn't remember anything about the evening.*

13 a Work in two groups.
   Group A: look at the picture story on page 126.
   Group B: look at the picture story on page 128.

   b What vocabulary do you need to tell your story? Use a dictionary/Ask your teacher.

   c Work in pairs. Tell your story to your partner and listen to your partner's story.

14 Look at the How to ... box again and write your story as an article of about 100 words. Divide it into three paragraphs.

9 Communication

Let's talk

1 Discuss with a partner.

In what situations do you 'negotiate'? E.g. with your boss for a pay increase; with your friends about what to do in the evening or with someone you live with about doing housework.

2 What should you do to negotiate successfully?

3 Look at the suggestions below. Do you agree with them? Can you add any more points?

The five-step negotiation plan

1 Be clear about what you want. Before you negotiate, decide: **a)** what you must have and **b)** what you would like but is not essential.

2 Make sure you have things to offer the other person, as well as things you want.

3 Keep calm and reasonable in your voice and behaviour. Do not let emotions take over. Be aware of your body language.

4 Listen carefully and ask questions. It's important to really understand what the other person is saying. Listening to someone shows respect. That person will feel valued and important and is more likely to listen to you.

5 Try to find a 'win-win' situation. Both sides should feel happy and successful when the negotiation is finished.

4 **9.6** Listen to this 'negotiation' and answer these questions.

1 What does each side do 'wrong'?

2 What advice would you give each of them to have a more successful 'negotiation'?

5 You are going to practise negotiating. Work in groups.

Group A: look at the information on page 126.

Group B: look at the information on page 128.

6 **a** Work in groups of four, two from Group A, two from Group B. Try to achieve as many of your targets as possible.

b When you have finished negotiating, read the targets of the other group. Who scored the most points?

can, could, be able to

Use *can* to say something is possible or someone has the ability to do something.

Form: *can* + infinitive

She can speak four languages.

Can you see the river?

They can't come to the party.

Use *could* to say something was possible or someone had the ability in the past.

Form: *could* + infinitive

She could speak French by the age of twelve.

Could you answer many of the questions in the exam?

I couldn't finish my report.

Use *will be able to* to say something will be possible or someone will have the ability in the future.

Form: *will be able to* + infinitive

She won't be able to come to the meeting on Tuesday.

You'll be able to pass the exam if you do all the homework.

Use expressions like *not at all/not very well/quite well/very well* to show degrees of ability

I can't cook at all. ✗✗

He couldn't swim very well. ✗

She could sing quite well. ✓

She'll be able to play the guitar very well with a few more lessons. ✓✓

Past Simple Passive

Use active verb forms like *gave*, *threw* and *made* to say what people and things did.

Sarah made a beautiful mirror for Sam's birthday.
 ↓   ↘
subject   active verb

We often use passive verb forms like *was cleaned, were taken, was made* to say what happens to things or people or what was done to them.

This camera was made in China.
 ↙   ↓
subject   passive verb

We often use the passive when the person or thing which causes the action is unknown or not important.

This house was built in 1745.

Form: *was/were* + past participle

➕ ➖	I/He/She/It	was wasn't ...	told ...
	You/We/They	were weren't ...	
❓	Was/wasn't Were/weren't	I/he/she/it you/we/they	promoted?
	Yes, No, Yes, No,	I/he/she/it you/we/they	was. wasn't. were. weren't.

Key vocabulary

Jobs

plumber   firefighter   fashion designer   lawyer receptionist   secretary   managing director sales rep.

Work

get promoted   run your own company   resign work long hours   have an interview   prepare a CV apply for a job   be offered a job   take a job employer   employee   interviewer   interviewee application form   CV   experience   qualifications salary   bonus   company   factory

Crime

judge   thief   jury   police officer   steal   arrest criminal   punishment   guilty   innocent   fine prison sentence

Make/do

Make: an effort, money, progress, a decision, a mistake, an appointment, a complaint

Do: business, research, nothing, homework, someone a favour, your best

1 Complete the sentences with *can('t)*, *could(n't)*, *will/won't be able to* and the verbs in the box.

> take   finish   help   play   stand
> sleep   tell   ~~lift~~

I *can't lift* this box. It's too heavy.

1 Alice has an amazing memory. She _____ you the capital city of every country in the world.

2 I didn't take my camera on holiday so I _____ any photographs.

3 _____ you _____ me with the housework tomorrow?

4 When Michael was younger, he _____ on his hands!

5 I hurt my leg last week so I _____ tennis tomorrow, I'm afraid.

6 **A:** You look awful.
   B: Yes, I _____ at all last night!

7 I _____ this report until Monday. I don't have all the statistics.

2 Make questions with *can, could, will be able to*. Use the verbs in brackets.

We're thinking of moving to Spain. (speak)
Can you speak Spanish?

1 Ellie would like to learn the saxophone. (read music)

2 We had a fantastic room in the hotel. (see the sea)

3 Pete wants to buy a car. (how much/afford)

4 Dave broke his leg skiing and is in a wheelchair. (when/walk again)

5 My dog is very clever. (what/do)

6 Jamie would really like to work for you next year. (when/start)

7 Tania loved speaking languages as a child. (how many/speak)

3 Make sentences from the words using the Past Simple Passive.

Several people/hurt/a fire/last night
Several people were hurt in a fire last night.

1 This letter/post/last Friday

2 The animals/give/some food

3 They/invite/Raul and Sharon's wedding

4 All the flights/cancel/because/the weather

5 This chair/make/Italy/sixteenth century

6 We/warn/stay indoors/until/morning

7 A lot of money and jewellery/steal/their house

4 Rewrite these sentences in the Past Simple Passive starting with the words given.

Somebody took the keys from my desk.
The keys *were taken from my desk.*

1 The police arrested more than fifty people.
More _____.

2 They opened the store at exactly 9a.m.
The store _____.

3 They paid me a lot of money to do the job.
I _____.

4 Nobody met us at the airport.
We _____.

5 They rescued everybody from the ship.
Everybody _____.

6 Somebody cleaned all the classrooms yesterday.
All _____.

5 In three of the sentences below, the word in italics is not correct. Replace the word with a more appropriate one.

Tom's been *promoted* to Sales Director. He's really pleased. *OK*

1 She's a very good *interviewer*. She's got every job she has applied for.

2 I don't have the right *experience* for this job. I don't have a degree in Mathematics.

3 They pay us a *bonus* of 20 percent of our annual salary if we reach our targets.

4 He's decided to *resign*. He wants to spend more time with his family.

5 A *secretary* is usually the first person you meet when you go in the building. So, they must make a good impression.

6 Put the letters in the correct order.

They all thought that a large *fine* would be the best punishment. (einf)

1 I'm going to _____ for the position of Head of the department. (yalpp)

2 There are normally twelve men and women on a _____. (yruj)

3 She's been voted '_____of the month'! She's met all her targets. (ymeeeolp)

4 I'd like to make a _____. Who do I speak to? (onatipmcl)

5 Could you do me a _____? I need to borrow some money. (ufvaro)

6 I'd like to run my own _____ and make all the important decisions. (ypncaom)

7 If you want to see the doctor, you'll have to make an _____. (nnpttoaimep)

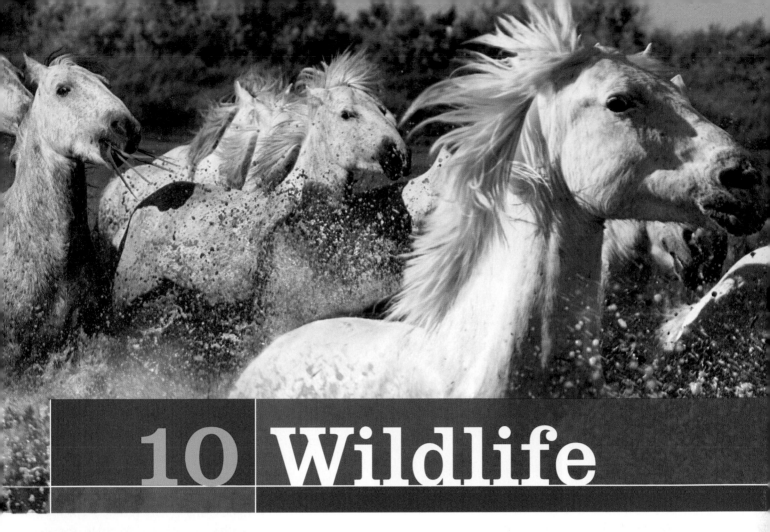

10 Wildlife

Lead-in

1 **a** Look at the photos. Which of the following animals can you see?

> tiger   lion   elephant   hyena   dog   cat   bear   wolf   snake
> horse   cow   zebra   spider   eagle   whale

b Divide the words above into: wild animals, domestic animals, insects and sea animals.

c Add two more animals to each list.

2 **a** Complete the expressions with a word from the box.

> fish   birds   horse   mouse   rat   cat

1   What's Claire doing? She's been *as quiet as a* _____ for the last hour!
2   We need to prepare lots of food for tonight. David *eats like a* _____ .
3   Forget about your ex-boyfriend. After all, *there are plenty more* _____ *in the sea*.
4   I hate working in the city and being part of the _____ *race*. I want to move to the country.
5   How did Tom find out about his present? Who *let the* _____ *out of the bag*?
6   I'd like to visit my old school and also see some friends who live nearby. That way I can *kill two* _____ *with one stone*.

b Discuss with other students. Do you have similar expressions in your language?

Grammar	phrasal verbs
Can do	talk about people who influenced you

Reading

1 Look at the people in the pictures. What do they have in common?

Raised by animals

There are a number of stories of children who are raised by animals. One of the earliest stories is about the twin brothers Romulus and Remus. They were the sons of the god Mars. When they were very young, they were left by the banks of the River Tiber. Luckily, they were found by a wolf. The wolf looked after them and fed them with her milk.

Later, a shepherd came across the boys. He took them home and brought them up as his own children. The boys grew up to be very strong and clever. They decided to build a town in the place where the shepherd found them.

Shortly after building the town, the twins had a big argument. Romulus killed his brother Remus in the fight. Romulus then became the first king of this town, which was named Rome, after him.

More recently, two young girls were discovered in the care of a wolf in 1920, in Godamuri, India. The girls (Kamala, 8, and Amala, aged 18 months) were taken to a children's home but they didn't like their new life there at all. They preferred to be with cats and dogs and they seemed to look up to animals, not people. They never got on with the other children and they sometimes bit and attacked them.

The girls slept during the day and were awake at night. They walked on their hands and feet and enjoyed raw meat. They had extremely good eyesight and hearing. The younger child, Amala, died one year later, but Kamala lived for nine years in the home. She picked up a small number of words but she remained very different from other children.

2 Read the text. How many examples of children raised by animals are mentioned?

3 Read the text again and answer these questions.
1 Who was the father of Romulus and Remus?
2 Where were they left when they were very small?
3 Who found them at first?
4 Who raised them?
5 What did the boys do when they became adults?
6 What was the result of the boys' argument?
7 Who was looking after Kamala and Amala when they were found?
8 How was the girls' relationship with other children?
9 What special abilities did they have?
10 What happened to Amala and Kamala?

4 Discuss.
1 Do you think the person who found Kamala and Amala should have left them with the wolf? Why/Why not?
2 Do you know of any similar stories in real life or in films?

Vocabulary | phrasal verbs

5 Match the <u>underlined</u> phrasal verbs from the text with the definitions below.

1 to change from child to adult = _____
2 to learn without trying = _____
3 to take care of = _____
4 to raise/educate children = _____
5 to find by chance = _____
6 to respect = _____

6 Complete these sentences with the correct form of the phrasal verbs from Ex. 5.

1 It's not easy to _____ children as a single parent.
2 All the children in my class _____ our History teacher. He was an amazing man.
3 We went to Spain on holiday and I was surprised at how much Spanish we _____ quite quickly.
4 Pete _____ a really interesting art gallery when he was walking around Venice.
5 I _____ in Manchester but then my parents moved to Edinburgh.
6 We're going on holiday for a few days. Could you _____ our dog while we're away?

7 a Complete the questions.

1 Where _____? (you/grow up)
2 Who _____? (bring up/you)
3 As a child, who _____ when you were ill? (look after/you)
4 As a child, who _____? (you/look up to)
5 Have _____ any English from TV or songs? (you/ever/pick up)
6 Have _____ any money in the street? (you/ever/come across)

b 🔊 **10.1** Listen and check your answers.

Pronunciation

8 a 🔊 **10.1** Listen to the sentences in Ex. 7a again. Which words are stressed in each sentence?

b Ask and answer the questions in Ex. 7a with a partner.

Lifelong learning

Keep a record (1)

It's important to keep a special vocabulary notebook of the new words that you learn. How do you organise it?

- Do you organise the new words by topic (e.g. animals), alphabetically or in another way?
- Do you write a definition?
- Do you write an example sentence?
- Do you write a translation?

Tell another student what you do.

Listening and speaking

9 a 🔊 **10.2** Listen to a woman talking about her childhood. Who were the two main people who influenced her?

b Listen again. Which statement is false?
1 She saw her father occasionally.
2 She grew up in Libya.
3 She feels close to her mother and grandmother.
4 She enjoyed school in England.

c Listen again and look at the How to ... box. How many times do you hear each phrase?

HOW TO ...	use conversational phrases	
	Say the same thing in a different way	*I mean, ...*
	Give yourself thinking time before you continue	*Well, ...*
	Go back to your original point	*So, anyway ...*
	Introduce an explanation	*You see, ...*

10 Tell another student about the people who most influenced you when you were growing up.

Grammar	countable/uncountable nouns
Can do	write a short contribution for a bulletin board

Reading

1 a Write a list of advantages and disadvantages of keeping animals in zoos.

b Compare with other students.

2 Look at the bulletin board messages. Is each person generally in favour of zoos or against zoos?

WILDLIFE WORLD
BULLETIN BOARD

Post your comments and questions here for everyone to see.

Are zoos a good thing?

Chris, London: Just been to the local zoo with my kids >>> awful! Hated seeing the animals locked up in those tiny cages. So little space. They looked really unhappy and it seemed quite cruel :-(.

Tania, Boston: Sorry Chris that you went to a zoo like that. Most zoos are quite good although that one sounds very bad. We have a fantastic zoo here :-). The animals have lots of space to move around. Actually, I think it's really important that children can see different animals face-to-face. Then they can learn about them. Also, nearly 12,000 species are in danger of extinction. Zoos can help save some of them!

Katie, Dublin: Although I think Tania's right in some ways, I mainly agree with Chris. Animals shouldn't be locked up. They should be free to go where they want. Yes, it's important that kids have information about animals but they can get that from the Internet and TV.

Dave, Manchester: Take my advice: have a break and go on a safari in Africa. See the animals in their natural environment. It's completely different to seeing animals in zoos! I don't think I could go to a zoo again.

3 Read the messages again and answer the questions.
1 Who is definitely a parent?
2 Who talks about using the Internet for education?
3 Who suggests taking a holiday?
4 Who is worried about how much room animals in zoos have?

4 Discuss. Which of the people do you agree/disagree with? Why?

Grammar | countable/uncountable nouns

5 **a** Look at the sentences. Which <u>underlined</u> noun is countable and which is uncountable?

1 The <u>animals</u> have lots of space.

2 It's important that kids have <u>information</u> about animals.

b Put the following nouns into the correct column in the Active grammar box.

> holiday travel furniture newspaper
> work news job advice money cheque

Active grammar

Countable	Uncountable
animal, _____	*information,* _____
Can be singular or plural.	Can only be singular.
Use *a few, some* or *a lot of* in positive sentences.	Use *a little/a bit of/a piece of, some* or *a lot of* in positive sentences.
Use *any* or *many* in negatives and questions.	Use *any* or *much* in negatives and questions.

see Reference page 103

6 Choose the correct alternatives.

1 This job will involve *many/a lot of* hard work.

2 We don't have *a little/much* furniture. Just a table and a few chairs.

3 I've got *any/some* bad news. There's going to be a train strike.

4 I have *a few/a little* cheques that I'd like to pay in to my account.

5 Can you help me? I need *a bit of/a few* advice about times and prices of flights to Krakow.

6 I'd like to buy a new CD player but I don't have *many/much* money at the moment.

7 Correct the mistake in the sentences.

1 Pete has just got new job. He's really happy.

2 We didn't see many wild animals. Just a few of lions.

3 I'd like to give you small piece of advice.

4 She hasn't got a lot money so she's going camping.

5 Can I write you cheque or would you like cash?

6 I've got any great news. We're moving to Spain.

Writing

8 Look at these examples and choose the correct alternative below.

1 *Although* there are a lot of arguments against zoos, they are a good thing.

2 Zoos are a good thing *although* there are a lot of arguments against them.

Although is followed by <u>a noun/ a clause</u>.

9 Make one sentence from two using *although*. Use *although* in two ways.

Dogs are fun. Looking after them is hard work.

Dogs are fun although looking after them is hard work. Although looking after them is hard work, dogs are fun.

1 We went to the zoo. We've been there before.

2 This book has been very successful. The author isn't well-known.

3 Our staff are getting a pay increase. We can't really afford it.

4 I want to take up sky diving. It's very dangerous.

5 He wants to study Zoology at university. He never reads any books.

10 **a** Read the bulletin board in the Writing bank on page 148. Do the exercises.

b Choose one of the topics below and start an 'online' bulletin board discussion (on paper). In pairs, write your opinions about this topic.

1 Are there good reasons for keeping animals in zoos?

2 Is it wrong to wear fur or leather?

3 Are animal sports wrong and should they be banned?

4 Is it necessary to use animals for scientific research?

c Pass your paper to another pair of students to continue the discussion.

10.3 Pet TV

Grammar	the definite article *(the)*
Can do	speculate about sounds and pictures

Reading and listening

1 Discuss.

Which of the following things do you think pets would like to watch on TV? Why/Why not?

snooker balls ☐   wolves howling ☐

cartoon characters ☐   cats mewing ☐

popular TV programmes ☐   balls of string ☐

2 Read the short text about a new TV programme. Answer as many of the questions as possible.

Pets get their own TV show

The BBC provides programmes for all tastes although they haven't made programmes for animals – until now. From next week, pets (and their owners) will be able to watch *Pet TV*. It is a programme full of sounds and images that might appeal to animals. The aim is to find out what animals respond to. What will your pet like?

1 What is the new TV programme from the BBC?
2 When does the programme start?
3 What different animals is the programme for?
4 What is the aim of the programme?
5 Where can pets take an intelligence test?
6 What did the advertisement show?

3 **a** 〔10.3〕 Listen to a radio programme about *Pet TV* and tick (✓) the things from Ex. 1 that you hear.

b Listen again and answer the rest of the questions from Ex. 2.

4 Discuss.

What do you think of the idea of *Pet TV*?

Vocabulary | verb + prepositions (1)

5 Match the sentence beginnings on the left with the endings on the right.

1	The starting date of *Pet TV* **depends**	a)	**to** many different kinds of animals.
2	The BBC think that *Pet TV* will **appeal**	b)	**to** an excellent series on the radio.
3	Do you really **agree**	c)	**on the results of** the trial.
4	Does your pet **respond**	d)	**about** our dog, Patch. He's not very well.
5	Six people have **applied**	e)	**on** my horse. He's very expensive to look after.
6	I can't believe how much I **spend**	f)	**with** Reena? You never have the same views!
7	My mum is **worried**	g)	**for** the job.
8	I've been **listening**	h)	**to** dogs barking?

6 **a** Add the missing preposition to the sentences below.

1 What kinds of people do TV programmes about animals appeal ____?
2 Some people seem to pick up a new language very quickly, others more slowly. What do you think it depends ____?
3 Have you ever applied ____ a job and lied about your qualifications?
4 Do you think TV advertising works? What kinds of people respond ____ it?
5 Do you ever listen ____ the radio? If so, what station?
6 What do you worry ____?
7 Which member of your family do you most often agree ____?
8 What do you spend most of your money ____ each month?

b Discuss the questions above with a partner.

Grammar | the definite article *(the)*

7 Match sentences 1–3 below to the rules in the Active grammar box.

1 And fish may want to watch TV ...
2 ... the cleverest cat or dog in the country.
3 ITV made an advertisement for Whiskas, a popular cat food. The advert consists of ...

Active grammar

a Use *the* with superlatives because there is only one.

*He's **the** youngest person in the company.*

e.g. sentence: _____

b Use *the* to refer to something or someone you have mentioned before.

*She has got a cat and a dog. **The** cat is nearly twelve.*

e.g. sentence: _____

c Don't use *the* to talk about things or people in general.

Children can be very funny.

e.g. sentence: _____

see Reference page 103

8 **a** Complete the sentences with *the* or nothing (–).

She's *the* most intelligent pet I've ever had!

1 Where shall I put _____ flowers that I brought?
2 _____ CDs are very expensive in the UK.
3 What was _____ name of that film we saw last weekend?
4 *Pet TV* is _____ strangest idea I've ever heard!
5 _____ oil is very expensive at the moment.
6 He's _____ young man I was telling you about.
7 Did you turn off all _____ lights?
8 _____ police officers seem younger and younger these days.

b 10.4 Listen and check your answers. What do you notice about the pronunciation of *the*?

c Repeat the sentences.

9 **a** Four of the sentences have mistakes. Find and correct them.

What's most interesting thing you've done recently?

What's the most interesting thing you've done recently?

1 Do you prefer the cats or dogs? Why?
2 Who's the funniest person you know?
3 How long have you known your best friend?
4 What age do you think the children should have to stay at school until?
5 Did you like the school(s) that you went to?
6 What's most beautiful place you have been to?
7 Do you think that the money makes you happy?
8 Is public transport expensive in your country?

b Ask and answer the questions above with a partner.

Speaking

10 a 10.5 Listen to an advert for cats. Use the How to ... box to say what you think each sound is.

HOW TO ...	**speculate**
	It looks/sounds like a ...
	Perhaps it's a ...
	It could be a ...

b Now look at the pictures on page 132. What do you think these might be?

Animal protection

1 Read the information about the charities and answer the questions.

   Which charity ...

   1 only works in England and Wales?
   2 teaches you about monkeys in the wild?
   3 works all around the world on a number of issues?
   4 offers you the chance to adopt an animal?
   5 accepts credit cards?
   6 has animal inspectors?

Who are we?

The Monkey Sanctuary in Cornwall has been home to woolly monkeys for over forty years. It provides a safe place in which the monkeys, many rescued from lonely lives in zoos or as pets, can live as naturally as possible.

What do we do?

Educate thousands of visitors each year about monkeys in the wild and in captivity. Advise other rescue centres around the world.

Campaign to stop trade in monkeys as pets.

How you can help ...

Thousands of young monkeys are taken from the wild every year. By adopting a monkey from only £2 per month you will help us give it a safe and happy home.

For more information go to: www.ethicalworks.co.uk/monkeysanctuary

WWF the global conservation organisation

WWF works on both global and local environmental issues.

- We protect animals in danger, e.g. tigers, great apes and whales
- We protect areas in danger, e.g. forests and seas
- We protect the planet from dangers, e.g. climate change and toxic chemicals

Make a donation by credit or debit card

Help support our conservation work by making a donation to WWF by credit or debit card.

For more information go to: www.wwf.org.uk

 The RSPCA (Royal Society for the Prevention of Cruelty to Anim

Action for animals

RSPCA inspectors in England and Wales work around the clock to save animals in distress. Last year inspectors investigated over 100,000 complaints of cruelty to animals.

Preventing cruelty

Our inspectors prefer to educate people rather than prosecute. They also offer help and advice about the care of animals in markets, pet shops, kennels and farms.

Our inspectors help animals in distress – last year they removed over 180,000 animals from danger or abuse and rescued over 11,000 injured or trapped animals.

Get involved

Your support can make the difference between life and death to an injured, sick or neglected animal.

For more information go to: www.rspca.org.uk

2 **a** Your class has recently won £1,000. You can give this money to one or more of the charities above. Or you can spend it to help animals in another way.

   b In groups of four, make a list of ways of spending the money. Then decide how you want to spend the £1,000.

3 Explain your decisions to other students. Listen to the ideas from the other groups. Are they similar or different to your group's decision?

Countable/Uncountable nouns

Countable nouns are words like *animal, child, zoo*. They can be singular or plural.

Uncountable nouns are words like *information, advice, news*. They are only singular.

Other examples of uncountable nouns

> accommodation behaviour bread furniture health knowledge luggage research salt spaghetti traffic travel trouble water weather work

The following nouns can be countable or uncountable.

> chicken chocolate coffee egg glass hair iron paper room space time wine

Compare: *Would you like a coffee?* and *I drink too much coffee.*

We use: *a/an, a few, some, any, many, a lot of* before countable nouns.

There weren't many people at the party.

They've got a lot of friends in Australia.

You should rest for a few days.

We use *a little/a bit of* (and sometimes *a piece of*), *some, any, much, a lot of* before uncountable nouns.

How much salt did you put in this?

We bought a lot of bread this morning.

Can you give me a piece of advice?

Some is most common in affirmative clauses; *any* is common in questions and negatives.

I'd like some information.

Have you been to any interesting places?

I didn't bring any money with me.

! We use *some* in questions if we expect people to answer *Yes*.

Could I have some more dessert, please?

We usually use *much* with singular nouns and *many* with plurals.

I haven't got much time.

Did you bring many CDs?

The definite article

We usually use *the* with superlatives because we are only referring to one and it is usually clear which one we are talking about.

*She's **the** best player in the team.*

We use *the* when we refer to something or someone we have mentioned before.

*I bought some ham and some chicken. We had **the** chicken for lunch.*

We also use *the* in a number of expressions referring to our physical environment.

*Would you like to live in **the country**?*

*Listen to **the rain**!*

*What do you think **the weather** will be like at the weekend?*

We do not usually use *the* to talk about things or people in **general**.

We use *the* to talk about **particular** people or things.

*People watch too much **TV** these days.*

*There's a problem with **the TV**. There's a picture but no sound.*

We do not usually use *the* with singular proper names.

*Which department does **James Cameron** work in?*

1 Complete the sentences with *a/an* or nothing (–).

Can I have _a_ glass of water?

1 Would you like _____ rice or potatoes with your dinner?

2 They say it will be _____ good weather this weekend.

3 This bed is made of _____ iron.

4 Have you seen _____ lion yet?

5 She's got _____ long, black hair.

6 I haven't got _____ room for your books in my bag.

7 Sue's _____ old friend from university.

2 Complete the sentences with *a/an*, *the*, or nothing (–).

What's _the_ longest river in South America?

1 I had _____ sandwich and _____ banana for lunch but _____ sandwich was awful!

2 Simon is looking for _____ job in publishing.

3 Did you pass _____ exam you took last month?

4 Listening to _____ music helps me relax.

5 I heard that yesterday was _____ hottest day of the year.

6 Yolanda is in _____ hospital. She is having an operation this afternoon.

7 Excuse me, where is the main entrance to _____ university?

3 Choose the correct alternative.

I only speak *a little/a few* words of Spanish.

1 We don't have *much/many* rain in summer.

2 She's got *a lot/some* of experience.

3 He gave me a very good *piece/lot* of advice.

4 I need *some/little* paper to write on.

5 Could I have *a little/few* more cake?

6 Do *many/much* tourists come to your town?

7 I don't have *a lot of/many* time this weekend.

4 Delete the extra and unnecessary word in each sentence.

I haven't got much ~~many~~ money at the moment.

1 Are you going to have a few summer holiday this year?

2 I don't need any more of advice.

3 We need some many new furniture for the living room.

4 She's really enjoying a work since she changed jobs.

5 Have you heard Tina's piece news? She's having a baby.

5 Complete the sentences with prepositions from the box. You will need to use some of the prepositions more than once.

for   on   to   with   about

My dog likes listening _to_ the radio.

1 I'd like to get a dog but it depends _____ the size of our new flat.

2 In our research, 70 percent of the animals responded _____ the *Pet TV* programmes.

3 I think we should get a cat but Tim doesn't agree _____ me.

4 It's amazing how much we spend _____ dog food each week!

5 Chris has just applied _____ a new job in Australia.

6 She's a bit worried _____ her horse. He's not been very well.

7 We feel that this advert will appeal _____ cat and dog owners.

8 Marcus often listens _____ the news on *Capital Radio* in the morning.

6 Complete the sentences with one missing word.

We've just bought our daughter a _horse_. She loves riding.

1 We're thinking of playing tennis tomorrow but it _____ on the weather.

2 It took me ages to pick _____ Spanish. I tried to learn it from tapes.

3 My dad wants me to work in advertising but I don't want to be part of the _____ race.

4 Could you look _____ our dog for a few days while we're away?

5 I hope I haven't let the _____ out of the bag. I told Julie that Simon's been promoted to Manager Director.

6 I really looked _____ to my father when I was a child.

7 Don't worry about him, Mary. There are plenty more _____ in the sea!

8 She was as quiet as a _____ when she was a child. She hardly ever said a word!

9 I don't think Sunita's parents brought her _____ very well. She behaves very badly.

10 I _____ up in Malawi, but my family moved to the UK when I was seventeen.

11 Travel

Lead-in

1 Find twelve forms of transport in the word search. The words go across or down.

A	M	O	T	O	R	B	I	K	E	B	L	A	N	E
R	O	N	A	T	E	U	S	S	Y	C	O	A	C	H
C	P	I	X	A	M	S	C	F	E	R	R	Y	A	O
A	E	B	I	C	Y	C	L	E	T	T	R	A	I	N
R	D	V	A	N	P	L	A	N	E	O	Y	C	A	P

2 **a** Match the verbs in the box with the forms of transport from the word search. Each verb can go with several forms of transport.

> go by   get on/off   get into/out of   catch   take   miss   ride

go by bus/train ...

b 〔11.1〕 Listen and check your answers.

3 **a** Correct the <u>underlined</u> mistakes in each question.

1 Do you ever go to work/school <u>on</u> bicycle?
2 Do you like <u>taking</u> a bicycle in cities? Why/Why not?
3 Have you ever got <u>in</u> a train without a ticket?
4 When did you last <u>ride</u> a taxi?
5 Have you ever got <u>out of</u> a moving train or bus?
6 Have you ever <u>lost</u> a plane?

b Ask and answer the questions in Ex. 3a with a partner.

Grammar	Present Perfect Simple with *just, yet* and *already*
Can do	find out if someone would be a good travel companion

Reading

1 Discuss.

1 Have you ever been on holidays with friends? What was it like?

2 What would annoy you most about a travel companion? Use the ideas in the box and your own ideas.

> he/she talks a lot   he/she is lazy
> he/she snores   he/she complains a lot

2 Read the extract from Lucy's travel diary. Which of the things above are mentioned?

Sat 3rd
I can't believe it! I'm in Rio, 3,500 miles from home, and I've just bumped into Andy, from my old school. We're going to travel to Salvador together. It's great to see him again!

Sun 4th
On the bus - 10.15 am. Bad news. Andy has already started to annoy me. He won't stop talking! Oh well ... I'm sure it'll get better.
3.30 pm! I can't stand it! He hasn't stopped talking yet. I now know everything about his friends, his family, even his neighbour's cat!
4.30 pm! Andy's just fallen asleep but now he's started snoring! Aggh!

Mon 5th
On the beach - 12.30 pm. I'm exhausted - I didn't get any sleep because of HIM. And I've just spent the whole morning listening to Andy complaining about the weather, the food, even the beach! What am I going to do?

Tues 6th
In a café - 2.30 pm. Now he's started singing to himself. I have to tell him I can't travel with him any more. He's driving me crazy ...

3 **11.2** Listen to a summary of Lucy's diary. Which three things are different from her diary?

4 **a** Lucy decides she doesn't want to travel with Andy any more. With a partner, write what you think she says and how he reacts.

b Practise your conversation.

c **11.3** Listen and compare your conversation with theirs. What is the same/different?

Grammar | Present Perfect Simple with *just, yet* and *already*

5 Look at the Active grammar box and complete the rules with *just, yet* or *already*.

> **Active grammar**
> _____
>
> You often use *just, yet* and *already* with the Present Perfect Simple.
>
> Andy has **already** started to annoy me.
>
> He hasn't stopped talking **yet**.
>
> He's **just** fallen asleep.
>
> a) _____ means a short time ago.
>
> b) _____ shows that something happened sooner than expected.
>
> c) _____ shows that the speaker expected something to happen before now.

see Reference page 113

6 Write *just, already* or *yet* in the correct place in each sentence.

I've had lunch. (I had lunch five minutes ago.)
I've just had lunch.

1 Simon's left the party. (It's only nine o'clock.)

2 Diana hasn't phoned. (I expected her to phone earlier.)

3 I've spent all my money. (I didn't expect to spend it all so early.)

4 Have you written any postcards? (I expect you wrote them before now.)

5 My parents have come back from holiday. (They came back two hours ago.)

Pronunciation

7 **a** **11.4** How do you pronounce the first sounds of *yet* and *just*: /dʒ/ or /j/? Listen and check.

b Say the sentences in Ex. 6 with the correct pronunciation.

8 Look at the picture on page 132. Say what Lucy's *just done* and what she *hasn't done yet*.

A

B

C

D

Vocabulary | holidays

9 **a** Match the photos with the types of holiday.

> sightseeing holiday   beach holiday
> camping holiday   skiing holiday

b Find the opposite pairs.

rent a car – use local transport

A	B
1 rent a car	a) unpack
2 pack	b) get a last-minute deal
3 go abroad	c) sunbathe on the beach
4 go sightseeing	d) use local transport
5 stay in hotels	e) go to bed early
6 book early	f) stay in your country
7 go clubbing	g) go self-catering

10 Test your partner. Say one word from one of the phrases in Ex. 9b. Your partner must say the whole phrase.

A: *minute*

B: *get a last-minute deal*

11 Tell your partner about a really good holiday. Use the How to ... box to help you.

<table>
<tr><td rowspan="8" style="writing-mode: vertical-lr">HOW TO ...</td><td colspan="2">talk about a holiday you've had</td></tr>
<tr><td>When ...?</td><td>I went on holiday last July.</td></tr>
<tr><td>What ...?
Where ...?
How long ...?</td><td>It was a two-week beach holiday in Portugal.</td></tr>
<tr><td>Booking</td><td>We got a last-minute deal.</td></tr>
<tr><td>Accommodation</td><td>We stayed in a lovely hotel.</td></tr>
<tr><td>Activity</td><td>We sunbathed all day.</td></tr>
</table>

Speaking and writing

12 **a** **11.5** You're going to find a travel companion. Listen and write down the questions you hear.

b Write two more questions to ask.

13 **a** Ask and answer the questions with other students. Make notes of their answers.

b Who is the best travel companion for you? Why?

c Write a paragraph about your best travel companion.

I think the best travel companion for me is Teresa. She likes very similar types of holidays to me.

Lifelong learning

Keep a record (2)

When recording new vocabulary, it can help to note down if the word has an opposite. That way you can double your knowledge!

11.2 | Customs worldwide

Grammar	verbs with two objects
Can do	make generalisations about customs

Reading

3 Work in two groups.

Group A: read the text below.
Group B: read the text on page 129.

Which of the things in Ex. 2a are mentioned in your text?

Vocabulary | greetings and presents

1 Match the words with the photos above.

> a handshake   a wave   a bow   a kiss
> a present or gift

2 **a** Try and complete the sentences using the correct form of the verbs.

> to shake hands (with)   to wave   to bow
> to kiss   ~~to give a present or gift~~

In Japan, you should ***give a present*** using both hands.

1 In most countries, people _____ when they say goodbye.

2 In most Western countries, people usually _____ when they meet in a business situation.

3 In Asia, people usually _____ when they meet in a business situation.

4 In the UK, men don't _____ on the cheeks when they meet in a business situation.

b **11.6** Listen and check your answers to Ex. 2a.

c Discuss.
Which of the customs above are true in your country?

ADVICE FOR UK BUSINESS TRAVELLERS

GIVING GIFTS

Japan
Unlike the UK, gift-giving is very important in Japan and it usually happens at the end of a visit. Pens are a good idea or something not available in Japan. If you give flowers, avoid giving four or nine flowers as these are unlucky numbers.

China
Chinese people will probably refuse your gift several times, but it is polite to continue offering it to them. Do not give clocks to Chinese people as the Chinese word for 'clock' is similar to the word for 'death'.

Middle East
Give gifts of highest quality leather, silver, or crystal. Remember to avoid alcohol and leather from pigs.

South America
Gift-giving is less formal in South America but still an important part of the culture. Avoid leather, as many of the world's best leather products come from South America.

Australia, Canada, USA and Europe
Gift-giving in these countries is informal and not always expected. However, it is polite to bring someone flowers, chocolates or wine when visiting their house. In some European countries, you should avoid red flowers (associated with romance).

4 a Group A read the text again. What is the significance of the following?

> pens   four flowers   a clock   silver goods
> a leather briefcase   red flowers

b Work with a student who read text B. Ask these questions about his/her text.

1 Should you use first names in Germany?
2 In which part of the world do people stand closest to each other?
3 Why don't American people like you to stand too close to them?
4 Should you show how strong you are when you shake hands?
5 Do Asian people ever shake hands?
6 Do business people kiss each other in Russia?

c Now answer your partner's questions about your text.

5 Read the saying below and discuss the questions.

'When in Rome, do as the Romans do.'

1 What does the saying mean?
2 Do you agree with it? Why/Why not?

Grammar | verbs with two objects

6 Read the Active grammar box. Write *to* in sentences 1–2, if necessary.

Active grammar

Some verbs can be followed by two objects.

*He **gave** his boss a present.*
    indirect object   direct object

The indirect object is usually a person and comes first. Two forms are possible.

a) verb + indirect object + direct object
b) verb + direct object + *to* + indirect object

Structure 'a' is more natural, especially when the indirect object is a pronoun (*me, him, them*, etc.).

1 *It is polite to **bring** ___ your host flowers.*
2 *It is polite to **bring** flowers ___ your host.*

Common verbs which take two objects are:
give, bring, offer, lend, owe, send, tell, promise.

---

see Reference page 113

7 a Find and correct the mistakes.

1 Our company more choice offers you.
2 I lent to him €20 about three weeks ago.
3 Could you bring that book me when you come?
4 He sent to her a huge bunch of flowers.
5 Would you like to tell to me anything?
6 We must a special gift give our hosts.

b [11.7] Listen and check your answers.

Person to person

8 a Look at the questions below. Write five more *Have you ever …?* questions. Use the verbs at the end of the Active grammar box.

1 Have you ever **lent** someone some money which they never paid back?
2 Have you ever **given** a present to someone that they really hated?

b Ask and answer your questions with a partner.

Speaking

9 a Prepare to talk about customs in your country (or a country you know well). Think about the topics below.

> giving gifts   visiting someone's house
> birthdays   an important national festival

b Tell your partner about the customs using the language in the How to … box to help you.

HOW TO …

make generalisations about groups of people

Use *the* + nationalities / adjectives	: The British, The young, The rich, …
Make generalisations	: … **tend** to talk about the weather. : … don't **generally** / **usually** give gifts.

Listening

1 Discuss.

Do you like travel books? Why/Why not?

2 **a** `11.8` Listen to the first part of an interview with a travel writer. Tick (✓) the things she talks about.

1 Travelling in her childhood ☐

2 How she started travel writing ☐

3 Other jobs she's had ☐

4 Something lucky that happened ☐

b Listen again and answer these questions.

1 How did she start travelling?

2 How did she start writing?

3 What was her first 'break' as a travel writer?

3 **a** `11.9` Listen to the second part of the interview. Mark the order (1–4) she talks about these things:

a Other travel writers ____

b Advice to people who want to be travel writers ____

c Difficulties about the process of writing ____

d Difficulties about travelling ____

b Listen again and answer these questions.

1 What is the most difficult thing for her when she's travelling?

2 What is the most difficult thing for her when she's writing?

3 Which travel writer influenced her the most?

4 What advice does she give to someone thinking of being a travel writer?

4 Discuss.

1 Do you agree that being a travel writer is a 'dream job'? Why/Why not?

2 Which country would you most like to travel to and write about? Why?

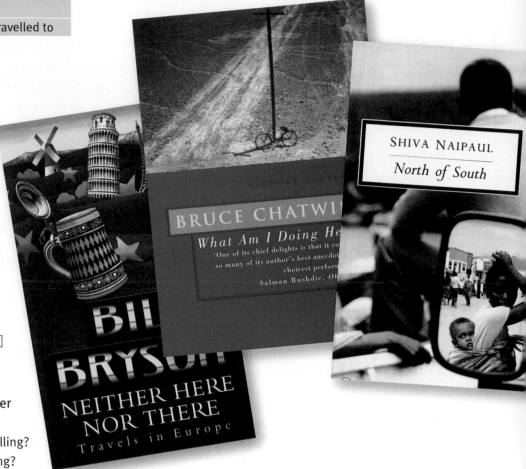

Grammar | Past Perfect Simple

5 **a** `11.10` Listen and complete the sentences.

1 By the time I was sixteen I _____ nineteen countries!

2 I _____ there very long when I got the job.

3 _____ any other books before this one was published?

b Look at the Active grammar box. Choose the correct alternative to complete the rule.

> ### Active grammar
>
> *By the time I was sixteen I had visited nineteen countries!*
>
> Use the Past Perfect Simple to talk about an action (or actions) that happened *before/ after* another action in the past.
>
> | I had visited nineteen countries | I was sixteen | now |
>
> Form: *had* + past participle

c Look at the first part of the tapescript on page 160 and find two more examples of the Past Perfect Simple.

see Reference page 113

6 Choose the best alternative.

1 We arrived at the cinema late. The film *began/had begun*.

2 I saw a car by the side of the road. It *ran/had run* out of petrol.

3 I was very tired so I *went/had gone* straight to bed.

4 A man came into the shop. I didn't *see/hadn't seen* him before.

5 I phoned Jack but he wasn't there. He *went/had gone* out.

6 Sorry I'm late. The car *had/had had* a puncture on the way.

7 It was my first time in Egypt. I *didn't go/hadn't been* there before.

8 She couldn't come to the party. She *arranged/had arranged* something else.

7 Put one verb in brackets in the Past Perfect Simple and one verb in the Past Simple in each sentence.

1 When I _____ (arrive) at the station, the train _____ (leave).

2 When the driver _____ (ask) to see my ticket, I realised I _____(lose) it.

3 When we _____ (get) there, we realised we _____ (not/pack) enough warm clothes.

4 I _____ (decide) to go back to the same place I _____ (be) for my last holiday.

5 I _____ (want) to read a book on the plane, but I _____ (forget) to buy one at the airport.

6 As soon as I saw Carolina, I _____ (realise) I _____ (meet) her before.

Pronunciation

8 **a** [11.11] Listen to sentences 1–3 from Ex. 7. How do you pronounce *had* in the Past Perfect Simple in each one?

b Repeat the sentences with good pronunciation.

Person to person

9 Discuss in pairs. For each picture, what do you think had happened before this?

He woke up late because he'd been out late the night before ...

Writing

10 **a** Look at the photo and read the text about Havana. Which of these things are mentioned?

> music   people   weather
> buildings   countryside
> transport   food and drink

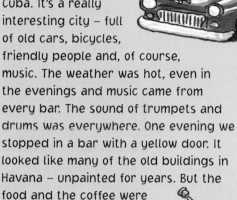

Last summer we went to Havana, the capital of Cuba. It's a really interesting city – full of old cars, bicycles, friendly people and, of course, music. The weather was hot, even in the evenings and music came from every bar. The sound of trumpets and drums was everywhere. One evening we stopped in a bar with a yellow door. It looked like many of the old buildings in Havana – unpainted for years. But the food and the coffee were fantastic. I had never tasted such delicious coffee before.

b Read the text again and find examples of:

1 adjectives; senses (taste, smell, etc.) and colours. What do they describe?

2 Past Perfect Simple. Why is it used?

11 You're going to do some travel writing. Follow these instructions.

1 Think of a place you have travelled to (e.g. a beach, a town) and make notes about the place. (Look at Ex. 10a.)

2 Tell your partner about your place and ask questions about your partner's place.

3 Write about your place. (Use about 100 words.)

11 | Communication

Single or return?

A

B

C

D

1 a Describe what you can see in the pictures.

b 🔊 11.12 Listen to four dialogues and match them with the pictures.

2 a Complete the dialogues 1–4 using the phrases in the box.

> pack your suitcase   I'd like to book
> One pound   like to pay   I'd like a return
> pieces of luggage   That's £18.50

Dialogue 1
A: _____ to Oxford, please.
B: Yes, of course. Are you coming back today?
A: Yes, I am.
B: _____, please.
A: Thank you.

Dialogue 2
A: How many _____ have you got?
B: One suitcase and one handbag.
A: Did you _____ yourself?
B: Yes, I did.
A: Does it contain any knives or scissors?
B: No.
A: Fine. Could you put it on here, please? OK … fifteen kilos.

Dialogue 3
A: Piccadilly Circus, please.
B: _____, please.
A: Thanks.
B: Thank you.

Dialogue 4
A: Victoria Coach Station. Can I help you?
B: _____ a single ticket to Edinburgh, please.
A: Yes … when would you like to travel?
B: Friday 14th March, in the afternoon.
A: OK … there's a coach at 5.45p.m.
B: Yes, that's fine. How much is it?
A: £45 for a single ticket. How would you _____ _____?
B: By Visa, please.
A: OK.

b Listen again and check your answers.

c Practise the dialogues with a partner. First, refer to the dialogues on the page. Then try again without looking.

3 Work in pairs.
Student A: look at the information on page 127.
Student B: look at the information on page 129.

Present Perfect Simple with *just, yet* and *already*

Use *just, yet* and *already* with the Present Perfect Simple.

Form the Present Perfect Simple with *has/have* + past participle.

Just means a short time ago.

Just usually comes between *has/have* and the past participle.

*I've **just** seen a really great film.*

*Have you **just** arrived?*

Already shows that something happened sooner than the speaker expected.

Already usually comes between *has/have* and the past participle or at the end of the sentence.

*You've **already** told me that.*

*He's taken his driving test six times **already**.*

Yet means 'until now' and shows that the speaker is expecting something to happen.

Yet usually comes at the end of questions and negative sentences.

*Have you seen Dave **yet**?*

*I haven't got the tickets **yet**.*

Verbs with two objects

Some verbs can be followed by two objects (a direct object and an indirect object).

The indirect object usually refers to a person and comes first:

verb + indirect object + direct object

He gave <u>his wife</u> <u>some earrings</u> for her birthday.

We can also put the indirect object **after** the direct object. In this case, we use *to* before the indirect object:

verb + direct object + *to* + indirect object

He gave <u>some earrings</u> <u>to his wife</u> for her birthday.

However, it is more natural to use: verb + indirect object + direct object, especially when the indirect object is a pronoun (*me, you, him, her, it, us, them*).

He gave her some earrings for her birthday.

! Common verbs which use the same constructions are:

give, bring, offer, lend, owe, send, tell, promise, buy, teach, show, write.

Past Perfect Simple

Use the Past Perfect Simple to talk about an action/ or actions that happened before another action in the past.

*When I saw him I realised **I'd met** him before.*

I had met him		I saw him	now

Form the Past Perfect Simple with *had* + past participle.

*By the time we got to the restaurant, I **hadn't eaten** all day.*

***Had you been** to that cinema before yesterday?*

! The Past Perfect Simple is common after verbs of saying/thinking:

I told her we had bought the tickets.

She realised she'd met him before somewhere.

The Past Perfect Simple is common after *when*:

When he'd finished the washing-up, he turned the TV on.

Key vocabulary

Transport
bicycle   bus   car   coach   ferry   lorry   moped   motorbike   plane   taxi   train   van

Verb phrases about travel
go by car/bus/train/plane/taxi/bicycle
get on or off a bus/train/plane/bicycle
get into or out of a car/taxi
catch, take or miss a bus/train/plane/taxi
ride a bicycle

Holidays
sightseeing holidays   beach holidays
camping holidays   skiing holidays   rent a car
use local transport   go abroad
stay in your country   stay in hotels
go self-catering   go sightseeing
sunbathe on the beach   pack   unpack   book early
get a last-minute deal

Greetings and presents
shake hands (with someone)   a handshake
bow (to someone)   a bow   kiss (someone)   a kiss
wave (to someone)   a wave   give a present or gift

11 Review and practice

1 Choose the correct word.

A: Where are you going on holiday this year?
B: I've haven't decided (yet)/already.

1 A: Do you want to see that film?
   B: No, I've seen it yet/already.
2 A: Have you booked the tickets just/yet?
   B: No, I'll do it today.
3 A: Why is your hair wet?
   B: I've just/already had a shower.
4 A: Have you cleaned the kitchen?
   B: No, I haven't done it already/yet.
5 A: Would you like some lunch?
   B: No, thanks. I've yet/just had some.
6 A: I'd like to buy Louise that new CD.
   B: She's yet/already got it.
7 A: Have you started jogging just/yet?
   B: No, I'll start next week.

2 Write sentences using the prompts. Make any necessary changes.

Tom's only seventeen and he/visit eleven countries. (already)

Tom's only seventeen and he's already visited eleven countries.

1 I hope Katya is OK. She/not phone me. (yet)
2 Do you like these flowers? Natalia/bring them. (just)
3 I'd love to see your new flat. You/move in? (yet)
4 The sitting room looks lovely. I/paint it. (just)
5 I really want to read that book. You/finish it? (yet)
6 A: Could I speak to Alex, please?
    B: She/go home. (already)
7 I hope it's not too late to invite Pietro. I/not ask him. (yet)

3 Put the words in the correct order.

anyone/You/money/shouldn't/to/lend
You shouldn't lend money to anyone.

1 all my secrets/told/I/him
2 owes/a lot of money/me/Juan
3 I/Can/some tea/you/offer?
4 a pay rise/He/this month/me/promised
5 always/me/My grandmother/really good advice/gives
6 the nurse who looked after me/I/some flowers/sent/to
7 the bill/us/Could/bring/please/you?

4 Put one verb in brackets in the Past Simple and one verb in the Past Perfect Simple in each sentence.

I *wanted* (want) to read something but I *hadn't packed* (not/pack) my book.

1 She _____ (want) to buy a bag she _____ (see) the day before.
2 When I _____ (arrive) at the airport, I realised I _____ (miss) my plane.
3 As soon as I _____ (close) the door, I remembered I _____ (leave) my keys inside.
4 When I _____ (eat) my breakfast, I _____ (feel) better.
5 When I _____ (see) the exam question, I realised I _____ (not/study) enough.
6 When she _____ (try) to pay for something in the shop, she realised she _____ (forgot) her credit card.

5 Six of the underlined verbs are in the incorrect tense. Decide which ones, then correct them.

I <u>went</u> to the ticket office to buy my train ticket. When I <u>had tried</u> to pay for the ticket, I <u>had realised</u> I <u>didn't have</u> my wallet. I <u>remembered</u> that when I <u>got off</u> the bus, someone <u>pushed</u> past me. I <u>had realised</u> that this person <u>took</u> my wallet.

6 Complete the sentences using the correct form of the verbs in the box.

have   get   go   shake   rent   wave
~~unpack~~

When I arrived at the hotel, I *unpacked* and put all my clothes in the wardrobe.

1 Should I _____ hands with the boss when I meet her?
2 Go on the Internet and see if you can _____ a last-minute deal.
3 Sorry I'm late. I _____ a puncture on the motorway.
4 When I was in Greece, I _____ a car to see the island.
5 The train left the station and we all _____ goodbye to them.
6 I usually stay in my country for holidays but this year I'm _____ abroad.

12 Money

Lead-in

1 What can you see in the photos? Discuss with other students.

2 **a** Complete the questions with the most appropriate words.

> earn   won   cost   withdraw   spending   borrowing
> lending   save

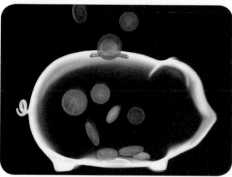

1 How do you feel about _____ money to friends?
2 How do you feel about _____ money from your friends or family?
3 Do you try and _____ any money each month? If so, is it difficult?
4 What do you enjoy _____ money on?
5 How much do nurses, teachers or lawyers typically _____ each year in your country? Do you think this is right?
6 How often do you _____ money from a cashpoint machine? Do you like using them?
7 How much does a short bus or train journey _____ in your country? How much do you think it is in the UK?
8 Have you ever _____ any money in a lottery or a competition?

b **12.1** Listen and check your answers.

c Ask and answer the questions in Ex. 2a with a partner.

Reading

1 Look at the photos. What can you see?

2 Read the text. Is it suggesting that:

a) people are honest?

b) people are dishonest?

c) people's honesty depends on the situation?

Honesty is the new policy!

Newsagents in train stations and other busy areas have a problem. How do you take small amounts of money (e.g. for newspapers) from a lot of people, but avoid long queues? WHSmith, a big newsagents in the UK, is trying a new idea. It has introduced 'honesty boxes'. You take the newspaper you want, put the exact money into an honesty box and walk away. Does it work? Well, according to David McRedmond, managing director for WHSmith, customers have been honest. 'We feel this idea is working very well.'

But before the big stores get too excited they should look at a recent 'honesty survey' done for a well-known TV programme. The programme arranged for a cashpoint to give out an extra ten pounds every time a customer withdrew money. A third of the people were honest and handed the money into the bank. The rest kept it. One man actually went back to the cashpoint twenty times to try and get rich quick!

It seems that people have an attitude of 'They can afford it' towards large banks and companies. In another test, shoppers were given too much change. It was found that in large supermarkets, people usually kept the extra change. However, in small shops, they would give it back.

(adapted from the *Independent on Sunday*)

3 Read the text again. Correct the sentences.

'Honesty boxes' are for people who want to buy cigarettes and newspapers.

' Honesty boxes' are for people who want to buy newspapers.

1 You put the money in an envelope and then drop it in the 'honesty box'.

2 David McRedmond doesn't know yet if the 'honesty boxes' are a success.

3 A big store organised an 'honesty survey'.

4 The pretend cashpoint gave customers twenty pounds too much.

5 Most of the customers gave the extra money back to the bank.

6 People seem to have the same attitude towards big organisations and small shops.

4 Discuss. Do you think the idea of 'honesty boxes' would work where you live? Why/Why not?

Vocabulary | money

5 **a** Check the meaning of the <u>underlined</u> words with a partner.

A	B
1 pay for something	a) on money that you borrow
2 leave a <u>tip</u>	b) when you retire
3 pay <u>interest</u>	c) for working a 35-hour week
4 get a <u>pension</u>	d) in <u>cash</u>
5 earn a <u>salary</u>	e) to the government
6 pay <u>tax</u>	f) in a restaurant

b Match the phrases in A to the phrases in B.

6 **a** Complete the sentences using the <u>underlined</u> words from Ex. 5a.

1 Do you always leave a _____ in a restaurant?

2 How often do you pay for things in _____, by cheque or by credit card?

3 How much _____ do you pay when you borrow money from a bank?

4 Do you think the _____ you pay to the government is too high?

5 How much is the state _____ for old people in your country? Is it enough?

6 What is an average _____ in your country?

b Discuss the questions above.

Grammar | Second Conditional

7 Read the examples in the Active grammar box. Choose the correct alternatives to complete the rules.

> ### Active grammar
>
> *If a cashpoint gave me too much money, I would tell the bank.*
>
> *If I won the lottery, I might go on a cruise.*
>
> *If* + Past Simple + *would* + verb
>
> 1 The Second Conditional refers to <u>imaginary</u>/ real situations.
>
> 2 The Second Conditional refers to <u>past</u>/ <u>present and future</u> time.
>
> 3 The *if* clause comes <u>first</u>/ <u>first or second</u>.
>
> 4 Use <u>would</u>/ <u>might</u> if you are less certain.

See Reference page 123

8 Put the words in the correct order.

1 had/you/If you/would/a dog/exercise/get/more

2 he/his exams/pass/worked/He/if/would/harder

3 She/if/much/her boyfriend/be/would/she left/happier

4 spoke/job/easier/German/I/much/my/be/If/would

5 If/a car/I/to/had/would/to work/I/drive

9 **a** Complete the second sentence in each pair so it has the same meaning as the first.

I don't have any money, so I can't buy a new car.

If I **had some money, I would buy** a new car.

1 I won't change my bank because it gives good rates of interest.

If my bank didn't _____ change it.

2 We're not going to Australia because it costs so much.

We'd go _____ so much.

3 You know the film *Wall Street*, so we won't watch it tonight.

If you didn't _____ watch it tonight.

4 We don't visit you more often because you live so far away.

We'd _____ so far away.

5 I'm afraid of water so I don't want to go on that boat.

If I _____ that boat.

b **12.2** Listen and check your answers. How many times do you hear contractions?

Person to person

10 **a** Look at the picture. What can you see? What would you do if you saw this happening?

b Work in pairs. Read the situations on page 132 and discuss. What would you do/say?

c Write two of your own situations. Ask other people in the class what they would do.

12.2 The price of success
| Grammar | reported speech |
| Can do | report what someone said to you |

Vocabulary | education

1 Complete the sentences with a verb from the box in the correct form.

> pass   take   retake
> fail   get

1 Mike's quite upset. He _____ his Maths exam yesterday.

2 My sister _____ all her exams with grades 'A's last week. We're so proud of her.

3 You usually _____ A-levels at the age of eighteen in the UK.

4 The school _____ very good results this year. Everyone was very pleased.

5 If you are not successful this time, you can _____ the exam in October.

2 a Discuss the difference in meaning between:

student/pupil
subject/topic
college/university
teacher/professor
reward/result
lesson/lecture

b Mark the main stress on each word.

student

c Check your answers on page 132.

3 Discuss.

1 Were you a good pupil at school? Why/Why not?

2 Who was your favourite teacher? Why?

3 What was your favourite subject? Why?

4 Do you think everyone should go to college or university? Why/Why not?

Listening

4 a Look at the picture. Describe what you think is happening, and why.

b 〔12.3〕 Listen to the news item and check your ideas.

5 a Listen again and answer the questions.

1 How much in total, has the school given to its A-level students?

2 How much did it give to each student who got to university?

3 What is Alison Frank's job?

4 Why does she particularly like this scheme?

5 Is the parent generally positive or negative about the scheme? Why?

6 Is the head teacher generally positive or negative about the scheme?

7 Is the student generally positive or negative about the scheme? Why?

b What is your opinion of this scheme? Discuss.

Grammar | reported speech

6 〔12.4〕 Listen to the end of the news item again. Complete the sentences in the Active grammar box below.

Active grammar

1 'More students have got places at university this year than ever before.'

_(He) told me that more students _____ places at university this year than ever before._

2 'I think it's a great idea.'

_She said that she _____ it _____ a great idea._

3 'I'm going to buy a new laptop computer.'

_She said she _____ a new laptop computer._

To report what someone said, use _say_ or _tell_.

He **said (that)** it was a good idea.

He **told me (that)** it was a good idea.

Change the tense in the reported statement:
present → past
past/present perfect → past perfect
will/can → _would/could_

Change the pronoun if necessary.
'He's our teacher.'

She said that he was their teacher.

---

see Reference page 123

7 Find and correct the mistakes in the sentences. One sentence is correct. Which one?

1 I said Simon what time the exam was.

2 He said that his parents had offered him money if he did well in his exams.

3 They said they know Tony since university.

4 My manager told to go to a meeting in his office.

5 She said she living with her parents in a flat in the centre of town.

6 He told me that he can't help me with the revision for my French exam.

8 Anna is talking to Pete. Change her direct speech to reported speech. Begin with the words given.

1
> I prefer studying in the evening.

Anna said …

2
> I'm working at the local university.

Anna told …

3
> Mark saw Terry in the bookshop.

Anna said …

4
> They haven't lived here for long.

Anna told …

5
> My revision notes were on the table.

Anna said …

6
> I'm going to speak to the Professor of Economics.

Anna said …

Speaking

9 Ask each question in the table to a different student. Note their answer. Always ask 'Why?'

Refer to the How to … box below before you give your answers.

QUESTION	PERSON	ANSWER
❶ Do you think it's a good idea to pay students to do well in exams?	_____	_____
❷ Do you think exams are necessary?	_____	_____
❸ Do you usually do well or badly in exams?	_____	_____
❹ Do you think children under ten should have to do exams?	_____	_____

HOW TO …

deal with difficult questions

If you don't want to answer	A: *How much money do you earn?* B: *I'd rather not say.*
If you didn't understand the question	A: *Could you lend me a tenner?* B: *Sorry, what do you mean?* A: *Could you lend me ten pounds?*
If you need time to think of an answer	A: *That's a good question. Can I think about it for a moment?*

10 Show your table to other students. Explain why each person gave their answers.

Charlotte thinks it's a good idea to pay students to do well in exams. She said that it would help them to work harder.

Writing

11 a Look at the formal letter on page 146 in the Writing Bank. Do the exercises.

b Look at the advert below. Write a formal letter to the university to ask for more information.

TRAYBRIDGE UNIVERSITY

Traybridge University is located in a beautiful part of the UK. We now offer students money to study some of our courses.
Study and earn at the same time!

For enquiries and to request a brochure, please write to:
The Admissions Department
Traybridge University
Traybridge
TRB5 H8P

where exactly?

how much?

which courses?

| Grammar | *both, neither, either* |
| Can do | describe similarities/differences |

Reading

1 Discuss.

1 What is the game in the photo?

2 What is the aim of the game?

3 Why do you think a baseball might be worth $1 million?

2 Read the text and answer this question.

What was the argument between Alex Popov and Patrick Hayashi about?

3 Read the text again and answer the questions.

1 What record did Barry Bonds break?

2 Why was the ball worth $1 million?

3 Who caught the ball first?

4 Why did he then lose the ball?

5 What did Hayashi get from the officials?

6 What did Popov do after the game?

7 How long did the court case last?

8 What did the judge decide?

4 Find the following words in the text. Look at the context, i.e. what comes before and what comes after. Say what you think the words might mean.

1 the stands (line 1)

2 home run (line 4)

3 to own (line 7)

4 an official (line 13)

5 to claim (line 15)

6 a fee (line 19)

7 to appeal (line 20)

5 Discuss.
Do you think the judge made the right decision? Why/Why not?

The strange story of the $1 million baseball

When Barry Bonds hit a baseball into the stands, he had no idea he was starting one of the strangest legal battles in sporting history. On 7th October, Bonds, who plays for the San Francisco *Giants*, completed his seventy-third home run of
5 the season, beating the existing record.

As he hit the ball towards the crowd, it instantly became worth a million dollars – and the fans knew it. The fight over who owned the ball began as soon as it was caught.

Alex Popov and Patrick Hayashi both said that they had caught the
10 ball. In fact, according to TV video recordings, Popov caught the ball first but it was then knocked out of his hands by other fans. Then Hayashi got it and held it in the air. He was taken away by officials. They gave him a certificate saying it was his.

However, Popov wasn't happy and took Hayashi to court. Popov
15 claimed that the ball was his. For four months Judge Kevin McCarthy considered the case. In the end, he didn't agree with either man and said that the ball belonged to neither of them. He told them to sell it and share the money. Unfortunately for the men, however, any profit will go to pay their lawyers' fees. Both
20 men say they will appeal.

Vocabulary | verb + prepositions (2)

6 Some verbs are often followed by a preposition. Look at the text again and find which prepositions often follow:

> play   agree   belong

7 Complete the sentences with the prepositions from the box. Check in a dictionary if necessary.

> for (x3)   on   to   at   with (x2)

1 Why don't you go and play football ____ your friends?

2 Why did you argue ____ that police officer?

3 Look ____ that crowd of people! What are they doing?

4 Sheila has applied ____ a job in New York.

5 I'd like to listen ____ the news at 9p.m.

6 Martin apologised ____ being rude to me last night.

7 I've been waiting ____ ages. Where have you been?

8 I'm not sure if we'll play tennis today. It depends ____ the weather.

8 Ask and answer these questions with a partner.

1 When was the last time someone apologised to you for something?

2 When was the last time you applied for a job? What was it? What happened?

3 Do you mind waiting for friends who are late? Why/Why not?

4 Do you like listening to the radio? Why/Why not?

5 Do you regularly play sports with friends? If so, what?

Grammar | *both, neither, either*

9 Look at the Active grammar box and complete the rules with *both*, *neither* or *either*.

Active grammar

Both men said they caught the ball.

Neither man will make any money from the ball.

Do you think either man will change his mind?

Use *both/neither/either* when talking about two things or people.

a) Use _____ with a singular noun. It means 'one **or** the other'.

b) Use _____ with a plural noun. It means 'one **and** the other'.

c) Use _____ with a singular noun. It means '**not** one and **not** the other'.

Both/neither/either can be followed by *of +* pronoun/*the/these*, etc.

Both of them decided to appeal.

Both of the men decided to appeal.

---

see Reference page 123

10 Some of these sentences have mistakes. Find the mistakes and correct them.

1 We can eat at both the Italian or the French restaurant tonight. I don't mind.

2 I liked neither of the last two books that I read.

3 Both of the boys likes swimming very much. They prefer football.

4 I don't like either of these jackets. They're ugly.

5 I'm away on either those days.

6 We went into two hotels but neither had any free rooms.

11 a Complete the sentences with *both*, *neither* or *either*.

1 I like _____ classical and pop music.

2 I don't play _____ football or tennis.

3 _____ of my two best friends are married yet.

4 _____ of my parents have always worked.

5 I enjoy going to _____ the cinema and the theatre.

b `12.5` Listen and check your answers.

Pronunciation

12 a `12.5` Listen to the sentences in Ex. 11a again. How are *both*, *neither* and *either* pronounced?

b Change the sentences so that they are true for you. Tell another student.

Speaking

13 a Work with another student. Find four things you have in common. Think about:

> playing the lottery   spending money
> borrowing/lending/saving money

b Tell other students what you found.

*Firstly, **both** of us like playing the lottery but **neither** of us are very good at saving money.*

Lifelong learning

Into the future

How will you continue to improve your English when this course ends? Discuss with a partner. Make a list of what you both are going to do.

Maria and I are both going to use the Catch-up exercises on the CD-ROM to revise and practise grammar.

Excuse me, but ...

1 **a** What do you think is the problem in each of the pictures?

b Discuss with other students. What would you do in each situation above?

2 Match the sentences below to one of the pictures.

1 Hello, I'd like to speak to someone about this sweater.
2 Excuse me, I think there's a mistake with the bill.
3 I'm sorry, but I gave you a twenty pound note.
4 We actually only had two coffees, not three.
5 Well, basically, the first time I washed it the colour came out.
6 I should have £14.60 change, not £4.60.
7 I'm terribly sorry, Madam, I'll just go and change it now.
8 You're quite right. Here's the correct change.
9 Can I ask what temperature you washed it at?

3 **12.6** Listen to three dialogues and check your answers to Ex. 2.

4 **a** **12.6** Listen again. Prepare to report the dialogues by writing down the main points as you listen.

b Work in groups of three.
Student A: report the main points of dialogue 1
Student B: report the main points of dialogue 2
Student C: report the main points of dialogue 3

First the customer told the waiter that there was a mistake with the bill, then ...

5 Practise one of the dialogues in pairs. Take turns to be the customer. First, the assistant/waiter should be helpful. Then, the assistant/waiter should be less helpful!

Second Conditional

Use the Second Conditional to talk about unlikely or imagined situations in the present/future.

Form: *If* + Past Simple, *would* (or *'d*) + infinitive

If I won some money, I'd go to Australia for a long holiday.

The *if* clause can come first or second.

I'd train to be a pilot, if I wasn't afraid of flying.

Compare with the First Conditional which we use for talking about possible situations in the future.

If I pass all my exams, I will go to university.

When we are less certain, we can use *might* instead of *would*

If I had more money, I might buy some new clothes.

Reported speech

Use 'reported' or 'indirect' speech to tell people what somebody said or thought.

Make the tense of the verb one 'step' further back into the past. E.g. a verb in the Present Simple will usually change to the Past Simple.

Direct Speech	Indirect reported speech
'I **have** £50.'	*He said (that) he **had** £50.*
'Janice **is living** in Spain.'	*She said (that) Janice **was living** in Spain.*
'She **went** home.'	*He said (that) she **had gone** home.*
'He **has worked** there since March.'	*He said (that) he **had worked** there since March.*
'I'm sure **she'll pass** her exams.'	*He said he was sure she **would pass** her exams.*

If somebody said something that is still true when it is reported, tenses don't always change.

'I don't like carrots.'

She said that she doesn't like carrots.

That is often left out, especially after the verbs *say* and *think*.

Say or *tell* are often used in reported speech. *Tell* must have a personal object. We *tell* somebody something. Compare:

She said she saw Gordon on Friday.

She told me she saw Gordon on Friday.

A change of speaker may mean a change of pronoun

*'**We** don't like Tony.'*

*She said that **they** didn't like Tony.*

Both, neither, either

Use *both*, *neither* and *either* to talk about two people or things. For example:

***Both** jackets are expensive.*

***Neither** jacket fits me very well.*

*I don't like **either** jacket.*

Use *both* with a plural noun. It means one and the other.

Use *neither* with a singular noun. It means not one and not the other.

Use *either* with a singular noun. It means one or the other.

When you use *neither, both, either + of*, you also need *the* or *these/those* or *my/your/his,* etc.

***Both of my sisters** are at university.*

***Neither of them** is married.*

*I haven't seen **either of them** for ages.*

We usually use *neither* instead of *both ... not*.

Neither of them came to the meeting.

We can use *both ... and*.

He's both intelligent and good-looking.

For the negative, we use *neither ... nor*. (It is quite formal.)

*He speaks **neither** Russian **nor** Polish.*

Key vocabulary

Money

borrow   lend   cost   save   win   earn   spend
withdraw   earn a salary   leave a tip   pay interest
get a pension   pay tax   pay in cash

Education

college   university   teacher   professor   student
pupil   lesson   seminar   subject   topic   reward
pass/take/retake/fail (an exam)
get (good/bad) results

Verb + prepositions (2)

belong to   play for/with   apologise for
argue with   look at   wait for

1 Find and correct the mistake in each sentence.

If I got stuck in a lift, I'd to be scared.

If I got stuck in a lift, I'd be scared.

1 I'd do things differently if I have my life again.
2 I'd buy a dog if I wouldn't live in a city.
3 What you do if you saw an accident in the street?
4 If Karla studied more, she might passed her exams.
5 If I would had Pete's address, I'd send him a birthday card.
6 People would understand me more easily if my English is better.
7 What would you take you were going on a cycling holiday in France?
8 If you would had more time, would you read more?

2 Make Second Conditional sentences by putting the verbs into the correct form.

We*'d move* (move) to the country if our jobs *weren't* (not be) in the city.

1 If I _____ (have) some money, I _____ (buy) this CD.
2 My job _____ (be) much easier if I _____ (speak) Spanish.
3 If he _____ (get) up earlier, he _____ (not be) late for work.
4 I _____ (feel) happier if my daughter _____ (phone) more often.
5 If you _____ (not work) so hard, you _____ (not be) so tired.
6 I _____ (do) an art course if I _____ (have) more time.
7 If I _____ (find) a wallet in the street, I _____ (take) it to a local police station.
8 If I _____ (fail) my exams, I _____ (retake) them in October.

3 Choose the correct alternative.

He *said/told* the police nothing.

1 They didn't *say/tell* Peter that I was at home.
2 She *said/told* him to go.
3 Why did you *say/tell* that you hated your job?
4 Nobody *said/told* that the station was closed for a month.
5 You shouldn't *say/tell* you want to leave school if you don't mean it.
6 Who *said/told* you that I was with Carmen?
7 She didn't *say/tell* them she was getting married.

4 Somebody says the opposite of what they said earlier. Complete the replies.

A: Tim likes chocolate.
B: I thought you said *Tim didn't like chocolate!*

1 A: I'm going home soon.
  B: I thought you said ...
2 A: We'll see Steve and Jim tomorrow.
  B: I thought you said ...
3 A: I don't have much time at the moment.
  B: I thought you said ...
4 A: They borrowed my car for the weekend.
  B: I thought you said ...
5 A: I've talked to Tara.
  B: I thought you said ...

5 Read the following sentences and decide if *both, neither, either* are used correctly. If not, correct the sentence.

Neither of them wanted to do the washing-up. *OK*

1 Both of men were wearing long black coats.
2 Neither hotels has a swimming pool.
3 I was invited to two parties at the weekend but I didn't go to either of them.
4 I think that both candidates for the job were very good.
5 I'm afraid the Maths teacher has had problems with either of your sons.
6 I don't think I like neither of her brothers.
7 I can't believe it. She's asked both of her ex-boyfriends to the party!

6 Complete each sentence with the correct word. There are three extra words.

> ~~belong~~   lend   depends   borrow   result
> apologise   argue   reward   pension   tax

Who does this bag *belong* to? There's no label.

1 My father has just retired and is getting a good company _____ .
2 Why do you always _____ with your brother? Can't you agree about anything?
3 I'm taking the children swimming this afternoon as a _____ for being good.
4 Can I _____ your car for the afternoon? I'll bring it back around 6p.m.
5 We might have the party outdoors. It _____ on the weather.
6 I think the government should increase the _____ on cigarettes. It might stop some people smoking.

Communication activities

Lesson 2.3 | Ex. 2a, page 20

Student A

Charlotte was born on 21st February 1986, in Cardiff, South Wales. In the early years, she had a normal life but she was clearly a talented singer. At the age of eleven, she appeared on, and won, a talent show on TV. She got a recording contract with Sony and her first album, *Voice of an Angel*, was an instant success. It came out in November 1998 and sold 600,000 copies. She sang all over the world in concerts for Bill Clinton, the Queen and even the Pope. She was just thirteen and life was good – extremely good.

Her second album, in 1999, was also an instant success, but there were problems. People said her parents were pushing her too hard. She argued with her manager and paid him £2 million to go. People said that it was the end of Charlotte's career. But she then employed her mother, Maria, as her manager and more album successes came in 2000 and 2001. Charlotte then decided to leave school and concentrate on her career. People said it was a bad decision, but with the help of a personal tutor, she passed all her exams with 'A' grades. Everything seemed unbelievably good for the young star.

Lesson 3.2 | Ex. 9, page 29

Student A

Explain these words to your partner. Your partner listens and says what word you are describing.

> knife   pilot   tea   ice cream   plate   cooker   salt

Lesson 7.3 | Ex. 8, page 71

Student A

Homoeopathy

You could try homoeopathy. Homoeopathy has two main beliefs. Firstly, homoeopaths believe you should treat the symptoms, not the disease. A homoeopathic doctor looks at the whole person in order to decide which medicine to give. Homoeopaths also believe you only need a very small amount of medicine to get better.

A typical session with a homoeopathic doctor lasts about an hour. He or she asks you about your medical history, your family's medical history and your personality. Homoeopathic medicine is usually in the form of small tablets to put on your tongue.

Millions of people around the world say that homoeopathy works for many kinds of illnesses. It is especially useful for skin problems. The only possible disadvantage of using homoeopathic medicine is the cost. A typical session costs around £60 in the UK. There are no side effects* and it is safe for everyone, including babies.

> **Glossary**
> * *side effect* = an effect that a drug has on the body apart from curing the illness

Lesson 5.1 | Ex. 2a, page 46

Student B

Isabel Jiménez, Spain

Isabel is in her last year at an inner-city Madrid secondary school. If she goes to university she will have at least five more years at home.

I live with my parents and my brother. My sister, who is nearly twenty-seven, left home a month ago. This means I don't have to share my bedroom anymore.

Our mother cooks and irons for us – she shouldn't do this but she enjoys it! She also works. We're all a bit spoiled, I suppose.

I'm in the last of my two years of baccalaureate. I want to study medicine at university because I want to become a doctor. I have to get very high marks to get a place on that course at a public university. You can get into a private university with lower marks but my parents can't afford that – especially as there are three of us.

I'd like to travel, but I think I'll always live in Spain. I'd love to get married and have children too. People in Spain don't have so many children now because of the cost, and everybody wants an easy, comfortable life.

Communication activities

Lesson 8.3 | Ex. 11a, page 81

Student As

Read the information below.

> A large number of CDs were stolen from a shop in your town between 4.30 and 6.30 yesterday afternoon.
>
> Both of you are suspects. The police are going to interview you separately about what you were doing during that time.
>
> In order to convince them that you are not the thieves, you need to prove that you were together during that time. You will need to tell them exactly the same things about what you were doing.

Prepare what you are going to say, e.g. *What you were wearing. What you were doing between those times. Where you went. Who you were with,* etc.

Get ready to be interviewed. Try and keep your stories the same.

Communication 9 | Ex. 5, page 92

Group A

You have worked for a small family company for two years. The company sells books over the Internet. You have worked hard for a small salary. Now you and your eight co-workers feel that conditions need to improve.

YOUR TARGETS:

- **increase salaries**
  - by 6–7% (5 points)
  - by 4–5% (3 points)
  - by 2–3% (1 point)

- **increase number of days' holiday per year (currently 15):**
  - by 6–8 days (5 points)
  - by 4–5 days (3 points)
  - by 2–3 days (1 point)

- **reduce weekly hours (currently 36 hours a week)**
  - by 4–5 hours (5 points)
  - by 2–3 hours (3 points)
  - by 1 hour (1 point)

- **introduce benefits for staff: free lunch, free coffee and cheap books**
  - all three benefits (5 points)
  - two of the benefits (3 points)
  - one of the benefits (1 point)

Lesson 9.3 | Ex. 13a, page 91

Group A

Lesson 1.3 | Ex. 9, page 11
Student B

Lesson 2.3 | Ex. 2a, page 20
Student B

When she was sixteen things started to go wrong again. The media attention was very difficult for her and her family. She had arguments with her mother about her boyfriend. She sacked her mother as manager and went to live with her boyfriend. The newspapers said she went clubbing every night. Everyone said that it was the end of Charlotte's career. But again, this intelligent and talented young woman remained calm. She looks back at her experience with amazing maturity. 'At times, I've behaved badly,' she says 'but I haven't done anything terrible, just normal teenage stuff, except that for me it's all in the news. It can be difficult but it's part of being famous. Yes – I've had arguments with my mother – but what teenager hasn't? We're very close and she's always been very supportive of me.' So, it seems that for this Charlotte things have worked out fine. She's rich and happy and still loves making music. People in the music industry say she can do anything she wants … and she probably will.

Lesson 3.2 | Ex. 9, page 29
Student B

Explain these words to your partner. Your partner listens and says what word you are describing.

> mineral water   pepper   soup   doctor   bowl
> fridge   fork

Communication 11 | Ex. 3, page 112
Student A

1   **a** You are a passenger buying a ticket at Victoria Station, London. Your partner is an assistant in the ticket office.

Before you buy your ticket, prepare what you need to ask using the information below.

> You want to go to Brighton on Friday after 5.30pm and come back on Sunday around 4.00pm. You want to pay by credit card.

b Buy your ticket.

2   **a** Now change roles. You are an assistant in the ticket office at King's Cross Station, London. Your partner is a passenger.

Before you help the passenger buy his/her ticket, prepare your answers using the information below.

TICKETS TO CAMBRIDGE

Prices:

Single: £11 / Day Return: £18.50
Weekend return: £16

Times of trains:

To Cambridge – Thursdays 10:22 / 10:52
To London – Thursdays 18:15 / 18:45

Method of payment:

Credit card, cheque or cash

b Help the passenger buy his/her ticket.

Communication activities

Lesson 8.3 | Ex. 11a, page 81

Student Bs

Read the information below.

> A large number of CDs were stolen from a shop in your town between 4.30 and 6.30 yesterday afternoon.
>
> Both of you are police officers. You are going to interview two suspects separately about what they were doing during that time.
>
> In order to try and prove that one of them committed this crime, you need to show that they are lying about the fact that they were together during this time. You will need to get as much detail as possible and then afterwards, compare their stories.

Prepare what you are going to ask, e.g. *What were you wearing? Where did you go first? Did you meet anyone?* etc.

Get ready to interview the suspects. Then, decide if they are guilty – are their stories the same?

Communication 9 | Ex. 5, page 92

Group B

You own and run a small family company which sells books over the Internet. You employ nine people. You started the company two years ago. After a difficult start, things are beginning to look more positive but the future is still very uncertain.

YOUR TARGETS:

- **avoid big salary increases for staff:**
  - salaries stay the same (5 points)
  - salary increase of 1–2% (3 points)
  - salary increase of 3–4% (1 point)

- **avoid big increase in number of days' holiday per year (currently 15)**
  - no increase (5 points)
  - increase by 1 day (3 points)
  - increase by 2 days (1 point)

- **increase weekly hours (currently 36 hours a week)**
  - by 4–5 hours (5 points)
  - by 2–3 hours (3 points)
  - by 1 hour (1 point)

- **no benefits for staff: no free lunch, no free coffee and no cheap books**
  - no benefits for staff (5 points)
  - one benefit for staff (3 points)
  - two benefits for staff (1 point)

Lesson 9.3 | Ex. 13a, page 91

Group B

Lesson 11.2 | Ex. 3, page 108

Group B

3 Group B read the text below. Which of the things in Ex. 2 are mentioned in your text?

ADVICE FOR UK BUSINESS TRAVELLERS

Forms of address

In most countries, business people use surnames when they talk to each other. In some countries (e.g. Germany and Switzerland) business people use surnames even when they know each other well. To be safe, continue using someone's surname until he/she asks you to use his/her first name.

Personal space

People in South America and southern Europe stand quite close to each other when talking. – about 60 centimetres apart, while in the Middle East they sometimes stand even closer – less than 30 centimetres apart. People from northern Europe and the USA stand further apart and feel uncomfortable if you stand too close. Their preferred distance is 75 to 90 centimetres apart.

Physical greetings

In most countries people shake hands when they meet in business situations. You should be careful that your handshake is not too strong or too weak. In Asia, the main form of greeting is the bow. When greeting Westerners, many Asians follow the bow with a handshake. Even in countries where it is common to kiss (e.g. Italy and Russia), it is usually only for people who know each other well.

4 a Read the text again. What is the significance of the following?

> surnames   first names   30 centimetres
> strong handshakes   bowing   kissing

b Work with a student who read text A. Answer your partner's questions about your text.

c Now ask your partner about his/her text.

1 When should you give presents in Japan?
2 What kind of gift should you give in Japan?
3 Is it OK to give four flowers in Japan?
4 Is it OK to give clocks in China?
5 Why should you be careful with leather products in South America?
6 Is it always OK to give red flowers in Europe?

Communication 11 | Ex. 3, page 112

Student B

1 a You are an assistant in the ticket office at Victoria Station, London. Your partner is a passenger.

Before you help the passenger buy his/her ticket, prepare your answers using the information below.

TICKETS TO BRIGHTON

Prices:

Single: £10 / Day Return: £18
Weekend return: £15

Times of trains:

To Brighton – Fridays 17:37 / 17:53
To London – Sundays 15:58 / 16:51

Method of payment:

Credit card, cheque or cash

b Help the passenger buy his/her ticket.

2 a Now change roles. You are a passenger buying a ticket at King's Cross Station, London. Your partner is an assistant in the ticket office.

Before you buy your ticket, prepare what you need to ask using the information below.

> You want to go to Cambridge on Thursday between 10.00 and 11.00am. You want to come back the same day after 6.00pm. You want to pay in cash.

b Buy your ticket.

Communication 7 | Ex. 3a, page 72

Total Stress Factor

10–15: You are one cool customer who is always calm under pressure. Well done!

16–25: Not bad... you're mostly stress-free – just a little hot sometimes!

26–35: Keep an eye on yourself. You are nearly at dangerous levels of stress... don't go there!

36–50: Watch out! You are getting too stressed, too often. You need to keep calm before you go completely crazy!

Communication activities

Lesson 5.1 | Ex. 2a, page 46

Student C

Gregor Kinski, Russia

Gregor is from Moscow. He is a sculpture student at Moscow University and lives with his parents and two brothers. He turned eighteen last month.

In Russia men aged eighteen usually have to go into the army and do military service. This should be optional but it's not. Fortunately, I don't have to go because I've got health problems. I'm actually quite happy about that! It means I can continue studying sculpture at university. Who wants to be a soldier when you can be a student?

In the future I want to stay in Russia. I know that you can earn more if you work abroad, but this is my home. You have to work hard to earn a good salary in Russia, but you can succeed.

In my free time I like listening to rock and hip-hop. I also like going to restaurants and bars, and concerts and playing football, like teenagers everywhere, I suppose.

Lesson 6.1 | Ex. 11, page 57

1   Draw a simple map of your country/region. Label the important geographical features.

2   Choose three of the places. What would you tell a tourist about them? Make notes.

3   What do you think is the future of tourism in your country/region? Make notes.

4   Finally, show other students your map. Tell them about tourism and the future of tourism in your country/region.

The beaches in my region are very popular. I think the number of tourists will increase because ...

Lesson 8.1 | Ex. 7b, page 77

1   85% of international phone calls are made in English.

2   In the US, more messages are carried by email than by post.

3   70% of websites aren't visited by anyone.

4   81% of the cars in the world are owned by people in the US, Canada, Europe and Japan. However, only 16% of the world's population live in these places.

5   Four million tons of junk mail are delivered every year in the US.

Lesson 7.3 | Ex. 8, page 71

Student B

Acupuncture

You could try acupuncture.
Acupuncture is based on two main beliefs. Acupuncturists believe we have lines of energy (called meridians) in our bodies. When these meridians are blocked*, your body cannot work properly. Acupuncturists also believe they can unblock the meridians so that energy can move around the body and you feel better.

During your first session, the acupuncturist discusses your symptoms and your general health. The acupuncturist treats illnesses by putting thin needles*_ into your body at points on the meridians. The treatment usually lasts about 45 minutes. Patients often get better after just one visit.

Millions of people use acupuncture. It is especially useful for stomach problems. Some people have an 'electric' feeling going up and down the meridians, but it doesn't usually hurt and it is also very safe. A typical session costs around £40 in the UK.

Glossary
1*blocked = when something cannot move in a narrow place
2* needle = a long, sharp piece of metal (e.g. used for sewing, acupuncture)

Lesson 8.3 | Ex. 4, page 81

'Why were you holding the dog?' he asked again.
'I like dogs,' I said.
'Did you kill the dog?' he asked.
I said, 'I did not kill the dog.'
He was asking too many questions and he was asking them too quickly ... The policeman said, 'I am going to ask you once again ...'
I rolled back onto the lawn and pressed my forehead to the ground again and made the noise that Father calls groaning. I make this noise when there is too much information coming into my head from the outside world.
The policeman took hold of my arm and lifted me onto my feet.
I didn't like him touching me like this.
And this is when I hit him.

Lesson 9.1 | Ex. 11, page 87

a Look at the three job ads and choose one.

b Think about these things:

Student A

1 Why would you be good for the job?
2 What experience or qualifications do you have?
3 Why do you want the job?
4 What questions might the interviewer ask you?
5 What questions do you want to ask the interviewer?

Student B

1 What does the job involve?
2 What kind of person do you want?
3 What questions are you going to ask the interviewee?
4 What questions might the interviewee ask you?

c Student B interview Student A. Then Student B should tell Student A if they got the job or not. Give reasons.

The International School of English

Receptionist wanted to deal with enquiries, give information and enrol students.

Horizon Children's Summer School

requires enthusiastic helpers to supervise groups (6–15) during afternoon activities (sports, drama, etc.) while in UK.

WESSEX UNIVERSITY DEPARTMENT OF LANGUAGES

is looking for foreign students to provide 1:1 speaking practice to university students learning foreign languages.

Lesson 9.2 | Ex. 2b, page 88

Churchill is 19, but he isn't famous or particularly 'cool'. In fact, he runs an IT empire. __B__

But success doesn't come easily. It involves long working days, doing business from 9a.m. to 7p.m., and sometimes making difficult decisions. He then spends two or three hours at night dealing with his programmers. __C__. He says, 'On one occasion I worked three days without stopping, – no sleep.' He smiles at the memory.

Is he happy with the progress the company has made? 'We've made some mistakes but it's all going pretty well now. I hope the business will be able to grow steadily over the next few years.'

So, how does he feel about all the money he's making. 'Well, I don't go out a lot like some of my friends, but it does mean I can do things that I couldn't do a few years ago. I've just bought a new car but that's about it really. __D__ You never know what will happen.'

Communication activities

Lesson 10.3 | Ex. 10b, page 101

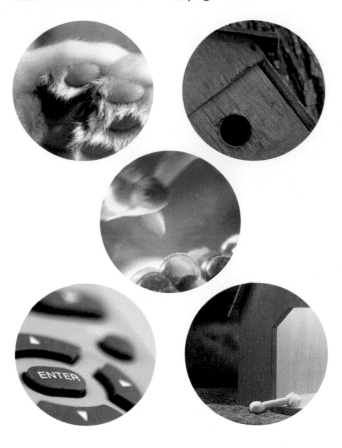

Lesson 11.1 | Ex. 8, page 106

Look at the picture. Say what Lucy's just done and what she hasn't done yet using the words in the box.

> fold/clothes   pack/bag   wash/hair   dry/hair
> make/bed   brush/teeth   have/shower
> write/postcards

Lesson 12.1 | Ex. 10b, page 117

1   A shop assistant gives you €5 too much change.
2   You find a wallet in the street. There is no name or address in it but there is €100 in cash.
3   A builder is doing some work on your house. He asks you to pay in cash, so he doesn't have to pay any tax.
4   A friend has just bought a new jacket. It was very expensive. You think it's awful. He/She asks you your opinion.
5   Your friend doesn't have much money. He/She suggests going on a train without paying.

Lesson 12.2 | Ex. 2c, page 118

A **student** can refer to someone who studies at school or university; **a pupil** only refers to a child at school.

A **subject** can refer to one of the things, e.g. Maths, History, that you study at school or university OR the thing you are talking or writing about; a **topic** just refers to the thing you are talking or writing about, e.g. The main topic of conversation was Saturday's party.

A **college** is where students study after they leave school, e.g. an art college; a **university** is a place where students study a subject at a high level in order to get a degree.

A **teacher** usually refers to someone who works in a school; a **professor** usually refers to someone who works in a university.

A **reward** is something, especially money, that is given to someone to thank them for doing something; a **result** can be the number or letter that shows how well you have done in an exam.

A **lesson** is a period of time in which a person or people are taught a subject or skill, e.g. at school; a **lecture** is a long talk given to a group of people on a particular subject, especially in universities.

1 Discuss.

1 What places can you see in the photos? What do you know about them?

2 Have you ever visited London? If so, what did you like/dislike about it? If not, would you like to? Why/Why not?

2 Do the quiz with a partner. Check your answers (at bottom of page.)

What do you know about London?

1 What is the population of Greater London (central London and suburbs)?

   A 12 million   **B** 7 million

2 How many visitors come to London from overseas every year?

   A 8.7 million   **B** 13.2 million

3 What is another name for London's underground system?

   A the Tube   **B** the Metro

4 What is the most visited tourist attraction in London?

   A The London Eye   **B** The British Museum

5 How old is Buckingham Palace?

   A About 100 years old   **B** About 300 years old

6 How many theatres are there in London's West End?

   A About 25   **B** About 50

3 In what order do you think these events happen on an average day in London?

A Shops in Oxford Street and Covent Garden open. ☐

B The afternoon rush hour begins. ☐

C Plays and musicals start in the West End theatres. ☐

D London's ancient markets open. 1

E Clubs (like the famous *Hippodrome*) open. ☐

F Tourists start to go sightseeing and to visit museums. ☐

G 'The Changing of the Guard' happens at Buckingham Palace. ☐

H More than 3 million office workers arrive in London. ☐

4 Watch the film and check the order of events.

5 Discuss.

1 Did you like the film? Why/Why not?

2 When you visit a large city, what do you like doing?

1 A   2 B   3 A   4 B (with 5.7 million visitors a year)   5 B   6 B

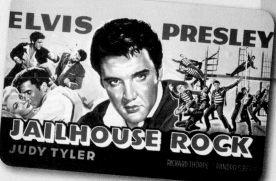

1 Look at the pictures and discuss the questions.

  1 Have you heard of any of these films? If yes, what do you know about them?

  2 Do you ever watch musical films or other films with pop stars in them? Do you have any favourites? What do you like/not like about musical films?

  3 Do you ever buy film soundtracks on CD? Why/Why not?

2 Complete the phrases below using the words in the box.

> brightly dream holiday two
> worries true laughter blue

  1 A summer _____
  2 A week or _____
  3 Fun and _____
  4 No more _____
  5 The sun shines _____
  6 The sea is _____
  7 Let's see if it's _____
  8 Make our _____ come true

3 Watch the film and check your answers.

4 Which of these things did you notice in the film?

  • musicians on a beach
  • London double-decker buses
  • people sitting on deckchairs
  • holiday-makers eating icecreams
  • people playing football
  • waves crashing onto the beach

5 Discuss with other students.

  1 What did you think of the song *Summer Holiday*?

  2 What did you think of the film extract? Does it make you want to watch the whole film?

  3 Do you usually go on holiday during the summer? At what other times do you go away? How do you feel about going on holiday?

3 Jamie Oliver

1 Look at the photos and answer the questions.

   1 Do you ever watch cookery programmes? Why/Why not?

   2 Do you know any celebrity chefs? What do you think of them?

   3 Have you learned any useful skills (e.g. cooking, DIY, etc.) from TV? If yes, what have you learned?

2 Look at these different stages for preparing barbecued salmon. Work with another student and put them in order.

	a) wrap the fish in newspaper
	b) serve with potatoes
	c) cover the fish with plenty of fresh herbs
	d) place the fish on the barbecue
	e) wet the paper to stop it burning too quickly
	f) put salt and pepper inside and outside the fish
	g) sprinkle fennel seeds over the whole fish
	h) put slices of lemon under, inside and on the fish

3 Watch the film and compare your ideas to what Jamie does.

4 Discuss.

   1 What do you think of this way of cooking salmon? Does it sound tasty?

   2 Did you enjoy watching this extract? Why/Why not?

   3 Do you like eating outdoors? Why/Why not? Can you remember a special occasion when you did this? What was the occasion? Who were you with? What happened?

   4 Do you have any favourite recipes? If so, what are they?

Ray Mears is a survival expert. He is known worldwide for his survival skills. In his TV series *Ray Mears' World of Survival*, he shows viewers how to survive in a wide variety of extreme situations, from the Arctic to the Sahara.

1 Look at the photos and read the information. Then, answer the questions.

  1 Do you have any survival programmes in your country? If yes, what are they like?

  2 Do you like watching this kind of programme? Why/Why not?

  3 What do you know about the Sahara desert?

2 Work in pairs. What do you think is the correct alternative in each sentence below.

  1 Desert covers $\frac{1}{5}$ /$\frac{1}{15}$ of the Earth's land surface.

  2 The Sahara/Gobi desert is the biggest desert in the world.

  3 Temperatures in the desert can go as high as 40°C/50°C.

  4 The first rule of desert survival is don't stay with/stay with your vehicle if you break down.

  5 The second rule of desert survival is get in the shade/look for water.

  6 It's important to drink your water/save your water.

  7 An 'S'/'V' sign in the sand is an international distress signal.

  8 You need to look out for snakes/scorpions in the desert.

3 Now watch the film and listen for the correct alternatives.

4 Think about what you learned in the programme. What advice would you give to someone who has broken down in the desert?

5 Discuss.

  1 Did you like the programme extract? Why/Why not?

  2 Would you be interested in watching this kind of programme regularly? Why/Why not?

  3 Would you like to spend time in the Sahara desert? Why/Why not?

5 | On Golden Pond

Every year around February the world's media begins to get excited about the Oscars. People start to guess who will win Best Actor, Best Actress, Best Picture, and many other awards. All the films in the photos have won a Best Picture Oscar and all of them are 'tearjerkers', (films that are sad and make you cry.) Tearjerkers are one of the most successful film types at the cinema and at the Oscars.

On Golden Pond

Titanic

The English Patient

Out of Africa

1   Look at the photos and discuss these questions.
   1   Have you seen any of these films? If yes, what can you remember about them?
   2   What other films do you know that have won an Oscar?
   3   Do you like watching tearjerkers? Do you have any favourites?

2   You're going to watch an extract from *On Golden Pond*. Who does these things: the mother (M), the father (F), the daughter (D) or the boy (B)?
   • gives someone a hug   *M and D*
   • is warm and welcoming
   • kisses someone on the cheek
   • is reserved and distant
   • takes his/her coat off
   • points at someone
   • introduces someone to someone else
   • shakes hands with someone
   • walks upstairs

3   Discuss.
   1   What can you tell about the relationships between the people in this film?
   2   What did you think of this film extract? Does it make you want to watch the whole film?
   3   What do you think happens in the rest of the film?
   4   How do you feel when you have to meet new people for the first time?

FILM
BANK

Belfast

Erie

Port of Spain

Perth

1   Look at the photos and discuss the questions below. Then check your answers (at the bottom of the page.)

1   Which language is spoken in all four places?
2   Which two of the places are capital cities?
3   Which place is on the edge of a lake?
4   Which place is in a bay at the mouth of a river?
5   Which two places are on the coast?
6   Which two places have a population of over 1 million?
7   Which two places have the hottest summers?
8   Which place has the coldest winters?
9   In which places do you drive on the left side of the road?

2   Watch the film and complete the chart about the four people.

	How long did she live there?	What did she like about it?	What can you do there?	Would she like to go back and live there?
Alison from Belfast		*the warm, friendly people*		*Yes*
Jennifer from Erie	*17 years*			
Kathleen from Trinidad				
Astrid from Perth			*go to the beach*	

3   Discuss.

1   Which of the four places would you most like to visit? Why?
2   Which of the four places is most similar to where you live? In what ways is it similar? What is different about it?

1 English   2 Belfast and Port of Spain   3 Erie   4 Belfast   5 Port of Spain and Perth   6 Port of Spain (1.2 million) and Perth (1.3 million) (Erie 102,000; Belfast 280,000)   7 Port of Spain and Perth   8 Erie   9 Belfast, Port of Spain and Perth

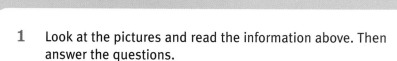
The *Carry on* series of British slapstick* comedy films includes classics such as *Carry on Doctor*, *Carry on Camping* and the first one, *Carry on Sergeant*, made in 1958. For over two decades, the *Carry on* films were among the most popular comedy films in Britain. Other more recent popular slapstick actors in Britain include Benny Hill in *The Benny Hill Show* and Rowan Atkinson as *Mr. Bean*.

*humorous acting in which the actors fall over, throw things at each other, get wet, etc.

1 Look at the pictures and read the information above. Then answer the questions.
1 Have you heard of the *Carry on* films, *The Benny Hill Show* or *Mr. Bean*? If yes, what do you know about them?
2 Do you like watching slapstick comedy films? Do you have any favourites?

2 Match words from column A and B to make verb phrases.

A	B
1 have	a) the blinds
2 go	b) the hoovering
3 do	c) an accident
4 take	d) a sip of tea
5 open	e) a syringe
6 prepare	f) a thermometer under someone's tongue
7 put	g) someone's face
8 wash	h) to hospital in an ambulance

3 All the events in the table above occur in the extract of *Carry on Doctor* you're going to watch. Before you watch it, with a partner try to imagine what happens.

4 Watch the film and check your ideas. Say in what order the events in the table above happen.

5 Discuss.
1 What did you think of the film extract? Does it make you want to watch the whole film?
2 Is this type of film popular in your country? Why/Why not?
3 If you are ill in bed, what do you like (a) doing (b) eating/drinking?

Quiz show

Current affairs programme

Drama

Comedy

1 Look at the different types of TV programme in the photos and discuss the questions.

1 Which type do you watch most?

2 Which type is most common on TV in your country?

3 Which type is most popular in your country?

4 Think of other types of TV programme. Make a list and compare with your partner.

2 You're going to watch a short current affairs programme about speed-dating. First complete the phrases below with a word from the box. Check your answers with a partner.

1 three-minute time _*slots*_

2 a good sense of _____

3 to exchange email _____

4 down-to-_____

5 stimulating _____

6 similar professional _____

7 to get to know each _____

other
~~slots~~
humour
addresses
background
conversation
earth

3 Watch the programme and decide if these things are said by the man, the woman or neither.

1a I'm a dentist.

b I'm 27 years old and I'm a journalist.

c I'm a 24-year-old IT consultant.

2a I'm up for new things.

b You get a good idea whether they interest you or not.

c Three-minute time slots are too short.

3a To be honest, I'm feeling very nervous.

b I'm bored of meeting the same people.

c You're not under any pressure.

4a ... someone from a similar professional background.

b ... someone who has the same hobbies as me.

c ... someone who can make me laugh.

4 Discuss.

1 Were you surprised that Darren and Kavita both ticked 'yes'? Do you think that they seem compatible? Why/Why not?

2 Do you have similar current affairs programmes in your country?

3 Look at the list below of different ways you can meet a girl/boyfriend or future wife/husband. What do you think the advantages and disadvantages of each one are?

• You can meet someone at work

• You can meet someone when you go out with your friends

• You can go speed-dating

1 **Discuss.**
1 Have you ever watched any teaching or training videos? If yes, what was their purpose? Did you think they were successful?
2 In what situations are training videos typically used?

2 Imagine you are going to make a training video to help people prepare for interviews. Which of the following points would you include in your video?
– make a good first impression
– wear appropriate clothes
– be enthusiastic and self-confident
– find out about the company you are applying to
– relax before you go in to the interview
– have some questions to ask the interviewers
– other points (say what)

3 What style of presentation would you use?
– someone talking to the camera and explaining what to do
– presenter asking people in the street their opinions
– examples of good and bad real interviews
– examples of humorous bad interviews
– another style (say what)

4 Watch the film and make a note of (a) which of the points from Exercise 2 it included and (b) what style of presentation it used.

5 **Discuss.**
1 Do you think it's a useful training video for people who are preparing for interviews? Why/Why not?
2 Which of the following do you think are characteristics of a good sales rep.?

> charming   fit   full of ideas   persuasive   good with numbers
> confident   brave   calm under pressure
> dynamic   artistic   good I.T. skills

3 Would you like to be a sales rep.?

1 **Discuss.**

  1 Are there any well-known programmes about animals in your country? If so, what are they? Do they have well-known presenters?

  2 Have you ever seen any cartoons, films or TV programmes about wolves?

  3 What do you know about wolves?

2 Work with other students. Decide if you think the following statements about wolves are true(T) or false(F).

  1 In children's stories, wolves are usually presented as dangerous and very intelligent.

  2 The word 'werewolf' means 'manwolf' because people who are normal during the day become werewolves at night.

  3 Wolves are very common in North America, Europe and Asia.

  4 They can 'talk' with other wolves 10km away.

  5 They tend to move and attack as individuals, not in groups.

  6 They rarely or never attack humans.

  7 Today, wolves are nearly extinct.

3 Now watch the film and check your ideas. Correct the information above if it is wrong.

4 **Discuss.**

  1 Did you like the film? Why/Why not?

  2 How many different programme types did you notice in the extract? Which of them do you like to watch?

  3 How do you feel about wolves after watching the extract? What new information have you learned?

1 Look at the photos and discuss these questions.

1 Do you know any travel programmes in your country? If so, what are they like?

2 Do you like watching this kind of programme? Why/Why not?

3 Do you think travel writers have an easy life? Why/Why not?

2 Try to complete what Gill says in the film. Use the phrases in the box.

> travel editor   two million readers   writing about them
> travelling   at my desk   scripts   film crews
> laptop computers

'I'm a travel writer and TV programme maker. I spend much of the year (1) _____, visiting countries and (2) _____. I work with (3) _____ to make programmes in amazing places. In fact, I've just come back from Antarctica. I'd like to travel most of the year but I need to spend time here (4) _____ writing stories for newspapers and (5) _____ for TV programmes. Many journalists today use (6) _____ but I prefer travelling light. I'm the (7) _____ of a British newspaper called the *Sunday Mirror*. Sometimes I have eight pages to write every week and sometimes we have (8) _____.'

3 Watch the film and check your answers. Make a note of the places that Gill mentions.

4 Which of the places is Gill referring to in each of these quotes?

A 'I haven't been to … yet.'

B 'It's the most amazing place I've ever been to.'

C 'They're the friendliest people I've ever met.'

D 'I was nearly eaten by an angry shark.'

E 'It's the coldest, driest, windiest continent on Earth.'

5 Discuss.

1 Did you like the film? Why/Why not?

2 Which of the places in the programme would you most like to visit?

3 Would you like to have Gill's job? Why/Why not?

12 The Ladykillers

The Ladykillers is a classic British comedy originally made in 1955 in which a little old lady (Mrs Wilberforce) takes in a lodger and then finds out he has committed a robbery with four friends. When the villains realise she knows everything they plan to kill her. But this little old lady isn't as harmless as she seems. This film was remade in 2004, starring Tom Hanks.

1 Look at the pictures and read the information above. Then answer the questions.

   1 Have you heard of this film? If so, what do you know about it? If not, what do you imagine it might be about?

   2 Do you ever watch old films? Do you have any favourites? What do you like/not like about them?

2 Look at the photos from the film again. What do you think is happening in each one? Who do you think the different people are?

3 Watch the film and answer the questions.

   1 What are the five men pretending to be?

   2 What are they in fact?

   3 What happens as they are leaving?

   4 Why do they go back to the house?

4 Work with another student. Discuss what you think happens next in the film. Tell another pair of students your ideas.

5 Discuss.

   1 Did you like the film extract? Did you find it funny? Why/Why not?

   2 Would you like to watch the rest of the film? Why/Why not?

Writing bank

Informal emails

Lesson 1.3 | Ex. 10, page 11

1 Read the email and answer these questions.

    1 What is Gaby describing?
      A her life now
      B her plans for the future

    2 What is Gaby doing ?
      A working in a school
      B working in a bank
      C studying

    3 Where is Gaby's flat?
      A in the countryside
      B near a town
      C in a town

    4 What does Gaby ask Enrico?
      A to come and stay
      B to write her an email

Writing skill | paragraphs

2 Match these descriptions to paragraphs 1–3 in the email.

    A Asking to hear about your friend's life around now ☐

    B Saying generally what you are doing around now ☐

    C Saying in detail what you are doing around now and your daily routine ☐

Informal letters

Lesson 3.2 | Ex. 10, page 29

1 Read the letter and answer the questions.

    1 Why hasn't Steve written to Sophie before now?

    2 What is the main reason for writing to Sophie now?

    3 How many people will be at the party?

    4 What does Steve want Sophie to do?

Informal language for greeting, e.g. *Hi Enrico*; *Hello Enrico*; *Dear Enrico*

Hi Enrico,

① I've got so much to tell you. Things are different for me now. I'm living in Canada at the moment! We're here for a year.

② James is working for a bank in Vancouver and I'm studying at the film school. We're staying in a lovely flat in the centre of town. There are lots of things to do in the city, but every weekend we go to the countryside. It's really beautiful!

③ What about you? I'd love to know what you're doing these days. Send me an email soon.

Love, Gaby xxx

Informal language for ending, e.g. *Love, Gaby*; *Lots of love, Gaby*; *All the best, Gaby*

Useful phrases

Give your general news	*I've got so much/lots of news to tell you.* *We're living in Canada!*
Give your news in detail	*I'm working at a bank.* *We're studying at college.* *I go to the cinema every weekend.*
Ask for your friend's news	*I'd love to know what you're doing.* *It would be great to hear your news/from you.* *Please write/email me soon.*

Introduction. Possibly apologise for not writing sooner/say what you have done recently.

Dear Sophie

Thanks a lot for your letter. I'm sorry I didn't reply sooner but I've been on holiday in Italy. I had a wonderful time and want to show you all my photos when I see you!

Explain main reason for writing.

Anyway, I was wondering if you'd like to come to a small dinner party at my house on Saturday 23rd at 8pm. Sam and Julie will be there and two other friends that you don't know. Do let me know if you can come. I hope you can!

Closing. Possibly refer to when you will next be in contact.

Looking forward to seeing you very soon.

Love, Steve

Writing skill | starting/
ending letters

2 Mark these ways of starting
and ending letters formal (F)
or informal (I).

- Dear Sarah ☐
- Dear Sir/Madam ☐
- Dear Mr. Davies ☐
- Yours faithfully, ☐
- Love, ☐
- Best wishes, ☐
- Yours sincerely, ☐

Formal letters

Lesson 12.2 | Ex. 11a, page 119

1 Read the letter and answer
these questions.

1 Why is Alberto writing this
letter?

2 What three things does he want
to know?

Writing skill | sequencers

2 Put the following words/
phrases into three groups of
similar meaning.

> firstly   lastly   secondly
> to begin with   next   finally
> I'd also like to know
> as well as this   to start with

Useful phrases

Introduction	Thanks a lot for your letter. It was really nice to hear from you. (I'm) sorry for taking so long to write/not writing recently.
Explain the main reason for writing	The main reason I'm writing is ... I was wondering if you ...
Closing	Write back soon and tell me your news. Hope everything's OK with you. Looking forward to seeing you soon. Give my love to your family.

How to start a formal letter if you don't know the name of the person you are writing to.

Your address

Recipient's address

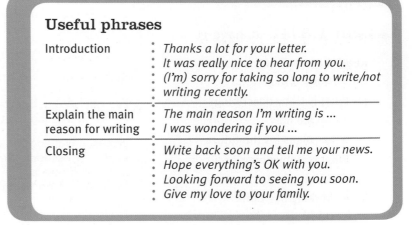

Blvd. Patrotas
Colonia Roma
México City 42811
México

Clifton School of English
Clifton
Somerset
CL8 92H

12 April 2005

Dear Sir/Madam,

I recently saw your advertisement for
Summer Intensive Courses and would like
some more information.

Firstly, can you tell me the specific dates
of the courses during July and August?
Secondly, do you know how many students
there will be in the classes?

Finally, can you tell me if you arrange
accommodation with local families or is that
something I have to do myself?

Yours faithfully,

Alberto Garcia Ramirez

Introduction.
Explain how
you know about
the person/
company and
the main reason
for writing.

Explain
exactly what
information you
would like.

How to end a
letter beginning
'Dear Sir/
Madam'.

Useful phrases

Explain the main reason for writing	I recently saw your advertisement in The Times. I'd be grateful if you could send me some information about your courses.
Explain exactly what information you need	Could you tell me how long the course lasts? I'd like to know more about the job. Could you send me a brochure about the courses your college offers?

Description

Lesson 6.3 | Ex. 12, page 61

1 Read the description and answer these questions.

1 What is special about the trees in Kingsgate Wood?

2 Why does the writer like this place when the weather is hot?

3 In which season does the writer prefer to be in the woods?

4 Does the writer live in a place which is similar to or different from the woods?

Writing skill | referencing words

2 Find these underlined words in the text and say what they refer to.

1 them (line 3):

2 there (line 4):

3 It (line 5):

4 it (line 6):

5 It (line 12):

6 there (line 14):

> **What/Where your favourite place is.**

> One of my favourite natural places is a wood near where I live called Kingsgate Wood. Many of the trees are very old – some of them have been there for hundreds of years.
>
> 5 It is a lovely place to go in every season and whatever the weather. When it's very hot, you can keep cool under the trees. I also like walking in the woods in the rain. My favourite time to go is autumn when the leaves are fantastic colours
> 10 – red, orange, yellow and gold.
>
> Kingsgate Wood is a very special place for me. It is an escape from the noisy, crowded city I live in. The wood is beautiful and peaceful and I always feel better when I go there.
>
> Gabriela Pisani

> **Why you like it/what you do there.**

> **Summarise why it's special for you.**

Useful phrases

Say what/where your favourite place is	*One of my favourite natural places is …* *One place which is very special to me is …*
Say why you like it/ what you do there	*It's a lovely place to go in autumn …* *I like/My favourite time to go there is in the early morning/when it's snowing …* *When it's very hot/cold/wet, you can …*
Summarise why it's special for you	*It's an escape from the city/stress/work …* *I feel happy and relaxed when I'm there.*

Short stories

Lesson 8.3 | Ex. 12, page 81

1 Choose the correct alternatives.

1 The writer felt *bored/excited* at his cousin's house.

2 He went for a walk *with his cousin/on his own.*

3 At the start of the walk, the weather was *good/bad.*

4 He didn't know the way *to his cousin's house/to the top of the mountain.*

5 The dog *was very quiet/ made a lot of noise.*

6 The writer *followed/took* the dog to his cousin's house.

7 The dog *stayed/didn't stay* with the writer.

> **Use narrative tenses**

> ① It all happened last summer. I was staying at my cousin's house in the mountains and I was bored. I really wanted something exciting to happen so I decided to go for a walk alone.
>
> ② At first, it was sunny, the mountains were beautiful and I felt happy. But time passed quickly and soon it was getting dark. I realised that I was a long way from my cousin's house and I was completely lost!
>
> ③ Suddenly, I heard a strange noise and saw a large dog. He was barking and he seemed to be asking me to go with him. So I decided to follow him. After a while, he took me to my cousin's house. He ran off into the night and I never saw him again.

> **Use interesting vocabulary**

> **Use phrases to show when things happened.**

Writing bank

Writing skill | organising your story

2 Match these descriptions to paragraphs 1–3 in the story.

  A Describe the main events of the story, e.g. a problem, a crime or a mystery.

  B Set the scene, including the place, the person/people and the feelings.

  C Say what happens in the end. Remember that an interesting ending is the most important part of your story.

Bulletin boards

Lesson 10.2 | Ex. 10a, page 99

1 Read the bulletin board and mark the statements true (T) or false (F).

  1 Paula doesn't think it is necessary to take anything.

  2 Craig disagrees with Paula.

  3 Craig will always take flowers.

  4 Kelly will take different things for different people. It depends on how well she knows them.

  5 Kelly thinks chocolates are good to take in formal situations.

Useful phrases

IMO – In my opinion
W/O – Without
BTW – By the way
F2F – Face-to-face
FAQ – Frequently asked question
LOL – Laugh out loud
TIA – Thanks in advance
YW – You're welcome

Writing skill | its/it's

When *its* is a possessive word (like *my* or *your*) there is no apostrophe. When *it's* is the contracted form of *it is* or *it has*, there is an apostrophe.

2 Decide for each example of 'its' below, if it needs an apostrophe (') or not.

  1 If I invite people to dinner, its because I want to see them.

  2 I think you should give the dog its food now.

  3 Every family has its own special way of celebrating Christmas.

  4 A: What time is the film on? B: I'm afraid its started already.

MODERN DAY POLITENESS BULLETIN BOARD

This is the place for your questions and replies.
What should you take when you are invited for dinner?

Paula, Newcastle: IMO, you don't have to take anything. If I invite people for dinner, it's because I want to see them, not because I expect anything!

Craig, Auckland: Come on, Paula! I think that's quite rude. I would never arrive for dinner W/O a small gift! I usually take something to drink and maybe flowers.

Kelly, Belfast: I think it all depends on who you're visiting. With really good friends who I see a lot, I probably wouldn't take anything … or maybe just a few chocolates. But if it's more formal, or people I don't know very well then I'd do the same as Craig – something to drink and flowers are always appreciated.

Using bulletin boards

Disagree politely: Give your opinion but please disagree politely and use reasonable language. Being rude to other people is not acceptable.

Keep personal information private: It's usually not a good idea to put your address or telephone number on the public message board. Also, do not ask for personal information from others.

Don't repeat yourself: Do not post the same message more than once on a message board. Duplicate messages can be frustrating for other members and will be removed.

No commercial messages: Do not post commercial messages advertising websites or products for sale in message boards. They will be removed.

Irregular verbs

Verb	Past Simple	Past Participle
be	was/were	been
beat	beat	beaten
become	became	become
begin	began	begun
bend	bent	bent
bite	bit	bitten
blow	blew	blown
break	broke	broken
bring	brought	brought
build	built	built
burn	burned/burnt	burned/burnt
burst	burst	burst
buy	bought	bought
can	could	been able
catch	caught	caught
choose	chose	chosen
come	came	come
cost	cost	cost
cut	cut	cut
dig	dug	dug
do	did	done
draw	drew	drawn
dream	dreamed/dreamt	dreamed/dreamt
drink	drank	drunk
drive	drove	driven
eat	ate	eaten
fall	fell	fallen
feed	fed	fed
feel	felt	felt
fight	fought	fought
find	found	found
fly	flew	flown
forget	forgot	forgotten
forgive	forgave	forgiven
freeze	froze	frozen
get	got	got
give	gave	given
go	went	gone/been
grow	grew	grown
hang	hung	hanged/hung
have	had	had
hear	heard	heard
hide	hid	hidden
hit	hit	hit
hold	held	held
hurt	hurt	hurt
keep	kept	kept
kneel	knelt	knelt
know	knew	known
lay	laid	laid
lead	led	led
learn	learned/learnt	learned/learnt

Verb	Past Simple	Past Participle
leave	left	left
lend	lent	lent
let	let	let
lie	lay	lain
light	lit	lit
lose	lost	lost
make	made	made
mean	meant	meant
meet	met	met
must	had to	had to
pay	paid	paid
put	put	put
read/riːd/	read/red/	read/red/
ride	rode	ridden
ring	rang	rung
rise	rose	risen
run	ran	run
say	said	said
see	saw	seen
sell	sold	sold
send	sent	sent
set	set	set
shake	shook	shaken
shine	shone	shone
shoot	shot	shot
show	showed	shown
shut	shut	shut
sing	sang	sung
sink	sank	sunk
sit	sat	sat
sleep	slept	slept
slide	slid	slid
smell	smelled/smelt	smelled/smelt
speak	spoke	spoken
spend	spent	spent
spill	spilled/spilt	spilled/spilt
spoil	spoiled/spoilt	spoiled/spoilt
stand	stood	stood
steal	stole	stolen
stick	stuck	stuck
swim	swam	swum
take	took	taken
teach	taught	taught
tear	tore	torn
tell	told	told
think	thought	thought
throw	threw	thrown
understand	understood	understood
wake	woke	woken
wear	wore	worn
win	won	won
write	wrote	written

Pronunciation bank

Part 1 | English phonemes

Consonants

Symbol	Key word	Symbol	Key word
p	**p**an	s	**s**ell
b	**b**an	z	**z**ero
t	**t**ie	ʃ	fre**sh**
d	**d**ie	ʒ	mea**s**ure
k	**c**ap	h	**h**ot
g	**g**ap	m	**m**et
tʃ	**ch**urch	n	**n**et
dʒ	**j**udge	ŋ	ra**ng**
f	**f**ew	l	**l**ed
v	**v**iew	r	**r**ed
θ	**th**row	j	**y**et
ð	**th**ough	w	**w**et

Vowels

Symbol	Key word	Symbol	Key word
iː	f**ee**t	aɪ	b**y**
ɪ	f**i**t	aʊ	br**ow**n
e	b**e**t	ɔɪ	b**oy**
æ	b**a**t	ɪə	h**ear**
ɑː	b**a**th	eə	h**air**
ɒ	b**o**ttle	ʊə	s**ure**
ɔː	b**ou**ght	eɪə	pl**ayer**
ʊ	b**oo**k	əʊə	l**ower**
uː	b**oo**t	aɪə	t**ire**d
ʌ	b**u**t	aʊə	fl**ower**
ɜː	b**ir**d	ɔɪə	empl**oyer**
ə	broth**er**	i	happ**y**
eɪ	b**ay**	u	ann**ua**l
əʊ	g**ol**d		

Part 2 | Sound-spelling correspondences

In English, we can spell the same sound in different ways, for example, the sound /iː/ can be 'ee', as in *green*, 'ea' as in *read* or 'ey' as in *key*. Students of English sometimes find English spelling difficult, but there are rules and knowing the rules can help you. The chart below gives you the more common spellings of the English sounds you have studied in this book.

Sound	Spelling	Examples
/ɪ/	i	this listen
	y	gym typical
	ui	build guitar
	e	pretty
/iː/	ee	green sleep
	ie	niece believe
	ea	read teacher
	e	these complete
	ey	key money
	ei	receipt receive
	i	police
/æ/	a	can pasta land
/ɑː/	a	can't dance*
	ar	scarf bargain
	al	half
	au	aunt laugh
	ea	heart
/ʌ/	u	fun sunny husband
	o	some mother month
	ou	cousin double young
/ɒ/	o	hot pocket top
	a	watch what want
/ɔː/	or	short sport store
	ou	your course bought
	au	daughter taught pause
	al	bald small always
	aw	draw jigsaw lawyer
	ar	warden warm
	oo	floor indoor
/aɪ/	i	like time island
	y	dry shy cycle
	ie	fries die tie
	igh	light high right
	ei	height
	ey	eyes
	uy	buy
/eɪ/	a	lake hate shave
	ai	wait train straight
	ay	play say stay
	ey	they grey obey
	ei	eight weight
	ea	break
/əʊ/	o	home phone open
	ow	show throw own
	oa	coat road coast
	ol	cold told

* In American English the sound in words like *can't* and *dance* is the /æ/ sound, like *can* and *man*.

Part 3 | Weak forms

In English, some words have two pronunciations – the strong form and the weak form, for example, Can (/kən/) you dance? Yes, I can (/kæn/). We usually use the weak form when the word is not stressed. Most of these words are 'grammar' words e.g. *a, an,* *than, have, been,* etc. Knowing weak forms helps you understand spoken English. The chart below shows some of the most common weak forms and examples of their use.

Word	Strong form	Weak form	Examples of weak forms in sentences
a, an	/eɪ/, /æn/	/ə/, /ən/	Did you bring **an** umbrella?
the	/ðiː/	/ðə/	He's **the** person who cleans our office.
are	/ɑː/	/ə/, or /ər/ before vowels	What **are** your phone numbers?
was	/wɒz/	/wəz/	He **was** an architect.
were	/wɜː/	/wə/	They **were** born in France.
been	/biːn/	/bɪn/	I've **been** to San Francisco.
do	/duː/	/də/	Where **do** you live?
does	/dʌz/	/dəz/	Where **does** he work?
have	/hæv/	/əv/	What **have** you got?
has	/hæz/	/əz/	Where **has** she been?
had	/hæd/	/həd/, /əd/	He **had** already gone. He'd already gone.
can	/kæn/	/kən/	She **can** sing very well.
you	/juː/	/jə/	How do **you** say that in English?
them	/ðem/	/ðəm	Let's take **them** to the cinema.
to	/tuː/	/tə/ (before consonants)	I want **to** go home now.
at	/æt/	/ət/	Let's meet **at** six o'clock.
of	/ɒv/	/əv/	There's a lot **of** food.
for	/fɔː/	/fə/	He's away **for** two months.
from	/frɒm/	/frəm/	She's **from** Brazil.
and	/ænd/	/ən/	I'd like a burger **and** fries.
but	/bʌt/	/bət/	She knows, **but** he doesn't.
than	/ðæn/	/ðən/	She's taller **than** Juan.

Tapescripts

Unit 1 Recording 1

P = Presenter

P: Everybody knows that cats like sleeping … they spend half their lives asleep and enjoy every minute of it. Other animals have very different sleeping habits, however. These horses may not look like they are asleep. But they are! Horses only spend about three hours asleep every day and they do it standing up! Fish sleep for about seven hours a day but they too have strange habits … they don't close their eyes to sleep.
So, what about us? Well, most people sleep for about a third of their lives. The number of hours you actually sleep, however, depends on your age. Newborn babies sleep a lot – usually about seventeen hours in every twenty-four. That's nearly 75% of their time spent asleep! As we get older we need less sleep. Children need about eleven hours and adults sleep for about eight hours every night. So, yes, on average you spend about 2,688 hours a year doing nothing - asleep in bed!
But you're not just asleep – you're not really doing nothing. Your body and your mind rest during this time, but a lot happens during sleep. Dreams are one way that the mind rests after a busy day. The average person spends about 20% of every night dreaming. That means you have about four or five dreams every night or about 1,800 dreams a year.

Unit 1 Recording 4

I=Interviewer W=Woman

I: Hello, madam. Welcome to Harrods.
W: Thank you.
I: I'm doing a customer survey. Can I ask you some questions?
W: Yes, of course.
I: Firstly, where are you from?
W: I'm from Valencia in Spain.
I: OK … and what are you doing in London?
W: I'm working as an au pair. I'm living with an English family for six months and looking after their children.
I: And what are you doing here in Harrods?
W: Well, I'm just looking really … I absolutely love this shop but everything is very expensive so I'm not buying anything …

I=Interviewer M= Man

I: Hello, sir. Can I ask you some questions for my survey?
M: Yes. No problem.
I: Where are you from?
M: I'm from Krakow in Poland.
I: OK, thank you. And what are you doing in London?
M: I'm here on holiday with my girlfriend. We're not staying long – just three days.
I: Oh, right. Are you looking for anything special in Harrods today?
M: Well, yes. My girlfriend is shopping for clothes at the moment and, this is a secret, I'm looking for a ring for her. Actually, it's an engagement ring.
I: An engagement ring? Wow!
M: Maybe you could help me. Which ring do you like?
I: Ummm … oh, I don't know … I'm not sure really…

I=Interviewer W=Woman

I: Excuse me, madam. Welcome to Harrods. Can I ask you some questions?
W: Oh, well, yes, OK.
I: First, where are you from?
W: England darling! I'm from Surrey.
I: OK … what are you doing in London today?
W: I'm shopping, darling. Shopping is wonderful, isn't it? So much fun.
I: Er, yes. And what are you doing in Harrods today?
W: I'm trying to find some clothes for a wedding … and some shoes … well, a whole outfit probably … maybe a hat too. I'm here with a friend you see and we always go shopping together … such fun. We'll probably go to the restaurant upstairs later I think … it's great … you can do everything here … we'll probably be here all day …
I: Oh, OK … mmmm … thank you … that's fine …

Unit 1 Recording 6

A=Antonio W=Woman:

A: OK … I've finished my wheel … can I tell you about it?
W: Yes, of course. Go ahead.
A: Well, let's start with grammar. Grammar is quite important to me, so I've put three for that.
W: And you're good at grammar, aren't you?
A: Yes, I am.
W: What about vocabulary?
A: Well, I've put four for that because it's important to me. But I think I need to improve my vocabulary because I'm not very good at remembering new words.
W: OK. So … reading?
A: Well, three for reading – it's quite important to me and I'm quite good at reading generally so I feel happy about that …
W: Are you good at listening too?
A: Pardon?
W: Very funny.
A: Umm … no, I'm not very good at listening because people usually speak so fast. But I've put four for that because it's very important to me. I really need to practise more.
W: Is speaking important to you?
A: Yes, it's very important. I've put five for speaking and pronunciation. I need more practice because I'm quite good but I'd … like … to … be … more … fluent.
W: And the last one… what about writing?
A: Well, I'm quite good at writing but it's not very important. I don't need to write in English much … just two for that …
W: Two for writing … OK … Can I tell you about my wheel now?

Unit 2 Recording 2

I=Interviewer R=Robin:

I: Tell me about your early life, Robin … where did it all start?
R: Well, I grew up in south London and when I left school I went to art college.
I: Art college? You didn't go to music college …

R: No. Art colleges were more exciting at that time and I was interested in art too.
I: How did you start in the music business?
R: I made my first record in 1969 but there were a few problems with my record label. I had some strong ideas about music and they didn't agree with me all the time.
I: So, it wasn't a good start. How did you feel at that time?
R: Well, I didn't feel very happy about my first record but life was still fun. I sang in small clubs and wrote songs in different musical styles. Then in the mid-seventies, I moved to Paris with my girlfriend Brigit. We formed a band with my brother, Julian, and called it M.
I: How did you think of the name M?
R: It was by chance. I looked out of the window of a studio in Paris and I saw the M over the entrance to the Metro station.
I: And was *Pop Muzik* M's first record?
R: No, it wasn't. The first one was *Moderne Man*. That came out in the summer of 1978. I think it was a great record but it wasn't successful. Then in February 1979, *Pop Muzik* finally came out after months of work.
I: Were you excited about it?
R: Yes, I was. It was great when people started buying it. It was popular all over the world.
I: What did you do next?
R: Well, after that, I worked with Ruichi Sakamoto in Japan and I continued making records, including an album with some African musicians. And of course, *Pop Muzik* came out again in 1989. I think the song is just a real classic and a lot of people have covered it.
I: So what about now? What are you doing?
R: I'm working with various artists and I want to do some live shows with them. You can find out more on my website, www.robinscott.org. There's information about …

Unit 2 Recording 4

1 I went to a fantastic concert last night.
2 Mozart wrote 600 pieces of music.
3 My brother played his guitar all day yesterday.
4 Ten years ago my favourite band was Oasis.
5 I made a compilation CD for my sister's birthday.
6 My dad taught me how to play the piano.
7 I bought three jazz CDs last week.

Unit 2 Recording 6

1 The concert finished at midnight.
2 I loved rock music when I was a teenager.
3 When I was a child, I wanted to be a pop star.
4 I worked in a CD shop last summer.
5 She moved her CD player into the living room.
6 I waited for three hours to see the lead singer.

Unit 2 Recording 8

relaxed; relaxation; tired; tiredness; energetic; energy; imaginative; imagination; intelligent; intelligence

Unit 2 Recording 9

1 **A:** I like rock music.
   B: So do I.
2 **A:** I've got a guitar.
   B: So have I.
3 **A:** I'm not keen on him.
   B: Neither am I.
4 **A:** I didn't go.
   B: Neither did I.
5 **A:** I often listen to rock music.
   B: I don't.
6 **A:** I've got a DVD player.
   B: I haven't.
7 **A:** I can't play an instrument.
   B: I can.
8 **A:** I don't like loud music.
   B: I do.

Unit 2 Recording 10

A: Have you ever won a competition?
B: Yes, I have. I won a singing competition when I was six.
A: Did you watch TV last night?
B: Yes, I did. I saw a documentary about child prodigies.
A: Have you ever met a famous person?
B: No, I haven't. But I saw Kylie in concert last year!
A: Have you ever played a musical instrument in public?
B: Yes, I have. I was in a band when I was a teenager.

Unit 2 Recording 11

I=Interviewer BK=Ben Knight:
I: On *My top three* today, we're talking to actor Ben Knight. What are his top three records? Imagine he is alone on a desert island for ten weeks. Which music would he want? Which three pieces of music would he take with him to this desert island? Let's talk to him and find out. Hello Ben – welcome to *My top three*.
BK: Hello, it's great to be here.
I: So, imagine – you're going to be alone on a desert island. You can only take three pieces of music. Which three do you want? First … tell us about number three …

Unit 2 Recording 12

I=Interviewer BK=Ben Knight:
BK: Well, it's very difficult to choose – but I think number three for me is *Dancing Queen* by Abba. I love it!
I: Yes. So do I!
BK: It reminds me of when I was at school. We finished our exams and then this song was on the radio all summer. It makes me feel so happy. I always want to dance when I hear it!
I: Well, let's hear it … … Great! so number three is Abba, what about number two?
BK: Number two for me is something completely different … it's a piece of classical music. It's got great memories for me. I heard it first when I was about 10 years old and I didn't know anything about classical music at that time. It's the fourth movement of Mahler's *Symphony number 5*. When I first heard it, it made me cry because it was so beautiful!! And I still love it.

I: OK … so here it is … the fourth movement of *Symphony number 5* by Mahler … … That really is lovely, isn't it?
BK: Yes …
I: So, number one … what's your all-time number one favourite piece of music?
BK: Well, I think my favourite song ever is *Angels* by Robbie Williams. He's got a fantastic voice. And I remember listening to this song when I was on holiday in Spain. It's so relaxing – I could listen to it every day!
I: Mmm … here it is … … A great choice! Thank you for coming in today to tell us about your top three, Ben …

Unit 2 Recording 13

BK=Ben Knight:
1 This song reminds me of when I was at school.
2 This music makes me feel so happy.
3 When I first heard this record, it made me cry because it was so beautiful.
4 I remember listening to this song when I was on holiday in Spain.

Unit 3 Recording 1

1 About once a week. I really like Italian and Japanese restaurants.
2 Not really. I think a lot of them are a waste of time. They don't really work.
3 Yes, I have. It was when I was a teenager. I didn't think it was right to eat animals.
4 Yes, there are lots. I really like Jamie Oliver. He makes cooking seem simple and fun.
5 Yes, chocolate! I eat far too much!
6 Yes, quite often and yes, I do use recipes. I like them to help me get new ideas.

Unit 3 Recording 2

I=Interviewer T=Trainee Chef
I: … so, have you enjoyed working in a restaurant in a big hotel?
T: Yes, it's been great. And I've been working for a top chef. I've learnt a lot but my contract finishes at the end of this month.
I: So, what are you going to do next?
T: Well, my dad has a friend who runs a small restaurant in the south of France. I'm going to work for him over the summer.
I: Wow … lucky you! Just the summer?
T: Yeah, but that's ok. I'm not going to stay there longer than a few months because what I really want to do is get a job in the States …

Unit 3 Recording 3

1 I'm going to start going to the gym.
2 Rachel isn't going to get a new job.
3 Are we going to visit your parents tomorrow?
4 They aren't going to come to dinner next week.
5 What are you going to do this weekend?
6 He's going to call you later.
7 Where are Peter and Tania going to stay?
8 Who's going to tell him the news?

Unit 3 Recording 4

M=Man W=Woman
M: So did you do much yesterday?
W: No, not really. I just stayed at home in the evening and got a video.
M: Any good?
W: Yeah, actually, it was great. It's called *Big Night*. Do you know it?
M: I think I've heard of it … I'm not too sure …
W: Well, it's set in the US in the 1950s and it's about two Italian brothers who live in New York. They own an Italian restaurant which isn't doing very well. It's the 1950s and the restaurant is called 'Paradise'. The brothers, Primo and Secondo, want to serve the very best Italian cooking. But, the big problem is that the customers just want spaghetti and meatballs so they don't get any customers and they don't have much money left!
M: Ok … so …
W: Well, next door to Paradise there's a restaurant where they serve terrible Italian food, but it's really popular. The owner's name is Pascal. The brothers think Pascal is their friend, but actually he isn't. Pascal has an idea for them to get more business. He thinks they should get Louie Prima, a famous jazz musician, to have dinner at 'Paradise'. The idea is that they will advertise that he's coming and lots of other people will want to come to the restaurant. So they start to prepare for the 'Big Night' and they spend their last money on the evening!
M: So, what happens? Is it a success, do they …
W: Ha, ha … I'm afraid, I can't say. Why don't you watch it yourself!
M: Oh no, you always do this, you …

Unit 3 Recording 7

M=Man W=Woman
M: So, Friday night, what are you doing tonight?
W: Well, you'll never guess what …
M: What?
W: I'm going out for dinner with Marcin.
M: Really? Who's Marcin?
W: He's a friend of my brother.
M: Wow, how exciting. Where are you meeting?
W: At a French restaurant in the centre of town.
M: And your brother?
W: Don't be silly, he's not coming with us! It's a blind date …

Unit 3 Recording 8

M=Man:
M: … Well, I'm renting this fantastic space … it's on the ground floor of this old factory. It's enormous … and I'm going to turn it into a really top quality restaurant. You see, there's almost nothing like that in this area. There are lots of fast-food chains selling burgers and so on … but no proper restaurants.
Basically, I'm going to divide the space into one third kitchen and two thirds restaurant and have big swing doors from the kitchen

into the restaurant.

I'd like to have about nine tables: three for two people, four for four people and two for six people. Of course, we can always put them together for bigger groups.

There's a small room on one side of the restaurant. We're going to turn this into toilets. Opposite this we're going to have the main entrance to the restaurant. I've also had a conversation with a local art gallery and we're going to put up pictures by local artists for sale ... and they'll change every month.

I've been thinking about the menu and I've decided that we're going to make it short and simple but change it every two weeks. We're going to always have three starters, three main courses and three desserts.

In our opening weeks we're going to have as starters: goat's cheese salad, tomato and orange soup and garlic mushrooms on toast. For the main course: vegetarian pasta, grilled salmon and new potatoes and roast chicken and vegetables of the day. Finally for dessert: apple tart with cream or ice cream, chocolate mousse and cheese and biscuits.

The food is going to be simple but delicious and we hope to have a friendly, lively atmosphere. Anyway, that's the plan. We'll have to see how it goes ...

Unit 4 Recording 1

1 To control your fear means to make yourself feel less frightened
2 To achieve your goal means to succeed in getting the result you wanted or hoped for.
3 A challenge is something new, exciting or difficult to do.
4 To rely on means to trust or depend on someone or something.
5 Physical and mental strength is the physical or mental ability to deal with difficult situations.

Unit 4 Recording 2

E.g. My brother is brave. His hobby is mountain climbing.
1 My aunt is generous. She gave me £200 at Christmas!
2 Jane is confident that she will pass her end-of-year exams.
3 Sarah is intelligent. She's got lots of qualifications.
4 Petra is reliable. She won't be late.
5 Joe is ambitious. He wants to be a manager.
6 My dad is determined. He's decided to run a marathon and I'm sure he'll do it.
7 Sam is talented as a writer. She won a short story competition in June.

Unit 4 Recording 3

Kurt is a bit taller than Pablo.
Pablo isn't as tall as Kurt.
The grey car is a bit more expensive than the blue car.
The blue car isn't as expensive as the grey car.
Teri is much funnier than Jan.
Jan isn't as funny as Teri.

Unit 4 Recording 4

DJ=David Johnson

DJ: Good evening and thank you for coming to find out about the Hillside Survival School. My name's David Johnson. I started the school and I'm the School's chief instructor. I learned my survival skills while I was in the army and since then I've used them all over the world.

Before starting the Hillside Survival School, I worked in other well-known survival schools. My real aim for this school is to help people discover nature and outdoor life but also to learn and to have fun.

We run a variety of courses but our basic survival course lasts a weekend and takes place throughout the year. This course teaches you the basic skills that you need to survive in the wilderness and during the course you have a lot of opportunities to practise these skills. This course costs £139 per person.

If you want an even bigger challenge, our extreme survival course takes place between November and February when the conditions are more difficult. These courses also last for a weekend and cost £149 per person.

The extreme survival course teaches you to survive in a cold and wet environment. The course offers you the chance to push yourself, both physically and mentally. No tents, no gas cookers, just you and the wilderness. You learn to find and prepare food and cook it over an open fire. You learn to build a shelter and then you actually sleep in it. Most importantly, you learn a lot about yourself and how well you can cope with unexpected situations.

A few final practical details. You have to be at least 18 years old to come on the courses. The full cost of the course needs to be paid at least 4 weeks before the course begins and remember that there are discounts for groups of 4 or more.

Well, I hope that gives you some idea of what we do. And now if there are any questions ...

Unit 4 Recording 5

E.g. This is the most comfortable chair in the house
1 This is the most exciting holiday I've ever had.
2 Everest is the highest mountain in the world.
3 What is the best department store in New York?
4 This is the wettest day of the year so far.
5 This is the most boring film I've ever seen.
6 Football is the most popular sport in Brazil.
7 This is the most difficult exam I've ever taken.

Unit 4 Recording 6

Dialogue 1

W=Woman B=Bus driver:
W: Do you go to Carson Street?
B: Yep.
W: How much is it?
B: £1.10

W: Can you tell me how long it takes?
B: About twenty minutes. I'll tell you when to get off.

Dialogue 2

S=Shop assistant C=Customer
S: Do you need any help there?
C: Yes, please. Can you tell me if you have this in a size 12?
S: One minute. I'll just have a look for you.
C: Thanks.

Dialogue 3

C=Customer B=Bank clerk
C: How much do you charge to change Euros into Pounds?
B: That's 3% with a minimum charge of £4.50.
C: Ok, thanks. I'd like to change 200 Euros please.

Dialogue 4

T=Taxi driver W=Woman
T: Where do you want to get to, love?
W: Queens Road please. It's near Victoria Station. Do you know it?
T: Yes, I think so. But do you know where it is exactly?
W: Yep. I'll tell you where to go when we get a bit nearer.

Dialogue 5

C=Customer W=Waiter
C: Could I have the bill, please?
W: Of course. One moment... Here you are.
C: Thanks. Do you take MasterCard?
W: Yes, that's fine.
C: Great.

Unit 4 Recording 7

E.g. Do you know how long the journey takes?
1 Can you tell me how much that is?
2 Do you know where I can get an application form?
3 Can you tell me if you have any 1st class stamps?
4 Do you know how far it is to the library?
5 Can you tell me if there's a post office near here?
6 Do you know what the time is?
7 Can you tell me where I get off the bus?

Unit 4 Recording 8

W=Woman M=Man

W: So ... Which of them do you think is the most important?
M: Well, it's not easy but I think we should take the blankets to keep us warm at night.
W: Ok ... so do you think they're more important than the penknife?
M: No, no ... not more important. We can have the penknife as well you know. We are allowed five things after all ...
W: That's true. So what else?
M: Well, in my opinion, we should take the matches so we can make a fire from all the wood you can chop up with the penknife!
W: Good idea and how about the tent?
M: Hmmm ... I'm not sure. Couldn't we make a shelter from the trees and leaves and things?
W: Well maybe you could!
M: Ok ... we'll have the tent ... and why don't we have the chocolate as number five

as a bit of luxury?
W: Perfect!

Unit 5 Recording 2

Dialogue 1
M=Man W=Woman
M: ... so then I met up with my brother and we had lunch in town.
W: How old is your brother?
M: He's eighteen.
W: Eighteen? So young.
M: Yes, but he's getting married in three months' time.
W: You're joking. And he's only eighteen? Mmm ... Well, I think eighteen is far too young to get married. I mean, you don't know what you want when you're eighteen. You haven't got any experience of life. What do you think?
M: Well, I'm not so sure ...

Dialogue 2
F=Father S=Son
F: ... of course, when I was your age it was different, you know. I had to do military service!
S: Yes, Dad, I know.
F: You know, in my opinion, military service is a good thing because it teaches you how to look after yourself.
S: But you can't even boil an egg!
F: Yes, but that's ... not important. The important thing is, young people should learn some discipline. Don't you think so?
S: Yes, Dad, you're probably right ... Dad, can I borrow the car?

Unit 5 Recording 3

T=Tina M=Martin
T: I'm so glad you emailed. It's been ages since I saw you!
M: I know. Well, I've been in Poland for almost two years. I'm teaching English there.
T: So, are you enjoying it?
M: Yes, it's great. Especially since I met this woman called Dorota. We've known each other for about six months now. She works in the same school as me.
T: Oh! ... That's great ... so when are you both coming to the UK?

Unit 5 Recording 4

N=Narrator
N: Average lifespan can be very different from one country to another. The country with the longest average lifespan is Japan. Women live to 82.5 years on average and men live to 76.2 years on average. This, of course, is much longer than the average lifespan 2000 years ago. That was just 26 years. Now, everyone expects to have a long and happy life. By 2050, around 20 percent of the population will be aged 65 or over.
If you would like to have a long life, there are certain things that seem to make a difference. On average, non-smokers live longer than smokers, married people live longer than single people and pet owners live longer than non-pet owners. So the message is don't smoke, get married and get a dog.

Unit 5 Recording 5

I=Interviewer E=Expert
I: Hello and welcome to *The Truth*, the programme that brings science into your home. Today our topic is The Truth about Ageing and expert Helen Foster is with us today ... Hello, Helen.
E: Hello.
I: So, what is the truth about ageing? Have scientists found a way to stop ageing and for us all to live longer?
E: Not yet! However, the question that many scientists are interested in is, 'why do some people live a long time and others don't?' ... Studies of the lifestyles of very old people don't really show a common pattern. Many of them drink and smoke and don't do much exercise ... In fact, the oldest person ever, a woman called Jeanne Calment, who lived to the age of 122, only gave up smoking when she was 120!!
I: Really?!
E: Yes ... so if lifestyle isn't the answer, then scientists think that it might be in our genes ... that some people are born with genes that protect them from ageing and diseases better than other people. For example, in the case of Jeanne Calment ... she probably had a gene that stopped her from getting cancer (caused by smoking) that other people may get aged 40 or 50 ...
I: Is there anything we can do about it then? Can we do anything to change the genes that we're born with?
E: Well, there are some experts who believe that the answer is in your diet ... specifically, a low-calorie diet. Experiments with mice show that when they eat one third fewer calories every day, they live 40% longer. In human terms, that's the same as living to 170 years old.
I: Oh well ... perhaps that's what we should all do?
E: I'm afraid there's no proof that it works in humans ... and I'm not sure that being hungry all your life is worth all those extra years!
I: No, you're probably right ... it's best to enjoy the days we've got!

Unit 5 Recording 6

Thomas used to do a lot of sport. Now he doesn't do any.
Thomas used to have a lot of hair. Now he doesn't have much hair.
Thomas used to be quite slim. Now he's overweight.
Thomas didn't use to have a girlfriend. Now he's married.
Thomas used to have a bicycle. Now he has a car.
Thomas didn't use to have much money. Now he gets a good salary.

Unit 5 Recording 7

P=Presenter
P: Welcome to *This is your life*. Our celebrity this week is the world-famous hero of the James Bond films. He was born in Ireland in 1953 but he has lived in California for over 15 years. He is married to Keely, and they have two sons. He is one of the most popular James Bonds ever.

Unit 5 Recording 8

P=Presenter
P: Pierce Brosnan is happy now but things used to be much different. When he was only a baby, his father left and his mother moved to London. He lived with his grandparents until he was six.
He left school when he was 16 and took various jobs to earn money, including washing dishes and driving a cab. For a while he was even a fire-eater in a circus. Though he looks cool now, at that time he had long hair and a beard.
Brosnan has been an actor since the age of 21. He finally found success in 1980 with the TV series *Remington Steele*. He was 27 years old. In 1995 he starred as James Bond in *Goldeneye*. The film was an instant hit and took $350 million at the box office – the biggest Bond film ever. But at home, Brosnan is a different man. His favourite hobbies are fishing and painting.

Unit 6 Recording 1

Spain; Spanish; Italy; Italian; Brazil; Brazilian; France; French; Japan; Japanese; Britain; British; Canada; Canadian; Egypt; Egyptian; Germany; German; the United States; American; Poland; Polish; Portugal; Portuguese; Australia; Australian; Kenya; Kenyan; China; Chinese; Mexico; Mexican

Unit 6 Recording 2

1 Ninety Mile Beach.
2 Tongariro mountain
3 Tasman Sea
4 South Pacific Ocean
5 Kawarau river
6 Lake Wakatipu
7 Stewart Island

Unit 6 Recording 3

T=Tour guide
T: New Zealand is a surprising country with a population of 4 million people and 40 million sheep. The capital city is Wellington but the largest city is Auckland. There are two official languages – English and Maori and the national symbol is a small bird called a kiwi.
New Zealand's tourist industry is based on outdoor sports. Go to the beautiful beaches of North Island if you like swimming, surfing or scuba diving. South Island is the place for you if you prefer mountain walking, skiing, or bungee jumping. There's plenty of culture too with ...

Unit 6 Recording 4

1 I think I'll stay in tonight.
2 My brother will help me with my homework.
3 In this class, David'll be rich in 10 years.
4 In this class, Michael'll get married soon.
5 I won't go on holiday this summer.
6 I want to go to New Zealand this summer.

Tapescripts

Unit 6 Recording 5

D=Daniel T=Tina

D: ... No, I missed it. What happened?
T: Well, three families had to live like Wild West settlers from the 1880s. They didn't have any modern things. No TV, no phone, no shampoo, very few clothes and the nearest store was 16 kilometres away. One family, the Clunes from California, had a very difficult time.
D: Why? What did they find difficult?
T: Well, Gordon, the father, did a lot of hard physical work and he lost a lot of weight. He chopped down trees and built the house when they first got there and basically he worked very hard all the time.
D: What about the mother?
T: She had a hard time too. She couldn't stand wearing the same clothes every day and she hated not wearing make-up. She had to cook, clean the house, wash clothes, etc, all without any machines. And they were always hungry.
D: Did the children enjoy it?
T: At first, they complained that there was too much to do. They had to help with the animals, cooking, chopping wood, etc. The teenage girls missed shopping and their friends and the younger boys missed the TV and skateboarding.
D: Did they change over the six months?
T: Yes. They all changed. Near the end of the six months, Tracy, who was 15, said she didn't care about make-up and clothes ... what is important is being with your family and friends and really getting to know them. I think they all felt the same.
D: So what happened when they went home to their modern life?
T: Well, back home in California ...

Unit 6 Recording 6

D=Daniel T=Tina

D: So what happened when they went home to their modern life?
T: Well, back in California, they loved seeing their friends again and wearing different clothes and stuff. But the children, especially the teenagers, were really bored.
D: Bored?
T: Yes. I think they realised that there is more to life than make-up, TV and clothes! They really missed having all the jobs to do. They missed being involved in ...

Unit 6 Recording 7

M=Man W=Woman

M: OK, so we've got to choose five machines we can't live without.
W: Yep.
M: And we're going to live in the Wild West for six months.
W: Yes ...
M: As now or as a hundred years ago?
W: To live as they did a hundred years ago.
M: OK, shall I start?
W: Go ahead.
M: Well, we could live without a mobile phone or answerphone but I'd like to choose a TV because it's good entertainment. And I couldn't live without a TV for six months!
W: Oh no. Not a TV! I think people watch too much TV and anyway we'll be too busy. I think we should take a radio.
M: A radio? Why's that?
W: Well, the main reason is that we can listen to music while we work – and you have to work hard in the Wild West. I always listen to the radio while I'm doing the ironing.
M: OK. Good point. What else? ... umm ... I'd choose a washing machine because I'm too lazy to wash clothes by hand.
W: Yes, I agree. OK, so that's two things. What else?
M: I'd also like to take a ... DVD player.
W: You're joking, aren't you! We're not taking a TV so how can we watch DVDs?
M: Good point. err ...

Unit 6 Recording 8

E.g. What's your town like?
1 Would you like to visit South Africa?
2 What's the weather like today?
3 What do you like doing at weekends?
4 Which famous person would you like to meet?
5 What sports do you like playing?
6 Do you look like your mum or your dad?
7 Where would you like to go on your next holiday?

Unit 6 Recording 9

H=Harry L= Linda

H: Well, what do you think? We're going in March so we need to get the tickets soon. Where would you like to go?
L: Umm ... I think Barcelona sounds really good or maybe Edinburgh ... I'm not sure. There are lots of great things to see and do in both places. What do you think?
H: Umm ... I think Edinburgh is too cold for me ... I like warmer weather ... 4° is too cold! Barcelona is a bit warmer. Is it warm enough?
L: Yes, I think so... it's warm enough for me ... I don't like it too hot.
H: Also, look ... I think Edinburgh's too expensive ... €60 a night ... that's too expensive.
L: Yes, you're right. OK, then ... I think we've decided on Barcelona ...
H: What's it like in Barcelona? Are there lots of interesting things to do?

Unit 7 Recording 2

M=Man W=Woman

M: Well, I think this person is really good-looking. He or she is tall and slightly overweight – you know, not fat, but big – and fairly muscular. Guess who?
W: OK, this person is ... very skinny actually. He or she isn't short ... In fact, I'd say this person is slightly taller than average. And he or she is a lot more attractive than most. Guess who ...?

Unit 7 Recording 3

P=Presenter

P: Don't be shy! Admit it! Men want to look after their skin as much as women do. How will you feel if you look in the mirror tomorrow morning? Will you feel happy with what you see? Or will you see that your face needs serious help? Don't worry! Help is here! New 'Face Saver' face cream from 'New Man Cosmetics' will save your skin from all the problems of modern living. If you use 'Face Saver' once a day, you'll soon have softer, fresher skin. And you'll certainly notice the difference if you use 'Face Saver' twice a day. Use it morning and evening to look years younger. Don't waste another day! Use 'Face Saver' from 'New Man Cosmetics' and save your skin before it's too late!

Unit 7 Recording 4

1 If you eat a lot of junk food, you'll put on weight.
2 You won't sleep well tonight if you drink all that coffee.
3 If he doesn't call you, what will you do?
4 He won't have any money left if he buys any more DVDs.
5 If you don't start training now, you won't be able to run the marathon.
6 Will you call me if your bus is late?

Unit 7 Recording 6

1 Are you ambitious?
2 Are you usually hard-working or lazy?
3 Are you more open or more reserved?
4 Are you an organised kind of person or disorganised?
5 Are you chatty or are you the quiet type?

Unit 7 Recording 7

H=Helen D=Daniel

H: Hi Daniel. Have you got five minutes to spare?
D: Yes, sure.
H: OK, I want to look at the shape of your fingers.
D: Why?
H: I'm going to tell you about your personality.
D: Oh, great. I love doing this kind of thing.
H: OK, there are three main things to look at.
D: What are they?
H: First, there's the length of your fingers. People with long, slim fingers are quite sensitive. People with shorter, thicker fingers, like yours, are more open. They talk about their feelings more.
D: Oh, I really enjoy talking about my feelings. I'm very open. This is great. What else?
H: Well, secondly, there's the shape of your fingers. Are you fingers straight?
D: They seem to be fairly straight.
H: Umm ... that means you're organised and reliable. Is that true?
D: Yes. I really think that's true about me.
H: Finally, the thumb is very important.
D: Oh really?
H: Yeah. Let's see if your thumb bends back easily.
D: What? Like this?
H: Yes ... mmm ... yours bends quite a lot which means you like talking – you're chatty.
D: I love talking!
H: Yes, I know. If it doesn't bend back it means you're more reserved – you avoid

telling people about your feelings or problems.
D: That's not me.
H: And a long thumb means you're ambitious. You've got quite a long thumb so I guess you're quite ambitious.
D: That's absolutely right! Hey, shall I do you now? Come on! Let me look at your fingers ...

Unit 7 Recording 8

K=Kate C=Chris
K: Hey, listen to these jokes! I think they're really funny.
C: OK. Go on.
K: 'Doctor, doctor, I've lost my memory.'
'When did this happen?'
'When did what happen?'
C: That's quite funny.
K: What about this one? 'Doctor, doctor, I get a pain in my eye when I drink coffee.'
'Have you tried taking the spoon out?'
C: ... I don't get it. Taking the spoon out? ... Oh! I see. Oh yeah, I get it.
K: OK. This is a good one. 'Doctor, doctor, when I press my finger on my stomach it hurts. Have I got food poisoning?'
'No, you've got a broken finger.'
C: Mmm ... That's very good.
K: Do you know any 'Doctor, doctor' jokes?
C: No, I can never remember jokes. They just go in one ear and out the other ...

Unit 8 Recording 1

1 Cheetahs can run at 112 kilometres an hour.
2 A Mclaren Formula One car has a top speed of 400 kilometres an hour.
3 The speed limit on motorways in Spain is 120 kilometres an hour.
4 The album *No strings attached* by *NSYNC is the fastest-selling pop album in the USA ever.

Unit 8 Recording 2

1 In what language are most international phone calls made?
2 In the US, are more messages carried by email or by post?
3 What percentage of websites are not visited by anybody?
4 What percentage of cars in the world are owned by people in the US, Canada, Europe and Japan?
5 How many tons of junk mail are delivered every year in the US?

Unit 8 Recording 3

1 The number of fast-food restaurants is going up steadily.
2 The quality of food that most people eat in the UK has got worse recently.
3 The amount of traffic has risen over the last few years.
4 The average speed in cities has fallen in the last 30 years.
5 The air quality in most cities is deteriorating rapidly.
6 The price of air travel has gone down in the last 10 years.

Unit 8 Recording 4

Dialogue 1
W=Woman M=Man
W: Hi ... my name's Melanie. What's your name?
M: I'm Steve – nice to meet you. What do you do, Melanie?
W: Oh, I'm a teacher. And you?
M: I'm an architect.
W: Oh, that's interesting. Do you enjoy your job?
M: Yes, I do. It's ... very interesting. Err, do you know much about architecture?
W: No, not really.
M: Oh. Have you done speed-dating before?
W: No. This is my first time. How about you?
M: Well actually, this is my third time but I haven't had much luck yet ...

Dialogue 2
W=Woman M=Man
W: Hello. I'm Rachel.
M: Hi Rachel. My name's Kieron.
W: OK, we've only got three minutes so ... how would your best friend describe you?
M: Well ... I think my best friend would say I'm friendly and open and that I love travelling.
W: Travelling? So what's the most amazing place that you've travelled to?
M: Oh, Canada, definitely. It's just so beautiful. Tell me something about you. What was the last CD you bought?
W: Well actually, it was a teach-yourself Italian CD. I'm learning Italian.
M: That's a coincidence because I'm learning Italian too!
W: Really? Why are you learning it?
M: Well, I really love the country and I want to be able to speak the language when I'm there ...

Unit 8 Recording 5

1 What were you doing this time last week?
2 He was driving so fast, he didn't see the dog.
3 They were having dinner when I phoned.
4 I met Sally when I was waiting for a bus.

Unit 9 Recording 2

Story 1
Charlie: My worst interview experience was about three years ago. I had a group interview for a sales rep. job with a big media company. I was fine at first but when the interviewer asked me a question I suddenly began to feel very nervous. My throat went dry and I couldn't speak. They offered me a jug of water and a cup. All 20 people in the room stopped and looked at me. I tried to pour the water into the cup but my hand was shaking so much that the water went everywhere. I was so embarrassed I had to leave the room. I still go cold all over when I think about it.

Story 2
Alison: Well, I think my worst experience was about two months ago. I had an interview for a job that I really wanted. I decided to drive but I got stuck in traffic and when I got there I was in a big hurry. By mistake, I parked my old car in the

Managing Director's parking place. He arrived as I was getting out of my car. He hooted his horn and asked me to park somewhere else. I ignored him and ran off to the interview. Unfortunately, he was the interviewer and he was so angry that he didn't even give me an interview.

Story 3
Kevin: My first interview after leaving college was for a trainee accountant job in a firm in Leicester. When I walked into the room the interviewer threw an ashtray at me. I quickly moved to one side and it missed. Unfortunately, I didn't get the job. They told me afterwards that the ashtray was to test how people react. The person who caught the ashtray and threw it back got the job! The people who moved to one side or caught it and put it back on the desk, didn't!

Unit 9 Recording 4

1 David can play the piano quite well now.
2 I couldn't get to sleep last night. I kept thinking about work.
3 I can't lift this box. It's too heavy. Can you help me?
4 Ann could write simple computer programs by the time she was 12.
5 They looked everywhere for Suzie's ring but they couldn't find it.
6 Could you hear what Paul was saying? It was very noisy in the restaurant.
7 I'm sorry but we won't be able to come to the party. We're on holiday in Spain that weekend.
8 Will you be able to help me move into my new flat on Saturday?

Unit 9 Recording 5

P: Presenter
P: .. and now to local news. A car thief started a six-year prison sentence last night after stealing 36 cars in order to clean them. All the cars were stolen from showrooms in the Midlands area and were worth more than £400,000. He was arrested by police at his home in Sheffield.
The court was told that Blain, a cleaner who doesn't own a car, walked into car showrooms and asked to test-drive a car. He then drove away from the showroom and didn't return. Every car was later found at the side of the road, absolutely spotless inside and out. Blain washed and cleaned each one before leaving it. He was once called 'the man you would most want to steal your car' by one judge.
Judge Alan Goldsack told Blain that he had to give him a long jail sentence. The judge told him, 'You get keys and drive off in expensive cars. You do not get any financial benefit but after driving around in them you leave them with the keys inside. It makes you feel important and you like to make people think you are a businessman with an expensive car. Clearly those who run businesses selling cars are at serious risk from your activities.' Blain was taken away by police to begin his sentence at Pentonville Prison.
Blain's wife, Mary, a 48-year-old nurse, said

after the case, that their 13-year marriage was now over. She told reporters, 'He looked after the cars better than me.'

Unit 9 Recording 6

D=Laura's Dad L=Laura

D: Morning Laura ... or should I say 'Afternoon!'?

L: Ha ha.... can you pass me the cereal, Dad?

D: So, what are you doing today?

L: Oh nothing ... going out ...

D: Fine but ... make sure you tidy up your room before you do. It's a complete mess.

L: Well, it's none of your business. It's my room.

D: Yes, well, this is my house ... and while you live in it, you do what I say. Got it!

L: Yeah right.

Unit 10 Recording 1

1 Where did you grow up?

2 Who brought you up?

3 As a child, who looked after you when you were ill?

4 As a child, who did you look up to?

5 Have you ever picked up any English from TV or songs?

6 Have you ever come across any money in the street?

Unit 10 Recording 2

W=Woman

W: Well ... I suppose I had a bit of an odd childhood really. I mean, it's very different to all my friends. My parents separated when I was really young ... errrr ... about three ... I think. They stayed friends so ... I saw my dad from time to time and that was fine ... but it was my mum who really brought me up. You see, she taught English and we lived abroad a lot. In fact, she spent a long time in Libya, in Tripoli ... and that's where I was born and really, where I grew up. I've always been incredibly close to my mum ... and also to my grandma. I really look up to my grandma. She's a wonderful person. I mean, she's incredibly kind and generous. We've all got on really well ... of course, we have the occasional row but ... that's normal I think. So, anyway, I came back to England when I was a teenager and went to school ... but I didn't really like any of my teachers. School wasn't easy for me ...

Unit 10 Recording 3

R=Radio Presenter

R: ... Pet TV is a new kind of TV programme from the BBC. The programme will have images and sounds that are repeated again and again. Examples of the images are: snooker balls on a snooker table, a frisbee flying through the air, and cartoon characters such as Top Cat.

The programme will also show extracts from popular TV programmes such as EastEnders, The Muppet Show and Animal Hospital.

The BBC says that Pet TV will appeal to many different kinds of animal including dogs, cats, birds and even fish. 'We think that Pet TV is a unique opportunity to find

out what are the pets' favourite shows,' the BBC said. 'We want to know if animals understand messages from the television. For example, does your pet respond to dogs barking, wolves howling or parrots talking in English?'

Responses like these are a sign of intelligence. Animal lovers who would like to know if they have the cleverest cat or dog in the country will also be able to give their pets an intelligence test on the BBC website.

This is not the first time programmes have been made for pets. ITV made an advertisement for Whiskas, a popular cat food. The advert showed 40 seconds of cats mewing, birds singing and mice squeaking, along with images including balls of string, birds and mice.

Unit 10 Recording 4

E.g. She's the most intelligent pet I've ever had!

1 Where shall I put the flowers that I brought?

2 CDs are very expensive in the UK.

3 What was the name of that film we saw last weekend?

4 Pet TV is the strangest idea I've ever heard!

5 Oil is very expensive at the moment.

6 He's the young man I was telling you about.

7 Did you turn off all the lights?

8 Police officers seem younger and younger these days.

Unit 11 Travel Recording 1

go by: bus, train, plane, taxi or car

get on or off: a bus, a train, a plane or a bicycle

get into or out of: a taxi or a car

catch: a bus or a train

take: a bus, a train, a plane or a taxi

miss: a bus, a train or a plane

ride: a bicycle

Unit 11 Recording 2

Lucy and Andy are friends from school. They are both in Rio de Janeiro. Lucy is worried because they are going to travel together. When they are on the train on Sunday, Andy annoys Lucy because he talks a lot. When he falls asleep in the afternoon, he snores very loudly.

When they are on the beach on Monday, Lucy is very tired. She is upset because Andy has complained about lots of things. On Tuesday afternoon, Andy is shouting and annoying Lucy. She feels she can't travel with him any more.

Unit 11 Recording 3

L=Lucy A=Andy

L: Andy, umm ... we need to talk ...

A: Yes?

L: Well, I was thinking ... I think we need to travel separately now ...

A: Oh! Really? I'm enjoying being with you so much... I think that would be a real shame ...

L: Well ... yes ... I like travelling with you too

... but ... I want to practise my Portuguese and when I'm with you, we just speak English all the time ...

A: Oh ... I promise I'll speak Portuguese to you ...

L: No ... I don't think that would work, do you?

A: No ... you're probably right ...

Unit 11 Recording 4

He hasn't stopped talking yet.
He's just fallen asleep.

Unit 11 Recording 5

P=Presenter

P: So, you want to find your perfect travel companion ... First, answer these questions ...

1: Do you like very hot places?

2: Do you like a chatty travel companion?

3: What kind of holiday do you prefer: sightseeing, beach, skiing or camping?

4: Do you like staying in hotels or going self-catering?

5: Are you interested in busy nightlife on holiday?

6: Do you like trying food from other countries?

Unit 11 Recording 6

E.g. In Japan, you should give a present using both hands.

1 In most countries, people wave when they say goodbye.

2 In most Western countries, people usually shake hands when they meet in a business situation.

3 In Asia, people usually bow when they meet in a business situation.

4 In the UK, men don't kiss on the cheeks when they meet in a business situation.

Unit 11 Recording 7

1 Our company offers you more choice.

2 I lent him €20 about three weeks ago.

3 Could you bring me that book when you come?

4 He sent her a huge bunch of flowers.

5 Would you like to tell me anything?

6 We must give our hosts a special gift.

Unit 11 Recording 8

I=Interviewer W=Writer

I: It's great to have you with us today. So... how did you start travelling?

W: Well, as a child, I travelled a lot with my family. We did some fantastic trips, like cycling through Europe, when I was 13. By the time I was 16 I had visited 19 countries!

I: Mmmm ... And how did you start writing?

W: When I travelled I always wrote a diary. I didn't want to forget all the things that I had seen and experienced. So I wrote it all down. At first, it was just facts. Then I added my feelings and stories about the places and the people.

I: It's sometimes difficult to get started as a writer ... What was your first 'break' as a travel writer?

W: It was luck really. I had lived in Turkey for about two years. Then a friend of mine, who worked for a travel company, said he needed someone to write a travel guide about Turkey. So I did it! Other writing jobs came from that.

Unit 11 Recording 9

I=Interviewer W=Writer
I: And what is the most difficult thing when you are travelling?
W: The language can be difficult. I love talking to people. But sometimes it's hard work when you can't speak the language.
I: And when you're writing ... What is the most difficult thing when you are writing?
W: When I get home from travelling I have notebooks full of notes. I often feel like writing about everything. The most difficult thing is deciding what to include and what to leave out.
I: Which travel authors or books have influenced you?
W: Some travel writers I like are Bruce Chatwin and Shiva Naipaul. But it was Bill Bryson who made me really want to be a travel writer. His books are so interesting and really funny.
I: What advice would you give to someone thinking of being a travel writer?
W: Firstly, read as many books as you can. And secondly, take notes of as many details as you can when you're travelling. Finally, go for it! Being a travel writer really is a dream job!

Unit 11 Recording 10

1 By the time I was 16 I had visited 19 countries!
2 I hadn't been there very long when I got the job.
3 Had you written any other books before this one was published?

Unit 11 Recording 11

1 When I arrived at the station, the train had left.
2 When the driver asked to see my ticket, I realised I'd lost it.
3 When we got there, we realised we hadn't packed enough warm clothes.

Unit 11 Recording 12

Dialogue 1
P=Passenger A=Assistant
P: I'd like a return to Oxford, please.
A: Yes, of course. Are you coming back today?
P: Yes I am.
A: That's £18.50 please.
P: Thank you.

Dialogue 2
C=Check-in clerk P=Passenger
C: How many pieces of luggage have you got?
P: One suitcase and one handbag.
C: Did you pack your suitcase yourself?
P: Yes I did.
C: Does it contain any knives or scissors?
P: No.
C: Fine. Could you put it on here, please? OK ... 15 kilos.

Dialogue 3
P=Passenger B=Bus driver
P: Piccadilly Circus, please.
B: One pound, please.
P: Thanks.
B: Thank you.

Dialogue 4
A=Assistant P=Passenger
A: Victoria Coach Station. Can I help you?
P: I'd like to book a single ticket to Edinburgh, please.
A: Yes ... when would you like to travel?
P: Friday 14th March, in the afternoon.
A: OK ... uh ... there's a coach at 5.45pm.
P: Yes, that's fine. How much is it?
A: £45 for a single ticket. How would you like to pay?
P: By Visa, please.
A: OK.

Unit 12 Recording 1

1 How do you feel about lending money to friends?
2 How do you feel about borrowing money from your friends or family?
3 Do you try and save any money each month? If so, is it difficult?
4 What do you enjoy spending money on?
5 How much do nurses, teachers or lawyers typically earn each year in your country? Do you think this is right?
6 How often do you withdraw money from a cashpoint machine? Do you like using them?
7 How much does a short bus or train journey cost in your country? How much do you think it is in the UK?
8 Have you ever won any money in a lottery or a competition?

Unit 12 Recording 2

1 If my bank didn't give good rates of interest, I'd change it.
2 We'd go to Australia, if it didn't cost so much.
3 If you didn't know the film *Wall Street*, we'd watch it tonight.
4 We'd visit you more often, if you didn't live so far away.
5 If I wasn't afraid of water, I'd go on that boat.

Unit 12 Recording 3

N=News presenter P=Parent
N: ... and finally... A school in Bristol has given £11,000 to its A-level students for getting good exam results. Before their exams, the school gave each student target grades to try and achieve. Now the results have arrived, St. George's 6th form college has given £500 to every student who got into university, and prizes of £20 to students who achieved their target grades. 'The results this year show the success of the scheme,' said Alison Franks, head of 6th form education. 'Unlike many schemes, this one rewards every student for doing well, not just the best students in the year.'
I asked people what they thought of the scheme. Firstly, I spoke to a parent of a student at the school and asked her how she felt about the reward scheme.

P: 'Well ... I'm not sure really. It feels a bit like bribery to me. I mean, young people should work hard for exams because they want to do well and have a good education. Not because they'll earn some money!'
N: Later I spoke to David Dobson, head teacher at St. George's. He was delighted with the scheme and told me that more students had got places at university this year than ever before.
Kelly, a student at St. George's said she had earned over £500 and was really pleased. She also said that she thought it was a great idea ... and that it'd made her work much harder. When I asked what she was going to do with the money, she said she was going to buy a new laptop computer. So, there we have it, a controversial approach but one that certainly seems to work for some students! And now ... over to Fiona in the weather studio ...

Unit 12 Recording 4

N: Later I spoke ... ... laptop computer.

Unit 12 Recording 5

1 I like both classical and pop music.
2 I don't play either football or tennis.
3 Neither of my two best friends are married yet.
4 Both of my parents have always worked.
5 I enjoy going to both the cinema and the theatre.

Unit 12 Recording 6

Dialogue 1
C=Customer W=Waiter
C: Excuse me, I think there's a mistake with the bill.
W: Oh really?
C: We actually only had two coffees, not three.
W: Oh yes, you're quite right. I'm terribly sorry, Madam, I'll just go and change it now.

Dialogue 2
C=Customer A=Assistant
C: Hello, I'd like to speak to someone about this sweater, which I bought a couple of weeks ago.
A: Sure ... what seems to be the problem?
C: Well, basically, the first time I washed it the colour came out and turned all my other clothes pink ... AND ... it shrank ... I mean, now look at it. It wouldn't fit a child.
A: Oh yes, I see what you mean ... Can I ask what temperature you washed it at?
C: Just a normal wash ... I think it's just very poor quality ... and I'd like a refund ...

Dialogue 3
A=Assistant C=Customer
A: Here's your book ... and ... your change.
C: I'm sorry but I gave you a £20 note. I should have £14.60 change not £4.60.
A: You're quite right. Here's the correct change. I don't know what I was thinking about ...

Pearson Education Limited
Edinburgh Gate, Harlow
Essex, CM20 2JE, England
and Associated Companies throughout the world

www.longman.com

First published 2005

Set in 10.5/13pt Meta Plus Book and 10/13pt Meta Plus Normal

Printed in Spain by Mateu Cromo, S.A. Pinto (Madrid)

ISBN 0582 841895 (Book only)
ISBN 1405 815620 (Book and DVD pack)

The publishers and authors are very grateful to the following people and institutions for piloting and/or reporting on the manuscript:
José Álvaro Álvaro, EOI de San Fernando de Henares, Spain; Elena Ruíz Aranda, EOI de Elche, Spain; Robert Armitage, IH Barcelona, Spain; Gonzalo Constenla Bergueiro, EOI de Santiago de Compostela, Spain; Juan Ignacio Costero de la Flor, EOI de San Fernando de Henares, Spain; Tony Dawson, University of Seville, Spain; Méabh Hopkins, EOI Toledo, Spain; Elizabeth Gregson, Italy; Liz Kalton, Keep Talking, Udine, Italy; Arantxa Pina Landeta, EOI Getxo, Spain; Ekaterina Lozhnikova, Russia; Celia Martínez Martínez, EOI Jesús Maestro, Spain; Andrea McMahon, United Kingdom; Alicia Nerguiziàn, Argentina; Sally Parry, United Kingdom; Ester Asunción Giner Prats, EOI de Valencia, Spain; MªSocorro Almagro Raya, EOI de Ciudad Lineal, Spain; Christopher Reakirt, United Kingdom; Pilar García Royuela, EOI de Pozuelo de Alarcón, Spain; Neide Aparecida Silva, Cultura Inglesa, São Paulo, Brazil; Jo-Ann Titmarsh, University of Venice, Italy; Matilde Seara Tortajada, EOI de Leganés, Spain; Agnieszka Tyszkiewicz-Zora, English Language Centre, Łodz, Poland; María Uribe, EOI Getxo, Spain

We are grateful to the following for permission to reproduce copyright material:
Dennis Publishing Ltd for the article 'Were school dinners really so bad?' published in The Week 3rd May 2003; Guardian News Services Ltd for an extract from 'Switched-on pets get their own TV show' by Jason Deans published in The Guardian 30th April 2004 © The Guardian; Independent News and Media Limited for an extract from 'Honesty gets a trial run' by Andrew Tuck published in The Independent 11th January 1998; ivillage. co.uk for an extract adapted from The Seven-Step Negotiation Plan published on www.ivillage.co.uk - The leading website for women; The Monkey Sanctuary Trust for information about The Monkey Sanctuary published on www.ethicalworks.co.uk/ monkeysanctuary/trust.htm; The Random House Group Limited for an extract from The Curious Incident of the Dog in the night-time by Mark Haddon published by Jonathan Cape; RSPCA for information about the RSPCA published on www.rspca.org. uk © 2004; Robin Scott for the text of an interview; Telegraph Group Limited for an extract from 'The man who stole cars from showrooms to clean them up' by Paul Stokes published in The Telegraph 8th April 2004 © Telegraph Group Limited 2004; Times Newspapers Ltd for an extract from 'The strange case of the $1m baseball' published in The Week 28th December 2002 © The Times 2002; and WWF-UK for information about WWF, the global conservation organization published on www.wwf.org.uk.

Cover design by Zeke Design

Illustrated by: Judy Brown, Noel Ford, Stephane Gamain (nb illustration), Neil Gower, Alex Green (Folio), Dominic Li (The Organisation), Sally Newton, Andrew Pavitt (The Organisation), Roger Penwill and Lucy Truman (New Division).

Photo Acknowledgements
We are grateful to the following for permission to reproduce photographs:
20th Century Fox / Kobal Collection for p. 134(tl), / Paramount / Kobal Collection / W Merie Wallace for p. 137(ml); AA World Travel Library for pp. 62(mb), 107(B); Actionplus for p. 88(l); Anthony Blake Photo Library for pp. 25(bl, mtl, mbl), 26(m), 32; AP Photos for pp. 78, 116(t), 121; BBC Photo Library for pp. 26(t), 135(t, m, b), 136(inset t), 140(bl); Steve Bloom Images for pp. 95(t), 102(l); Brand X Pictures for p. 26(br); Britain On View for p. 133 (tl, bl);Buzz Pictures for p. 35(t); Camera Press for pp. 36(inset r), 98(t); Canal + Images UK Ltd for p. 144; Capital Pictures for p. 20(tr); Celador Productions / Ronald Grant Archive for p. 140(tl); Corbis for pp. 5(mtl), 7(t), 20(l), 45(t), 48, 65(bl), 68(C), 76(r), 85(t, mbl), 95(mbl), 98(m), 107(D), 119, 125, 130, 136(t), 138(tm, br), 143(m); © Disney Enterprises, Inc for pp. 96(b), 142(t); Education Photos for p. 45(bl); Mary Evans Picture Library for pp. 95(tl), 96(tr); Eye Ubiquitous for p. 85(bl); Foodcollection.com / Alamy for p. 28(b); Jim Forrest Photography, photographersdirect.com for p. 10(br); Getty Images for pp. 7(b), 12, 30(l), 38(l), 46(br), 50(l), 65(t), 68(A), 75(mtl), 108(bl), 116(b); Sally & Richard Greenhill for p. 46(m); Robert Harding Picture Library for pp. 15(t), 25(t), 30(m), 46(tl), 106; Triona Holden for p. 57; Image100 / Alamy for p. 108(tr); Imagebroker / Alamy for p. 36(inset l); Imagesofbirmingham.co.uk / Alamy for p. 30(r); Imagestate for pp. 10(t), 35(mbl), 36(l), 45(mtl), 72(m), 90(r), 92(tr, l), 108(tl & inset tr), 132(br); International Photobank for pp. 62(br), 133(mtl), 138(tr); Ashley Karyl / Alamy for p. 68(B); Frank Lane Picture Library for pp. 95(mbl), 142(m, b); London Stills for p. 133(mbl); MGM / Kobal collection for p. 134(bl); Magnum Photos for p. 110(r); Miramax Films / Ronald Grant Archive for p. 134(mtl); Motoring Picture Library / Alamy for p. 90(l); Natural Visions for p. 132(tr); New Line Cinema / Ronald Grant Archive for p. 56; PA Photos for pp. 35(mtl), 60; Panos Pictures for p. 46(bl), Andrew Paterson / Alamy for p. 132(bl); Photofusion Picture Library for pp. 50(m, r), 92(br); Photolibrary. com for pp. 65(mbl), 75(t), 105(mbl), 132(m); Bob Pisko Photography, photographersdirect.com for p. 38(r); Powerstock for pp. 10(bl), 15(mtl), 75(mbl), 107(A & C), 115(t, bl); Punchstock for pp. 141 / Brand X Pictures, 38(t) / Creatas, 75(bl) / Corbis, 5(bl),15(bl), 22, 62(tr), 115(mtl), 140(mtl) / Digital Vision, 5(t), 132(tl), / Photo Alto, 15(mbl) / Thinkstock; Courtesy of Random House for pp. 80(t), 110(l, m); Courtesy of RSPCA for p. 102(inset br); Retna Pictures for pp. 66(b), 72(tl); Rex Features for pp. 5(mbl), 35(bl), 45(mbl), 52(l, br, tr), 66(t), 71(tr), 72(tr), 88(r), 89, 100, 102(br), 105(mtl), 115(mbl), 137(tl); Peter Rogers Productions for p.139(t); SC Photos / Alamy for p. 105(t); Courtesy of Robin Scott alias 'M' for p. 16(t, inset t); The Irish Image Collection for p. 138(tl); The Monkey Sanctuary for pp. 102(tr & inset tr); The Travel Library for pp. 55(bl), 62(mt, l); Tiger Moth / Miramax / Kobal Collection / Phil Bray for p. 137(bl);Timpano Productions for p. 28(t); Peter Titmuss / Alamy for p. 105(bl); Topfoto for pp. 55(mbl), 58, 65(mtl), 76(l), 85(mtl), 108(m), 139(m); Scott Tuason / imagequestmarine.com for p. 36(r);United Artists / Ronald Grant Archive for p. 134(mbl); Universal / Kobal Collection for p. 137(br); John Warburton-Lee Photography for p. 55(t); Courtesy Warner Bros / Ronald Grant Archive for p. 96(m); Webstream / Alamy for p. 98(b); Gill Williams for p. 143(b); Woodfall Wild Images for p. 95(bl); Working Tiltle / Ronald Grant Archive for p. 139(b); World Wildlife Fund for p. 102(inset l); YTV / Ronald Grant Archive for p. 140(mbl);Saul Zaentz Company / Kobal Collection for p. 18; Zefa for p. 68(D).

Cover images by Lonely Planet Images (tr); Punchstock / Corbis (l); Punchstock / Photodisc (b).

Picture research by Kevin Brown

Location photography by Gareth Boden